The American Short Story Cycle

Jennifer J. Smith

EDINBURGH
University Press

Edinburgh University Press is one of the leading university presses in the UK. We publish academic books and journals in our selected subject areas across the humanities and social sciences, combining cutting-edge scholarship with high editorial and production values to produce academic works of lasting importance. For more information visit our website: edinburghuniversitypress.com

© Jennifer J. Smith, 2018

Edinburgh University Press Ltd
The Tun – Holyrood Road,
12(2f) Jackson's Entry,
Edinburgh EH8 8PJ

Typeset in 11/13 Adobe Sabon by
IDSUK (DataConnection) Ltd

A CIP record for this book is available from the British Library

ISBN 978 1 4744 2393 9 (hardback)
ISBN 978 1 4744 2394 6 (webready PDF)
ISBN 978 1 4744 2395 3 (epub)

The right of Jennifer J. Smith to be identifiedastheauthorofthisworkhasbeenasserted
in accordance with the Copyright, Designs and Patents Act 1988, and the Copyright and Related Rights Regulations 2003 (SI No. 2498).

Contents

Acknowledgements	iv
Introduction: Forming Provisional Identities	1
1. Locating the Short Story Cycle	12
2. The Persistence of Place	37
3. Writing Time in Metaphors	60
4. Tracing New Genealogies	87
5. Resisting Identity	113
6. Atomic Genre	141
Coda: Novellas-in-Flash and Flash Cycles	170
Selected American Short Story Cycles	178
Works Cited	182
Index	191

Acknowledgements

In writing my acknowledgements, I am reminded of a scene from the television show *30 Rock*. When Kenneth-the-page is fired, he drunkenly staggers onto the scene of a wedding and grabs the microphone. Everyone braces for the worst as Kenneth announces, 'You people you are my best friends, and I hope you get everything you want in life. So kiss my face! I'll see you all in heaven!' He flashes a thumbs up, throws the microphone down, and walks away. Reaching the end of something, he realises how wonderful it's been. I know how he feels.

I am indebted to my insightful and gracious first readers: George Hutchinson, Purnima Bose, Margo Crawford, and Vivian Nun Halloran. George has an incredible talent for being able to conceptualise the big picture even as he zooms in on a single sentence. Both in his critiques and in his writing, he taught me the merits of clear and compelling prose. Purnima has been my most resistant reader, and, for that (and much more), I thank her. The push past the formal impulse is, in large part, due to her. Margo asked questions about identity and art that shape my work; her rigour and encouragement made this project better. I am likewise deeply indebted to Vivian; she has influenced my framing, choice of texts, argument, and countless other elements. We talked about drafts in her office, in coffee shops, in classes, and in her home; her generosity as a scholar is inspiring.

An army of English teachers and professors made this book and my career possible; I thank all of them. My work has been supported by the Booth Tarkington Dissertation Award; the English Department at Indiana University; a National Endowment for the Humanities Summer grant; a faculty development grant at Concordia University Chicago; and a Rinker, Dietz, and Runkle grant from Franklin College. I thank all of these institutions for their support. My colleagues at both Franklin College and Concordia University Chicago have been my great friends and readers these past seven years.

Sections of this book have appeared in earlier iterations in several venues. A section from Chapter 1 appeared in *Journal of the*

Short Story in English in 2011 in volume 57. A section of Chapter 1 also appeared in *Critical Insights: American Short Story*, published by Grey House Press in 2015 and edited by Michael Cocchiarale and Scott D. Emmert. An earlier version of Chapter 2 appeared in *Sherwood Anderson's Winesburg, Ohio*, released by Brill in 2016 and edited by Precious S. McKenzie. Thank you to my editors and the anonymous readers who sharpened and refined my arguments in those chapters. I offer my sincere gratitude to the anonymous readers from Edinburgh University Press, who pushed me to make the book more ambitious and clear. EUP's entire editing team, especially Michelle Houston, Adela Rauchova, and Rebecca Mackenzie, are all wonderfully supportive.

My project has also benefited from colleagues who read and discussed my work on the short story cycle: Erin Pryor Ackerman, Callista Buchen, Martha Carpentier, John Casey, Elke D'hoker, Mathijs Duyck, Adrian Hunter, Helena Kadmos, John Paul Kanwit, Aimee Krall-Lanoue, Jameelah Lang, Patrick J. Maley, Annika Mann, Jenny Mann, Andy Oler, Robin Roberts, George Phillips, David Settje, Maura J. Smyth, and Rishona Zimring. My special thanks to Cathy Day for granting me an interview and for her work on linked stories, both in and out of the classroom. I also want to thank all of my lovely friends for making life and work fun.

My largest debt of gratitude goes to my family. To Matt, Katie, Kiersten, Patrick, and Aaron, thank you for offering support and giggles. To my sister and best friend, Julie, thank you for being a more generous listener than I deserve, and to Jason, thank you for being the only one deserving to share the title of Julie's best friend. To my extended Smith and Craig families, I owe you so much in the way of love and enthusiasm. And especially to Bruce and Joan Montague and Edwin and Betty Smith; I am thankful to have had the years I did with you and wish there had been more.

Andy and June Craig have transformed my life. Andy read and gave me his thoughts on every part of this book and listened to me talk interminably about it over the years. June often forced the computer closed while yelling 'outside!' She was right to do so. And, by the time this book appears, a new baby will be here.

Finally, my loudest thanks go to those two individuals to whom this is dedicated – James and Michelle Smith, my parents. Their unwavering love and support have made this, and every accomplishment I have ever had, possible. They are, quite simply, the best.

'You people are my best friends, and I hope you get everything you want in life.'

*For James and Michelle Smith,
with love and gratitude*

Introduction

Forming Provisional Identities

H. L. Mencken, a clamorous advocate for modern American literature, remarked of Sherwood Anderson's *Winesburg, Ohio* (1919) that 'nothing quite like it is to be found in our literature' (qtd in Mann 1989: 163). Of Ernest Hemingway's *In Our Time* (1925), Edmund Wilson wrote that 'in the dry composed little vignettes . . . [Hemingway] has almost invented a form of his own' (qtd in Mann 1989: 163). Malcolm Cowley claimed that William Faulkner's *Knight's Gambit* (1949) 'belongs to a genre that Faulkner has made peculiarly his own by the artistic success of such earlier volumes as *The Unvanquished* and *Go Down, Moses*' (qtd in Mann 1989: ix). These three titans of early twentieth-century criticism claimed for each author the invention of a genre. They celebrated each book as utterly original. Each time a volume of loosely connected short stories appeared, critics and tastemakers heralded it as unlike anything that had come before.

Several possible explanations arise for their claiming the genre for each author, even among Anderson, Hemingway, and Faulkner, who clearly read and responded to each other. A fair amount of boosterism pervades critical responses to modernist texts, and more than a fair share recurs in authorial statements about creation and originality. In an era that held Ezra Pound's injunction to 'make it new' as sacrosanct of a modernist commitment to innovation, genre promises one such avenue for invention. By writing in an unfamiliar genre that echoes the uncertainties and ambiguities of modernity, each author could theoretically be crowned the originator of a form. These books were unlike the novels and short stories readers were most familiar with, and reading them smacked of a sense of revelation and liberation. Although these authors did not invent a genre, it matters that they seemed to. The boasting reveals that these volumes somehow captured elemental truths about modernity. The disjointed, recursive form of volumes like *Winesburg*, *In Our Time*, and *Knight's Gambit* represents the contingency and flux of modern life. This form, the short story cycle, composed of autonomous yet interconnected stories, is a persistent force in and on American fiction – before, during, and after the height of modernism.

The short story cycle gets claimed as new in each period, crystallising how much originality has mattered as a measure of greatness throughout literary history. Critical and popular reception of short story cycles reveals a longstanding celebration of innovation that evinces the influence of a modernist commitment to newness. The history of the cycle also demonstrates how little critics have attended to this tradition, which accounts for the consistent claims of novelty. Even now, each new short story cycle inspires great debates about what to call this apparently unclassifiable genre – a theme I treat throughout this book but especially in the final chapter on Jennifer Egan's *A Visit from the Goon Squad* (2010). Egan's popular and acclaimed volume provoked divergent declarations about its form akin to those made by Wilson, Cowley, and Mencken almost one hundred years earlier.

Scholars of the genre debate which term to use and which books fit and which do not. Robert M. Luscher and J. Gerald Kennedy separately advocate for short story sequences to 'emphasize its progressive unfolding and cumulative effects' (Kennedy 1995: vii); Kennedy's preferred term, and the collection of essays that accompany his introduction to the form, acknowledges the heterogeneity of fiction that spans from the short story collection to the fragmented novel, including works such as J. D. Salinger's *Nine Stories* (1953) and Raymond Carver's *Cathedral* (1983) as short story sequences. In his essay 'Towards a Poetics of the Short Story Cycle' (1988) Kennedy rightly critiques the emphasis on unity that dominated early criticism on short story cycles, arguing that any coherence that emerges from such volumes has as much to do with the reader's perception as it does with authorial intention or formal design. Luscher makes a compelling case for sequence by highlighting the 'form's kinship with the sonnet sequence and the modern poetic sequence' (1989: 149). He argues that the sequence invites the singularity of the story, the diversity of the novel, and the harmony and distillation of lyric poetry.

Conversely, Maggie Dunn and Ann Morris lobby for composite novel to highlight the genre's association not with the short story but with the novel. They assert that such volumes have 'whole-text coherence' (Dunn and Morris 1995: 1), and they critique short story cycle as a term because it conjures the story's inferior position to the novel in the marketplace and often in readers' estimation. Occasionally, the volumes themselves include subtitles supporting Dunn and Morris's sense that market forces drive how such volumes get packaged. In the chapters that follow, I often include books that carry various subtitles, for instance Rebecca Barry's *Later, at the Bar: A Novel in Stories* (2007). Others include the inscription 'A Novel', such as Russell Banks's *Trailerpark* (1981) and Amy Tan's *The Joy Luck Club* (1989), and still others, such as Cathy Day's *The Circus in Winter* (2004), get around such generic distinction by subtitling the work 'Fiction'. The repetition of such labels certainly indicates publishers' anxieties that short stories do not sell and that readers need to know how to read these volumes.

However, in their eagerness to have these volumes read and studied, Dunn and Morris miss how formative the short story is to such books, so much so that Rolf Lundén argues for short story composite. His study rightly attends to the tensions between unity and fragmentation that distinguish the genre, and he argues that not every such volume features cyclicality or sequencing. Lundén makes a compelling case that the emphasis on unity in critical debates emerges from a 'post-Kantian, Coleridgean ideal of esthetic organicism' (1999: 8). That is, from the eighteenth and into the twentieth centuries, scholars and readers alike privileged 'totalized prose forms such as the social-realistic novel' at the expense of 'more openly constructed forms of narrative' (Lundén 1999: 8). Aesthetic unity and coherence became the measure of great art, and disjointed and open works were often dismissed as flawed or uninteresting. To address this, Lundén advocates for short story composite, which attends to the constitutive significance of the short story as well as the volumes' openness, while still recognising the effects of accretion that go into making a volume. He argues that cycle is a problematic label for many of these books, which lack cyclicality, an emphasis on which would seem to continue the New Critical, post-Kantian emphasis on unity worked out through irony and juxtaposition.

And yet, cycle has emerged as the dominant metaphor to describe the genre, beginning with Forrest Ingram's foundational study from 1971. Ingram was the first to study the genre's attempts at coherence, by attending to compositional history and authorial intention, and defines the cycle as '*a book of short stories so linked by their author that the reader's successive experience on various levels of the pattern of the whole significantly modifies his experience of each of its component parts*' (1971: 19; original emphasis). Ingram employs the term short story cycle as do studies by Susan Garland Mann (1989), Rocío Davis (2002), James Nagel (2001), Mark Whalan (2007), Michelle Pacht (2009), and Benjamin Forkner (2012) (some with, and others without, the hyphen). In a 2013 special issue on the genre in *Short Fiction in Theory and Practice*, Elke D'hoker argues that formal and reader-oriented approaches dominate current criticism (2013: 155). D'hoker looks to international scholarship, which often treats the cycle as part of much larger shifts in narrative style, as presenting Anglo-American criticism with a 'potentially liberating shift away from problems of definition, terminology and taxonomy' (2013: 156). Although it is an imperfect term and there are many variants, short story cycle has become the primary and best descriptor for the genre, because it most accurately captures the recursiveness central to the genre and privileges the short story as its formative element. Concerns about authorial intention, readerly experience, revision, paratextual framing, generic distinctions, and the stories themselves all contribute to these scholars' debate over the terms. Such debates, while often fascinating in the context of a single text, ultimately obscure a longstanding, wide-reaching tradition, so my book is more interested in what these books do than in what we call them.

Moreover, genre itself has always been a fluid, hybrid element of compositional and reading practices. Histories of the novel, for instance, have long revealed the incredible diversity of the origins for, manifestations of, and experimentations with the novel. The prose poem provides a parallel to the short story cycle. The prose poem is akin to the cycle in its hybridity and flexibility and in its apparent novelty yet longstanding tradition. It seems to have exploded in recent decades with the proliferation of creative writing programmes and a turn toward distilled forms like flash fiction, but its origins include Charles Baudelaire, James Joyce, and Gertrude Stein, among many others. Michel Delville, who has written a foundational study of the genre, makes the argument that attempts to arrive at a 'monolithic definition of the genre' fall short because there are 'almost as many trends as there are poets practicing it' (1998: 1). Likewise, the cycle, by whatever name, enjoys the kinds of formal diversity of the novel or the prose poem. Rather than narrowing, my book broadens the scope of the genre by treating volumes that others call sketchbooks, novels, collections, composite novels, and short story sequences, similar to histories of the novel that examine the picaresque, the bildungsroman, the gothic, and even the anti-novel.

In cycles, stories can be read singly but gain meaning together, drawing on both the power of particularity and the explosive energy of fusion. Since the early nineteenth century, increased mobility and personal choice have made community, kinship, and temporality ever more open to interpretation. The genre transforms these subjects into its very form, atomising and then linking its stories through place, family, and time. Therefore, genre is both historical and theoretical. Cycles reflect in form and content a central narrative problem of modern literature: how to articulate subjectivity. Examining the myriad iterations of short story cycles reveals that authors from different periods, ethnic and national traditions, stylistic practices, and ideological viewpoints find the cycle powerfully suggestive for depicting cultural and personal upheaval.

The cycle is particularly apt for rendering what Paul March-Russell calls the 'historical mess of lived experience' (2009: 111), which is why the genre proliferates in moments of communal or national change, such as industrialisation, war, or decolonisation. In these contexts, cycles challenge the 'authenticity of historical narrative' (March-Russell 2009: 115) by embracing multiple points of view, non-linear chronologies, as well as complex kinship structures and communal affiliations. One example of this is Tim O'Brien's *The Things They Carried* (1990). Following in the tradition of Hemingway's *In Our Time*, O'Brien's stories render the trauma of participating in conflict about which one feels ambivalence. These cycles reflect the individual – even autobiographical – and collective violence done to and by a generation through interconnected stories that stand alone and yet, when taken together, portray quotidian and extraordinary pain. Their stories capture the 'mess of lived experience' during and after World War I and the Vietnam War, respectively, in a form that allows for a lack of resolution and embraces multiplicity. As ideas and institutions that unite a group or provide meaning for the individual destabilise, prove inadequate, or cause alienation, writers turn to the cycle to capture the narrative power that arises from uncertainty. In periods of great cultural and ideological upheaval, the cycle presents a form to express fragmentation and recurrence but not unity.

One common feature of the genre is its rejection of progression and resolution, as in *Winesburg, Ohio* and James Joyce's *Dubliners* (1914), often cited as archetypal short story cycles. Prior to their publication, short stories had tended to involve plot twists and neat resolution, made popular by O. Henry (William Sydney Porter) among others. Joyce and Anderson diverged from an emphasis on plot to focus on the inner lives of their characters. Edgar Allan Poe, in reviewing Nathaniel Hawthorne, famously celebrates the short story as the greatest artistic genre because tales have a 'unity of effect' arrived at through the 'totality' of experiencing a story in a single sitting (1984: 571, 586). Joyce and Anderson exploded this definition of the story by refuting totality; their characters often remain stunted and the plots – such as they are – go unresolved. Spiritual emptiness and economic hardship become driving forces for the short story in the wake of Joyce's and Anderson's cycles. Narrative itself attempts to fulfil the loss of faith – in God, progress, each other – that accompanied modernity, as Joyce explains to his brother in a letter: 'there is a certain resemblance between the mystery of the mass and what I am trying to do . . . to give people a kind of intellectual pleasure or spiritual enjoyment by converting the bread of everyday life into something that has a permanent artistic life of its own' (qtd in Scholes and Litz 1996: 250). Joyce's fifteen stories, which trace disparate characters through youth, adolescence, maturity, and death, do not culminate in meaningful action; rather, they reflect the modernist sense that a belief in progress is destructive. They articulate that teleological narratives are no longer apt for describing modern life.

Short story cycles are dissimilar from song cycles or sonnet cycles, often characterised by an organic relationship to time that results in symmetrical repetition. A more accurate metaphor might be that of the helix, as the stories circle around a common framework without exact repetition. The linking structures – of place, time, and family – serve as axes around which the stories curve. The genre favours episodic, non-chronological narratives. The cycle's spiralling structure disorients, creating a kind of vertigo offset by sharp moments of insight. That the insight from one story may or may not affect other stories is typical of the genre; the cycle does not, ultimately, conclude that narrative – and, by extension, life – gains clarity and unity.

The short story cycle's form enables a radical challenge to singularity in point of view by repudiating the idea that a single narrative voice or characterisation should drive a text. Even in a cycle ostensibly grounded in such a figure, authors introduce multiple points of view and stories unrelated to the central figure. This decentring promotes the idea that no single individual has a monopoly on knowledge and experience. Thus, communal groupings are paramount in the cycle, suggesting that structures of time, family, and place comprise human identity. Thereby, the genre paints a picture of identity in process; subjectivity attains a kind of flux and restlessness. By taking place, family, and time as linking devices that only occasionally result in unity, the prevalence of the genre suggests that these bases for identity are always conditional. The form of the cycle enables the expression of identity without fixity – what I call 'provisional identities' – that is, flexible, dynamic identities that emerge within a story or series of stories but which are neither rigidly defined nor fixed. Reflecting the conflicts between autonomy and belonging, such constructions allow stories to assert a momentary, contingent sense of a character's self without insisting that it remain so across the stories.

Proliferating from the nineteenth century to the present, the short story cycle constitutes an expansive history which includes influential writers and texts in American and global literatures. The preponderance of the genre across different movements from realism to modernism and postmodernism signals the continuity of the crises of coherence and legibility across these different periods. Story cycles date to the earliest written narratives, and their origins span the globe: Homer's *Odyssey*, Ovid's *Metamorphoses*, Boccaccio's *Decameron*, Chaucer's *The Canterbury Tales*, the Indian *Panchatantra*, the Arabian *A Thousand and One Nights*, Malory's *Morte d'Arthur*, and the Icelandic sagas (Ingram 1971: 17; Nagel 2001: 1–2; Lundén 1999: 7). Nineteenth-century volumes, such as Mary Russell Mitford's *Our Village* (1824–32), Honoré de Balzac's *The Human Comedy* (1830–54), Ivan Turgenev's *A Sportsman's Sketches* (1852), Émile Zola's *Natural and Social History of a Family under the Second Empire* (1871–93), and Gustave Flaubert's *Three Tales* (1877), highlight the importance of cyclical volumes to international realism and naturalism. *Dubliners* is an exemplar among modernist cycles, and more recent cycles, such as Alice Munro's *Lives of Girls and Women* (1971), Laura Esquivel's *Like Water for Chocolate* (1989), and Edwidge Danticat's *Krik? Krak!* (1995), continue to shape the genre's global presence. Although its antecedents extend to some of the earliest narratives across the globe, the modern iteration of the short story cycle proliferated from the nineteenth century because it questions the logic of progress and rationality, so central to modernity, directly in its form.

The history of the short story cycle exposes that the genre emerges and proliferates in places and at times of new identity formations: nineteenth-century Europe, turn-of-the-century America, and in recent decades in the Caribbean, to name just a few. The noted correlations between the cycle and national, gendered, and ethnic formations suggest that the genre repeatedly emerges during moments of embattled identity-making. The problems of coherence intrinsic to the cycle – of being both singular and connected – comport with an anxiety of unity formative, but not unique, to US culture. In scholarship and among authors, a pattern emerges: to claim that the genre is analogous to national and regional identities. The tendency to want to see the cycle as distinctive to a place reveals that the genre has flexibility and multiplicity. Lundén argues that the form resonates with 'the conjunction of centripetal and centrifugal forces in American society and the American "character"' (1999: 108). Gerald Lynch (2001) asserts that Canadian cycles make one from many, paralleling the way provinces contribute to Canadian national identity. Julie Barak (1998) claims that the cycle mirrors the creation of Caribbean identity from many distinct national and cultural identities, which reflect the geography of the archipelago. The model of standing alone but being more meaningful together, enacted in the genre, offers a compelling analogy to the pluralism of many geopolitical bodies. These critics get it right: authors do see the form as opening up new possibilities for national and local expression. And yet, it must also be acknowledged how international and transportable this form is. Like the modernist critics who insisted on authorial originality, these scholarly responses suggest that ostensibly new genres contribute to the formation of (trans)national traditions simultaneously.

Other critics, such as Margot Kelley (2000), Karen Weekes (2002), Rachel Lister (2007), and Helena Kadmos (2014), argue that the form, for reasons both practical and conceptual, is especially conducive to illuminating the experiences of women writers. From the mid-nineteenth century, women working in the genre have been pre-eminent. Because of the short story's ability to be published in magazines as well as in book form, it fulfils the demands of both magazine and book publishing. Critics argue that those writers with competing demands on their time (including parenting, pursuing a Master of Fine Arts, and working other jobs) find the cycle amenable to the immediate conditions of their work and long-range goals in producing a book. In the cycle, selfhood develops not out of autonomy and sustained realisation but from interconnectedness. It engages with decentralised narration and resistance to teleology, going against characteristics often associated with the novel and masculinity. Kadmos argues that the genre 'provides rich material through which to explore multi-layered representations of women's lives in a variety of roles as wives, mothers, aunts, daughters, sisters, and neighbours, as bearers of knowledge, as teachers who are resourceful and resilient' (2014: 2). The cycle is not the special province of women, and yet it has been a richly generative form for women, which I tackle in Chapters 1 and 4 especially.

Critics, particularly James Nagel and Rocío Davis, also attend to the marked correlation between ethnic minorities and the cycle. Nagel (2001) carefully focuses on the multivalent ethnic ties in constructing story cycles, turning first to Louise Erdrich's engagement with the multivoiced narrators of Chippewa gossip in *Love Medicine* (1984) and then examining the revisions to divergent cultural forms in writers such as Jamaica Kincaid, Susan Minot, Tim O'Brien, and Robert Olen Butler, among others. He frames this 'ethnic resonance' as inspiring writers of the 1980s and 1990s. Davis turns her attention to Asian American and Asian Canadian story cycles to argue that the genre is the 'formal materialization of the trope of multiplicity' (2002: 19) for writers such as Sara Suleri and Toshio Mori, among others. A formal analysis of the short story cycle, with an eye to how it reflects the creation and deployment of ethnic identities, exposes the continuous presence of such formations from its very beginnings. Davis turns to genre as a way to break the monolith of ethnographic approaches that dominated the study of ethnic literatures in the 1980s and 1990s, finding that the cycle 'illustrates the general process of multiethnic literature toward plurality, multiplicity, polyphony, and fragmentation' (2002: 17). An outcome of this has been the integration of autobiography and children's fiction into the genre, as well as an expansion of what a short story is, as many of these books contain one-page vignettes and others include eighty-page novellas.

I, too, engage a comparative approach to 'reveal the extent to which various ethnic literatures that are now often studied in isolation share a repertoire of available literary language' (Sollors 1995: 303). The cycle proves to be a productive piece of that repertoire because the stories within can draw from comparative ethnic experiences without losing specificity. For instance, conflicts over the precarious place of an indigenous nation within the United States condition the representation of Ojibwe identities and experiences in Louise Erdrich's *Love Medicine*. Julia Alvarez's depiction of Dominican identity and experiences in *How the García Girls Lost Their Accents* (1991) has a great deal in common with Erdrich's treatment but differs sharply with Junot Díaz's depiction of Dominican life in the United States in *Drown* (1996) and *This Is How You Lose Her* (2012). The cycle resists essentialism. By displacing a central protagonist, these texts achieve a brand of collective experience and history largely unavailable in the novel and impossible in the story.

When I began this project, I had a suspicion that cycles were apprentice works. I thought that if I could understand the cycle,

I could understand the battles for authority and narration that characterise novels by Faulkner, John Dos Passos, Kurt Vonnegut, and Toni Morrison. Cycles were a footnote on my way to more important works. I think this false impression resulted from a sense that *Winesburg* matters mostly because it influenced the high modernist experimentation of Hemingway and Faulkner. I think this also resulted from an early reading of Hemingway's *In Our Time* and a general sense that his novels mattered more to his literary reputation. Moreover, it derived from a general consensus – hard to pinpoint but nonetheless powerful – that novels are harder to write and therefore more worthy of study. Story cycles do not require the unity or the commitment to characterisation of the novel, and they can give the impression of an author learning how to write a novel through a cycle. What I found in my research, though, is that the techniques that define modernist expression were most often fully realised in the cycle. I found that modernist novels bear the imprint of the cycle. I now think that *In Our Time* is the height of Hemingway's achievement, *Winesburg* is certainly the height of Anderson's, and Faulkner's multivoiced novels are only possible because of the cycle.

I also came to realise that I was placing modernism on a pedestal. And that, if I did not make modernism the height of expression, as I and others too often do, then the short story cycle deserves an even more prominent place. Cycles in the nineteenth century profoundly interrogate the meaning of industrialisation and the interplay of the community and individual. Cycles, from the mid-twentieth century to today, constitute a vital, heterogeneous genre. They engage in formal and linguistic experimentation that their modernist predecessors would celebrate, but they also have their own contributions to make. They offer multiple responses to the nature of subjectivity and render beautiful and grotesque the desire to belong.

This book offers a reappraisal of modern American fiction by examining the history of the short story cycle – a form which fostered aesthetics of fragmentation, disjunction, and recurrence. Bringing together archival materials, such as correspondence and manuscript revisions, and critical and popular reception, I delineate how both authors and readers conceive of this genre as the ideal form for articulating the contingency of modernity. The short story cycle offers a powerful articulation of subjectivity and formal hybridity, which we miss if we only look at poetry or novels. Our ideas about the formation of identity that emerge from texts like *Leaves of Grass* or *Moby Dick* focus too narrowly on the creation of singular (albeit very complex) individuals such as Whitman's speaker, Ishmael, or Ahab. In contrast, the cycle advances the proliferation in points of view and temporalities as a way of multiplying potential models for American cultural identity. Characters like Mrs. Spring Fragrance, George Willard, Ike McCaslin, and Yolanda García depict the flux and range endemic to identity formation. The cycle merits a larger scholarly discourse, akin to that on the development of the novel. We just need more people to tell its story. What follows is my version.

Chapter 1

Locating the Short Story Cycle

> Suddenly I decided to go back to the *Winesburg* form. That is really a novel. It is a form in which I feel at ease. I invented it. It was mine. ('To Roger Sergel', in Anderson 1984: 220)

> I have even sometimes thought that the novel form does not fit an American writer, that it is a form which had been brought in. What I wanted is a new looseness; and in *Winesburg* I had made my own form. (Anderson 1942: 289)

In the summer of 1938, Sherwood Anderson began work on a new novel, but he was unhappy with the result. He decided to 'go back to the *Winesburg* form' (Anderson 1984: 220). According to him, when *Winesburg, Ohio* appeared in 1919, its form was wholly new – he had invented a new genre, named it for his volume, and claimed ownership. In his *Memoirs* (1942), Anderson links his formal innovation to an idea of US nationhood, which bolstered his sense that creating a national literature was paramount to the artistic projects of his time and circle; this sentiment repeats throughout his essays, memoirs, and letters. His reputation as a pioneer grew in proportion to his influence on other modernists, including most famously Ernest Hemingway, William Faulkner, Jean Toomer, and John Steinbeck. Anderson, seen so often as the arbiter of the genre, would chase the genre's magic for decades. His claims reveal the genre's power in capturing what seemed to be new experiences and ideas about storytelling.

Anderson's disparate statements on the volume's form – that it is and is not a novel – reveal a lack of language available to describe its seemingly unique position between novel and short story collection. The interplay between independent and interconnected tales generated new ways to tell stories, especially as authors increasingly concluded that 'Life is a loose, flowing thing. There are no plot stories in life' (Anderson 1942: 289). In *A Story Teller's Story* (1924), Anderson crystallises his intent: 'What was wanted I thought was form, not plot, an altogether more elusive and difficult thing to come at' (1989: 352). The lack of certainty about what to call this form and the sense of innovation remain with the cycle even today. Anderson's *Winesburg, Ohio* remains a touchstone, even standard-bearer, for the genre.

His claims to utter originality are, however, a bit false. Fiction had long exhibited an aversion to unity, clarity, and resolution and sought new ways to express fragmentation, confusion, and indecipherability. Anderson made innovations to the form, maximising its expressionist possibilities and engaging an appreciation for local places and quotidian events that would inspire Faulkner, Steinbeck, and the rest. Yet, *Winesburg* follows a long tradition of volumes that had exactly the kind of 'new looseness' Anderson claims for his own volume, including modernist works that directly preceded his own such as Gertrude Stein's *Three Lives* (1909) and Edgar Lee Masters's poetic cycle *Spoon River Anthology* (1915). The particular device of using a common setting for a series of prose tales, as in *Winesburg*, dates to at least the mid-nineteenth century in the United States and Europe. This chapter corrects the long-held assumption that the form began with modernist blockbusters and instead suggests that modernist writers revised a vibrant regionalist tradition to their own uses. I trace the development of the cycle from a regionalist tradition often marked by an attention to those living on the fringes of America. Scholars, due in part to a modernist investment in newness and in part because of the writers he influenced, have tended to take Anderson too much at his word. Instead, *Winesburg* cast modernity in terms of a mode of literary expression invested in both realism and the newest avant-garde practices, generating a watershed moment in an already dynamic genre.

The short story cycle's treatment of a particular place descends from nineteenth-century village sketchbooks – what Sandra Zagarell (1988) terms, in her seminal essay, 'narrative[s] of community'. Such volumes privilege a singular setting, emphasise localised language and practices, obfuscate linear/chronological development in favour of process, render the quotidian in episodic tales, and depict narrators who are 'participant/observers' (Zagarell 1988: 503). According to Zagarell, a 'Narrative of community thus represents a coherent response to the social, economic, cultural, and demographic changes caused by industrialism, urbanization, and the spread of capitalism' (1988: 499). Zagarell isolates the genre's core conventions in the works of Elizabeth Gaskell and Sarah Orne Jewett, among others. However, the volumes do not evince a wholly coherent, positive preindustrial ideal but instead are deeply entrenched in the alienation that accompanied urbanisation and industrialisation. Zagarell, too, reconsidered the wholly positive depiction of community she examined in her original essay to acknowledge the 'many-valenced' treatments of community. Almost twenty years after the publication of her original essay, Zagarell wrote of these communities that 'Some are sustaining, some destructive; all are contingent on the specific history, racial and ethnic circumstances, gender relations, sexual norms, and other factors which inform them' (2007: 434).

My own term for this organising principle, 'limited locality', reflects the cycles' ambivalence to the promises of community. Limited locality refers to the ways in which such texts depend upon the construction of a restricted geographic terrain to contain and ground the narratives. They are limited because they take as their focus a bounded geography and because the texts emphasise descriptions of particular, selected features of that geography. Short story cycles are not linked exclusively by setting. In *Winesburg*, for instance, recurring characters, a shared temporal setting, and the central figure of George Willard further integrate the stories. Yet, the story of the cycle in American literature begins with locality because the connections between regionalist and modernist concerns are especially explicit and pronounced in these cycles. The long history of cycles linked by locality reveals that preoccupations with the nation and nostalgia persist into modernism, as Anderson's comments intimate, and that experimentation with form as a response to modernity is present in the earliest cycles.

Mapping Genre, Guiding the Emigrant

From the earliest volumes centred on locality in the 1820s to the publication of *Winesburg* in 1919, the United States underwent a massive transformation in its very shape and scope. The regions depicted in these cycles were often actually new to the nation's geography, and the localities they depicted were distanced from metropolitan centres. As Paul Giles shows, states such as Nebraska, the Dakotas, and California entered the union during this period; geography became a compulsory course in school; and the United States began to be referred to as a singular rather than a plural noun (2007: 41–4). Under these conditions, the literature of this period 'tends not only to be saturated in locality but also to understand that locality as a guarantee of its own authenticity and its patriotic allegiance' (Giles 2007: 45). The ubiquity of limited localities indicates the extent to which these narratives particularise and integrate these places.

From the genre's earliest phases, writers and reviewers alike questioned whether the diversity of the United States could be expressed in the novel, and Anderson's comments suggest that this notion persisted among modernists. Book reviews and popular essays of the nineteenth century often debated the suitability of the novel to the United States. As a tastemaker, William Dean Howells's comments are illustrative: 'In most American novels, vivid and graphic as the best of them are, the people are segregated if not sequestered, and the scene is sparsely populated ... we excel in small pieces with three or four figures, or in studies of rustic communities, where there is propinquity if not society' (1910: 253). He continues: 'I am not sure that the Americans have not brought the short story nearer perfection in the all-round sense than almost any other people' (Howells 1910: 254). He attributes this refinement to a national temperament of 'hurry and impatience' and a robust magazine industry (Howells 1910: 254). The modern short story cycle emerged from the rise of the short story in magazines and a simultaneous demand for longer books. The sketchbook – and later the cycle – allowed for the diversity and refinement of the short story and the ambition of the novel.

Published in 1839, Caroline Kirkland's *A New Home – Who'll Follow? or Glimpses of Western Life* exemplifies the extent to which formal concerns intersect with anxieties of national and local integration in early volumes. In 1837, the same year that Michigan attained statehood, Kirkland and her husband acquired eight hundred acres in Michigan and set out to establish a village. The village, Pinckney, became the basis for the fictional town of Montacute in *A New Home*. This volume, composed of sketches and descriptive vignettes, introduced readers to the rigours and challenges of frontier life in the partially settled region. In the preface, Kirkland announces that her original impulse was to adhere to life but that fiction intervened:

> I claim for these straggling and cloudy crayon-sketches of life and manners in the remoter parts of Michigan, the merit of general truth of outline. Beyond this I venture not to aspire. I felt somewhat tempted to set forth my little book as being entirely, what it is very

nearly – a veritable history; an unimpeachable transcript of reality; a rough picture, in detached parts, but pentagraphed from the life; a sort of 'Emigrant's Guide:'. . . But conscience prevailed, and I must honestly confess, that there be glosses, and colourings, and lights, if not shadows, for which the author is alone accountable. (Kirkland 1990: 1)

Kirkland maintains that the book approximates a 'veritable history', indicating the extent to which she intends for A New Home to be read as a guidebook to the would-be traveller. That most of her readers would never venture to Michigan is irrelevant, because the book, as the preface makes explicit, strives to introduce this place to the national imagination. Thus, she needs to impress upon her readers the veracity of her descriptions.

A New Home subscribes to the belief that sustained geographic proximity fosters a sense of positive communal affiliation. In 1887, Ferdinand Tönnies gave a name to this nineteenth-century vision of organic and authentic community, *gemeinschaft*, which opposed artificial, industrial affiliation, *gesellschaft*. Characterised by 'locality, which is based on a common habit', the logic of *gemeinschaft* maintains that 'The proximity of dwellings, the communal fields, and even the mere contiguity of holdings necessitate many contacts of human beings and cause inurement to and intimate knowledge of one another' (Tönnies 1957: 42–3). Tönnies theorised that shared land and interests generated genuine communal commitment. A New Home narrates the process by which this unsettled land becomes a community and, by extension, part of the nation. In Kirkland's Montacute 'something new is born, a pluralistic, polyphonic culture that honors the original viewpoints and practices of each constituent group and may well represent the future of America itself' (Zagarell 1990: xxix). A New Home models an inclusive vision of the nation, made up of such communities; this model embraces the wanderlust of moving West while maintaining an elegiac mood for a disappearing landscape. Kirkland describes the dangers of traversing 'Michigan mud-holes' and the beauties of the forest's 'gosling-green suit of half-opened leaves' (1990: 5). Descriptions of such geographical features render these unfamiliar places legible. Thus, these texts function not only to depict the uniqueness of place, as Kirkland suggests in her preface, but also to help constitute the nation's image of itself through descriptions of the land's physical features.

The circumstances surrounding the Kirklands' founding of Pinckney and the composition of *A New Home* indicate that her volume is meant to be an attempt at a national form. In the first sketch, Kirkland describes 'the remote and lonely regions' as being 'beyond measure delicious to one "long in populous cities pent"' (1990: 5). Quoting Milton, Kirkland attempts to persuade her reader that the Michigan landscape is worthy of the great English poets. She charges that 'We must have a poet of our own' and speculates that Shelley, Charles Lamb, or Bulwer might be up to the task (Kirkland 1990: 6). These descriptions of the landscape and the call-to-pens essentially amount to a defence of this new territory's incorporation. Instead of poetry, though, the national form is, for Kirkland, the sketch volume. Kirkland acknowledges that her work is indebted to Mary Russell Mitford, whose chronicles of life in a small English hamlet, *Our Village*, 'suggested the form of my rude attempt' (1990: 2). This self-effacement reveals not just the popularity of an international sketch tradition but also the extent to which this American author saw herself in conversation with it. For Kirkland, this reliance on an English model did not detract from the American-ness of her own volume. *A New Home* is extraordinary in its explicit announcement of itself as an 'Emigrant's Guide' and in the conditions of its production. The volume portends the fascination with community and nation that dominates nineteenth- and twentieth-century short story cycles. It also dramatises the extent to which nation is defined by both regional ties and transnational exchanges. Her allusions to quaintness and the tone of sentimental retrospection initiate a mode of nostalgia that celebrates the particularity of a place. A number of early cycles embrace nostalgia and substantiate their seriousness through claims of realism in the manner of Kirkland's, including Augustus Baldwin Longstreet's *Georgia Scenes* (1835) and Eliza Buckminster Lee's *Sketches of a New England Village, in the Last Century* (1838). These early volumes centre on integrating distant, often cloistered, locales into the national imagination at a time when the very shape of the nation was changing radically, moving West and reshaping commerce and life in the East.

All of these volumes followed in the wake of Washington Irving's enormously popular *The Sketch Book of Geoffrey Crayon, Gent.* (1820), which initiated the unifying figure and the significance of travel, heralding the construction of nation in relation to international traditions. In a preface to the American edition, Irving cautions readers that his book lacked pretensions to 'finished composition', explaining instead that the sketches 'partake of his own thoughts and feelings; sometimes treating of scenes before him, sometimes of other purely imaginary, sometimes wandering back with recollections to his native country' (1930: xvii). Part deprecation and part instruction, this preface is typical of authorial introductions of the nineteenth century. Most significantly for the history of the cycle, it frames the subsequent stories as flexible and connected but not always easily unified. Mary Weatherspoon Bowden's study of Irving goes so far as to claim he is not 'a short-story writer but a composer of books: thus, a story in one of his books is more than that story alone, for it gains meaning from what came before and gives meaning to what will follow' (1981: 9). Kennedy shows how Irving's volumes 'were atypical of later short story collections, since from the outset he anticipated book publication and crafted his narratives for homogenous effects' (1988: 10) unlike later volumes by Balzac, Hawthorne, and Turgenev, who wrote tales individually for magazines before collecting them. Linked by the personality and charm of its ostensible author, Irving's book assembles story, essay, tragedy, and satire into one volume of stories that can be read singly (as stories such as 'Rip Van Winkle' and 'The Legend of Sleepy Hollow' routinely are) but mean more when taken together, especially as they provide a view of place.

For American readers, Irving offers glimpses into English rural life; for British readers (Irving's book was one of the first American bestsellers in England), Irving constructs New England legends, often through the recurring figure Diedrich Knickerbocker. In the essay 'English Writers on America', he even tries to broker a literary ceasefire between English and American writers by calling for a transnational exchange of literature that would seek artistic worth over national origin. Originally published serially in seven parts, it was later put forth as a book. In this, *The Sketch Book* aligns with contemporary publishing practices, as selected stories or even whole books are published in magazines before being arranged and edited into a cycle. Irving continued to work in the genre in *Bracebridge Hall* (1822) and *Tales of a Traveller* (1824).

Romanticism and Realism at the Crossroads of Genre

Although Irving's volume has more generic diversity and less cohesiveness than an archetypal short story cycle, it paved the way for the modern American short story cycle, which emerged from two, overlapping, strands of nineteenth-century fiction: the metaphysical and moral quandaries that animate American romanticism and the fascination with the quotidian and local that ground regionalist sketches. Nathaniel Hawthorne's and Herman Melville's short story collections, produced in the context of and embracing American romanticism, reveal thematic and artistic continuity that influenced the rise of the short story cycle. Hawthorne is a particularly fascinating case in the history of the short story cycle. By 1834, Hawthorne had conceived of and written three short story cycles that were never published in the connected form he intended: *Seven Tales of My Native Land*, *Provincial Tales*, and *The Story Teller*. Remnants of these early cycles would be published in *The Token*, a gift periodical, and later included in *Twice-Told Tales* (1837), but publishers were averse to releasing them as single, connected volumes. Hawthorne knew that linked tales would demand greater literary and public respect than a collection or discrete tales.[1] Anxieties about literary influence and longevity in relation to form recur in Hawthorne's *Mosses from an Old Manse* (1846).

In the opening story, 'The Old Manse', the narrator hopes that his time in the house, based on the home in Concord, Massachusetts where Hawthorne lived for the first three years of his marriage, would lead him away from 'idle stories' and toward 'a novel that should evolve some deep lesson and should possess physical substance to stand alone' (Hawthorne 2003: 4). The opening is replete with moments that apologise for having produced only stories, yet the biographically inflected frame tale also establishes that the stories, taken together, provide the 'deep lesson' and 'substance' of a novel. Hawthorne theorises this as he discusses the American Indian artefacts that await discovery on the property: 'Their great charm consists in their rudeness and in the individuality of each article, so different from the productions of civilized machinery, which shapes everything on one pattern' (9). Here he comments on how the idiosyncratic loveliness of an artefact or a story offers a reprieve from the monotony of industrial production; this is rather ironic given that the story flourishes because the factory and railroad made possible the production and transportation of the very magazines and newspapers that would print such tales. Hawthorne blends romanticist ideas about spontaneity and reflection – after all, the opening story reads like a spontaneous walk through the grounds, even as it is retrospective – with the emerging conditions of the industrial age. Indeed, Hawthorne celebrates the 'newspaper scribblers and almanac makers' who 'throw off in the effervescence of a moment' (16) art more real and true than the many generations of parsons who occupied the house before him.

Hawthorne and Melville, in *The Piazza Tales* (1856), both begin their volumes with frame narratives set in antiquated houses that are being made new by the writers, who serve as narrators. Hawthorne's tale follows the author-narrator rambling through the estate, considering the ways in which the collective past shapes his present. His rambling suggests a way of reading the subsequent stories. Melville's opening tale, likewise, describes the author-narrator's home as he recounts adding a piazza to a seventy-year-old structure to capture the sunlight and views in the Hoosac Mountains of Massachusetts. 'The Piazza' offers a new vantage to look at Melville's past work – just as the piazza in the story reframes the old farmhouse and invites fresh views of its environs. In both collections, all of the stories, save these opening tales, had been previously published. These original framing pieces, which locate the composition of the subsequent stories in a place and time, announce an authorial vision of connection for the volumes.

Hawthorne and Melville envisioned their works having thematic and textual continuity, if not unity. Even as he apologises for not producing the novel or philosophical treatise he had hoped, Hawthorne explains that 'With these idle weeds and withering blossoms, I have intermixed some that were produced long ago – old, faded things, reminding me of flowers pressed between the leaves of a book – and now offer the bouquet' (2003: 26). Like a bouquet, these tales are beautiful singly but even more lovely when they play off each other. Both collections draw on the interplay of extended, allegorical stories that meditate on the often sinister aspects of humanity and the relief of lighter, humorous sketches. Moreover, the volumes include 'Smaller clusters of three of more stories' (Kennedy 1988: 16) that are more highly integrated than the volume as a whole. In Hawthorne's volume, a sequence of stories including 'Legends of the Province House', 'Howe's Masquerade', 'Edward Randolph's Portrait', 'Lady Eleanor's Mantle', and 'Old Esther Dudley' all 'variously sugges[t] the legacy of that grim architectural emblem of royal government' (Kennedy 1988: 16). In Melville's volume, the ten sketches that comprise 'The Encantadas' produce a similar sequence within a cycle. In doing so, Hawthorne and Melville set a precedent for cycles within collections that many contemporary writers continue, including John Updike, Amy Bloom,

Junot Díaz, and Jhumpa Lahiri, whose *Unaccustomed Earth* (2008) takes its title and epigraph from Hawthorne.

The stories in Melville's and Hawthorne's volumes gain further coherence as they examine the relationship between nature and the domestic, announced in their travels through their estates in 'The Piazza' and 'The Old Manse'. That each author-narrator haunts a place that inspired so much writing anticipates stories that depict characters who are haunted by the tensions between nature and art, reality and the imagination, perception and knowledge – recurring themes that link the stories (Lordi 2006: 324). Melville's opening is especially concerned with issues of perspective; as a fictionalised authorial figure recounts a visit to his only visible neighbour, he meditates on how one's life looks from another's perspective. His house, a relatively modest farmhouse, looks like a palace through the 'mirage haze' (Melville 2006: 108) of the intervening mountain space. His neighbour sees it as the home of 'a happy being'; the narrator, knowing that his home is not the place of idyllic joy his neighbour imagines, simply confesses that 'well could I wish that I were that happy one of the happy house you dream you see' (112). Melville concludes with this moment of wistfulness undercut by reality, which is a central tension in the regionalist writing that emerges in the mid- to late nineteenth century.

Regionalism – evident in Hawthorne's and Melville's opening stories' emphases on locality and Irving's twin treatments of rural English life and New England – was the popular mode of much short fiction in the nineteenth century before and after romanticism. Hawthorne and Melville blend a regionalist fascination with place and romanticist concerns with creativity, the natural world, and the individual. The cycle is an especially rich mode for depicting the local, quotidian practices in the expanding nation before and after the Civil War. Later cycles of the nineteenth century, such as Hamlin Garland's *Main-Travelled Roads* (1891), Sarah Orne Jewett's *The Country of the Pointed Firs* (1896), Mary E. Wilkins Freeman's *The People of Our Neighborhood* (1898), Zona Gale's *Friendship Village* (1908), and Sui Sin Far's *Mrs. Spring Fragrance* (1912), reflect a desire to unify the nation in the wake of the Civil War by appealing to a sense of lost rural traditions and incorporating new populations into the nation. These complicated cycles are not mere nostalgia; rather, they capture a place's response, often ambivalent, to modernity. The loose form of the cycle allows the authors to depict multiple responses to the forces changing these communities, rather than articulating a singular, conclusive statement.

Critical Nostalgia at the Turn of the Century

Early volumes explicitly announce – but implicitly trouble – a belief that geographically based community presents an antidote to the poisons of industrialisation and modernisation. Claims of verisimilitude in prefatory materials distinguish the earliest stages of the cycle, spanning from the mid- to late nineteenth century, whereas a greater emphasis on fiction and invention mark cycles published in the last decade of the nineteenth and first decade of the twentieth centuries. The emphasis remains on portraying a particular place, such as Dunnet Landing in Jewett's cycle, the small New England town of Freeman's volume, and the titular Wisconsin town of Gale's book. Though more explicitly fictionalised and increasingly fragmented, later cycles maintain some sense of Kirkland's 'Emigrant's Guide'. Even as they continue to treat place-based community, later cycles move increasingly toward disjunction, both in terms of their representation of communal affiliation and in their formal construction. Earlier cycles celebrate the possibility of *gemeinschaft*, but turn-of-the-century short story cycles increasingly treat geographically based community not as an armistice to the conflicting forces of modernity but rather as another battle site. Nostalgia becomes a weapon in that battle.

The language of nostalgia serves two purposes. First, it establishes a narrative mode that reacts to the very conditions of modernity, which 'involves a powerful vortex of historical conditions that coalesce to produce sharp ruptures from the past' (Friedman 2006: 433). Susan Stanford Friedman claims this rapid change produces 'a gamut of sensations from displacement, despair, and nostalgia to exhilaration, hope, and embrace of the new' (2006: 434). The second purpose of nostalgia is to advance locality as simultaneously the site of, cause of, and solution for the ruptures that accompany modernity. Late nineteenth-century cycles deploy a self-conscious sentimentality, or what I call 'critical nostalgia', to signal and respond to the issues of nation and formal experimentation that pervade the genre. Critical nostalgia refers to the creation of a wistful simplification that is undercut within the stories themselves. Cycles linked by limited locality deploy nostalgia as a sincere mode of expression, an evocation in defence of a certain locality, or a mode of expression ripe for satire and subversion. Often, and increasingly by the turn of the twentieth century, they engage these different uses of nostalgia simultaneously.

The nostalgic celebration of bygone, frontier, or unknown localities replaces the earlier cycles' emphasis on introduction and incorporation. Produced in the context of 'postwar reunion' following the Civil War, volumes by Jewett, Freeman, and Gale were apt vehicles for transporting a nostalgic sense of national cohesion because their settings gave 'the appearance that local communities were disengaged from national politics' (Joseph 2007: 11). Svetlana Boym uncovers nostalgia's historical basis as a medical ailment, largely among soldiers fighting far from home in Europe in the seventeenth century. In the US, nostalgia did not appear until the Civil War. Boym traces how nostalgia, once invaliding soldiers and inspiring poets, came to dominate how nations imagined themselves into being (2001: 14). She argues that 'Nostalgia itself has a utopian dimension, only it is no longer directed toward the future. Sometimes nostalgia is not directed toward the past either, but rather sideways' (Boym 2001: xiv). Given the frequency with which authors engage nostalgia in not-so-distant pasts (often, these cycles are set just a decade before their publication), the cycle's recursive form and engagement with critical nostalgia articulates the fragmentation and contradictions of this moment of making modernity.

A thwarted desire for places untouched by national turmoil permeates these story cycles, as is the case with Stephen Crane's *Whilomville Stories*, which were published serially in *Harper's* in 1899 and posthumously as a book in 1901. The title draws on the term 'whilom', meaning 'some time before or ago', evoking the nostalgic sense of place that resonates in the stories (Brown and Hernlund 1978: 116–17). Turn-of-the-century cycles capture the feeling of places rapidly being lost to industrialisation, although their ability to circulate in multiple forms to large audiences was only possible because of that same industrialisation. As noted, such regionalist writing arose, in part, from the proliferation of magazines and the economic opportunities they presented. The serialisation of stories often suggests the economic conditions under which many were produced. The publication of the Whilomville tales, for instance, helped to alleviate Crane's financial crisis and medical expenses. Similarly, following her parents' deaths, Freeman's stories appeared in *Harper's* and initiated her financial autonomy. The stories in *The People of Our Neighborhood* first appeared in *The Ladies' Home Journal* between December of 1895 and December of 1897. That these stories appeared in magazines before being collected into cycles indicates the autonomy of their individual tales as well as the material advantages of cycles and collections drawn from previously published pieces. While these cycles maintain what Raymond Williams calls the 'fly-in-amber quality' of regionalism, they do so in highly self-conscious ways (1982: 61).

Such cycles maintain the connection between locality and community but increasingly expose the isolation of the individual. For instance, in *The Country of the Pointed Firs*, Dunnet Landing functions as a dual metaphor for loneliness and community, which are posited as two responses to the impending changes facing the cloistered locale. The specific geography of the place correlates to the lives of the town's citizens; the citizens of Dunnet Landing are 'human analogues to the pointed firs, possessing the will to flourish with the incoming tide and the strength to stand tall at its ebb' (Dunn and Morris 1995: 39). Much like Kirkland's emphasis on mud-holes, Jewett's emphasis on specific features of the landscape introduces that distanced locale into the national imagination. Jewett's cycle opens with an introduction of the place:

> These houses made the most of their seaward view . . . the small-paned high windows in the peaks of their steep gables were like knowing eyes that watched the harbor and the far sea-line beyond, or looked northward all along the shore and its background of spruces and balsam firs. When one really knows a village like this and its surroundings, it is like becoming acquainted with a single person. (Jewett 2000: 3)

The personification of the houses suggests the community's solidarity and perceptiveness. The specific geographical feature of the firs resonates with the tenacity of the people. The sea, in its strength and brutality, symbolises change. Dunnet Landing suggests how persistently, if not universally, cycles represent localities as outposts, distanced from other places or marginalised by economic conditions. The final statement – that the town resembles a singular person – establishes a tension between the individual and the community that the narrator's position over the course of the stories dramatises.

The friendship between the narrator and Mrs. Todd, the interconnections and affinities amongst the townspeople, and the general affection the narrator feels toward the place and its people make Dunnet Landing seem like a communal paradise. As they relate the journey to and the events of the yearly Bowden family reunion, the highly integrated stories 'The Great Expedition', 'A Country Road', 'The Bowden Reunion', and 'The Feast's End' depict what appears to be an idyllic rural community. According to Frances M. Zauhar, Jewett's volume minimises the 'independence and rugged individualism' of much American fiction and instead celebrates 'domesticity and friendship', which are constituted not by courtship and marriage, hallmarks of the domestic novel, but by 'a vision of mature friendship and mutually recognized affiliation' (2007: 412). In Jewett's volume, the trope of the tourist or emigrant narrator remains. She initially acts like the narrator of Irving's *The Sketch Book*, but the narrator in *Country* demonstrates that the tourist must become a member of the community and not merely flit outside its edges (Zauhar 2007: 414–15). As they leave the reunion, the narrator 'came near to feeling like a true Bowden, and parted from certain new friends as if they were old friends; we were rich with the treasure of new remembrance' (Jewett 2000: 117). The narrator's position at the end of the book appears to be a complete and total immersion into the community. The narrator celebrates her intimacy with the place and its inhabitants, especially sharing asides with Mrs. Todd that shape and confirm their friendship.

While Mrs. Todd's personal disclosures about the members and practices of the clan have been read largely in terms of her affinity for the narrator, the content of these disclosures often suggests the isolation omnipresent in Dunnet Landing. Thus, Jewett depicts a limited locality that offers only a provisional community to the narrator and denies community to some of its own members. The narrator spends a long section of the reunion describing the procession of Bowdens as they make their way to the site of the picnic. Led and organised by Santin Bowden, a man bent on military service but denied the opportunity, Mrs. Todd and Mrs. Caplin discuss the nature of Santin's proclivity for war, alcohol, and 'poor gloomy spells' (109). Mrs. Todd compares Santin's particularity to a certain 'sprig of laurel' (110) that will not bloom despite a welcoming landscape. She says of the laurel, "Tis a real Sant Bowden, out of its own place' (110). The narrator adores Mrs. Todd's botanical metaphors, which draw on her trade and familiarity with place, but Mrs. Caplin just 'looked bewildered and blank' (110) before moving on to more gossip about his odd ways. She does not understand the connection between the laurel sprig and Santin. This small moment highlights the lack of understanding available to Santin and between the women.

As much as the narrator enjoys Mrs. Todd's stories, there are hints that Mrs. Todd can be domineering and dismissive. During the procession, the narrator remains almost entirely silent, taking in the scene and enjoying the insights offered. When the topic of Captain Littlepage comes up – a person with whom the narrator has enjoyed some moments of disclosure and discourse – she writes, '"The stories are very interesting," I ventured to say' (111). The generality of the statement and the choice of 'ventured', as if she is testing the waters, suggest that Mrs. Todd is not exactly open to input. Indeed, Mrs. Todd immediately shuts her down, offering her take on Captain Littlepage's stories. The narrator characterises Mrs. Todd as knowledgeable, generous, and affectionate, but the stories reveal that those qualities are balanced by her often harsh judgement, railroading of others, and commitment to disingenuous conventions. Of a distant relative, she says, '"I hate her just the same as I always did; but she's got on a real pretty dress. I do try to remember that she's Nathan's cousin"' (112). Throughout the day, she isolates certain individuals for her disapproval, and her joy from the day comes as much from pointing to others' flaws as from seeing beloved friends and the old folks.

The recurrence of such moments and the narrator's final statements on Mrs. Todd's changed demeanour reveal that Dunnet Landing is not, after all, a communal paradise:

> As the feast went on, the spirits of my companion steadily rose. The excitement of an unexpectedly great occasion was a subtle stimulant to her disposition, and I could see that sometimes when Mrs. Todd had seemed limited and heavily domestic, she had simply grown sluggish for lack of proper surroundings . . . More than one face among the Bowdens showed that only opportunity and stimulus were lacking, – a narrow set of circumstances caged a fine able character and held it captive. (Jewett 2000: 113–14)

The narrator recognises that the place itself makes full, sustained communal feeling impossible. The annual Bowden reunion offers a regular but infrequent opportunity for the citizens of Dunnet Landing to be fully engaged with each other. The narrator hears 'the words "next summer" repeated many times, though summer was still ours and the leaves were green' (116). That they look forward to next year even in the midst of the reunion suggests that such occasions are the exception rather than the rule. Their nostalgia, which Boym would call 'sideways', for the event and its people while it is still happening reveals that nostalgia can be deeply ambivalent. To say that Dunnet Landing represents a coherent, positive community prior to industrialisation and urbanisation captures only a part of the place Jewett maps.

Jewett's cycle depicts how nostalgia often embraces a false simplification and sentimentalism that the content of the stories contradicts. For instance, Hsuan L. Hsu shows that *The Country of the Pointed Firs* sets forth a 'theme of prior cosmopolitanism' in that the narrator 'seek[s] a quiet retreat from urban life' but 'Ironically, the local colorist's nostalgia for a "prelapsarian" and homogenous region that "excludes historical change" leads her to discover the sea captain's own nostalgia for a historically prior period of cosmopolitan mobility' (2005: 39–40). In her conversation with the sea captain, the narrator learns that Dunnet Landing was once more highly interconnected to international trade networks than it is at the time of her visit. The Captain's nostalgia centres on the halcyon days of wide and frequent travel. Jewett's inclusion of the tale pokes holes in the narrator's (and often, the readers') desire to imagine Dunnet Landing as a quaint, isolated place only now being introduced to large-scale economic practices. Dunnet Landing is emblematic of localities that are represented as secluded outposts, distanced from other places or marginalised by economic conditions, but nonetheless entrenched in national and international networks. As this example from Jewett's cycle suggests, a brand of critical nostalgia saturates the cycles' treatment of the eponymous settings. Jewett's cycle makes especially clear how late nineteenth-century cycles borrow from the conventions of earlier cycles, such as romantic renderings of the geographical features and the use of tourist narrators; however, they also initiate the irony, scepticism, and disjunction that figure largely in *Winesburg* and later modernist texts.

Stunted Growth, Fractured Form

The extent to which *Winesburg* departs from the earlier cycles is evident in its opening. Whereas nearly all of the earlier cycles begin with a description of the place, *Winesburg* begins with a character sketch of one the 'grotesques' that populate the town. The man's hermetic life initiates the alienation and disjunction that the stories explore. Anderson's cycle, set in the 1890s, evokes a sense that the railroad and World War I radically changed the small town. However, the elegiac tone is undercut by the recurring depictions of characters whose lives are marked by those qualities, such as alienation, dislocation, and frustrated expression, usually associated with modernism. Critical nostalgia allows the texts to have it both ways: they appeal to the sentiment that things were better once while also showing that they are always the same. Critical nostalgia recurs in Anderson's focus on George Willard, the notion of progress, and the place itself.

The townspeople of Winesburg transfer onto George a romantic sense of youth, possibility, and lost opportunities. For example, his former schoolteacher fixates on his potential: 'Kate Swift's mind was ablaze with thoughts of George Willard. In something he had written as a school boy she thought she had recognized the spark of genius and wanted to blow on the spark' (Anderson 1999: 131). Kate is far from alone in this regard; his neighbours, parents, and peers all assign a kind of specialness to him that is tinged with nostalgia for their own misspent potential. The depiction of George in *Winesburg* suggests that communities rely on representative individuals for validation. To the extent that the development of George Willard creates an overarching thread, this cycle is akin to the *bildungsroman* or, more particularly, the *künstlerroman*. According to Franco Moretti, the development of the *bildungsroman* arose from a need for a symbol of modernity; the practitioners of the genre and their readers made youth that symbol and 'mobility' and 'interiority' its hallmark traits (1987: 3). Youth thereby renders modernity meaningful. *Winesburg* aligns with this tendency: faced with the mutability of modernity, these outposts, perceived as outdated or marginal, rely on George's growth to give meaning and stability to social conditions. However, in its emphasis on youth, *Winesburg* represents a significant departure from the earlier cycles, which focus largely, although not exclusively, on older travellers. Although George is a native of the town, his sensibilities and position as a newspaper reporter allow him to maintain the distance that Kirkland's and Jewett's emigrant narrators enjoy. The narrators' positions as participants/observers portend modernism's tendency to privilege an insider/outsider narrative voice.

Although George figures as a central organising figure in *Winesburg*, the cycle complicates his primacy through the emphasis on surrogate characters. The stories obscure the distinction between major and minor characters by having the latter function as protagonists in individual stories. For instance, Helen White, Enoch Robinson, and Seth Richmond are the protagonists of their own stories, and they often explicitly comment on why George has been singled out over them. While George appears to be a powerful unifying force, Anderson displaces some of his centrality onto the populace, questioning the possibility for textual and symbolic unity through an individual. The stories critique the aggrandisement of a single individual and challenge the overt nostalgia often aligned with George. The sheer multiplicity of such alternatives intimates that this glorification is often arbitrary and violently minimises the potential of other promising figures, many of whom are artists (for instance, Enoch paints). Making George carry the burden of the localities' dreams parallels the burden of making him the centre of the story; the cycle suggests the caprice inherent in both. While *Winesburg* ultimately devotes more textual attention to George's acts of writing, it nonetheless shows the tenacity and choices made by those that stay and continue, often writing or painting for no audience. One effect of making minor characters the equal of the protagonist is to offer multiple answers to the simultaneous yet contradictory impulses of a modern, industrialised, and capitalistic society: a glorification of the autonomy of self and the romanticising of communal obligation and spirit.

Winesburg modifies the conventions of the *bildungsroman* by implying maturity rather than depicting it. In Anderson's cycle, the exact nature of George's maturity remains vague. Unlike the traditional *bildungsroman*, marriage does not represent a viable solution for demonstrating a commitment to social responsibility. The stories introduce and reject many suitors for George, including Helen White, Kate Swift, and Louise Trunnion; that the stories cast off so many options shows the inadequacy of this resolution. Rather than marking maturity and social commitment through an event, this cycle leads the reader to infer that maturity has taken place outside of the stories from the moments where the narrative voice most resembles George's retrospection. This extra-textual maturation represents a substantial 'gap' within the stories and solidifies that 'Important events occur off-stage' (Kelley 2000: 298). Major events often occur through implication; the specifics remain ambiguous despite their ramifications being felt in the stories.

For example, in 'Nobody Knows', an asterisk marks the major event in the story, sex between George and Louise Trunnion, about whom George has heard 'whispered tales' (Anderson 1999: 40). As he longs 'to talk to some man', the unstated events help establish George's attitudes toward women, sex, respectability, and even communication (41). While George takes heart in the fact that 'Nobody knows' (41) of his tryst, the phrase acquires ironic meaning. The mention of gossip and 'whispered tales' implies that, of course, people will know, as they already seemed to have known about Louise's past; the story depicts the power and ubiquity of gossip, the evidence for which is the fact that George listens to such hearsay. In this scene and throughout, the cycle portrays the pitfalls of conjecture. George's misreading of this and other situations registers the impossibility of omniscience, even for a character granted special access to the lives around him.

Disjunction is central even to the explicitly paired stories 'The Strength of God' and 'The Teacher', which focus on neighbours Curtis Hartman and Kate Swift, respectively. The characters' stories take place feet apart on the same night and are sequenced together in the text. The extent to which they overlap appears to be proof of affiliation in *Winesburg*; however, disruption exists even in this highly integrated pair of stories. The characters remain oblivious to the others' struggles and desires, and the very division of the tale into two stories 'signals an important separation of consciousness' to the extent that 'Between them there is no compassion, no communication, no sense of community' (Kennedy 1995: 199). In these stories, connection is available exclusively – and only to a limited degree – to George.

However, hubris undercuts even George's affiliation. As Kate Swift sets out on an 'unpremeditated walk', the narrator reflects, 'It was as though the man and the boy, by thinking of her, had driven her forth into the wintry streets' (Anderson 1999: 128). Of this moment, Mark Whalan argues that 'the fantasy of being able to write one's own life story, and write other people in and out of it at will, is momentarily indulged in during a moment where the imperative of wish fulfilment seems to override the literary codes of realism' (2007: 54). This moment signals Anderson's move away from sheer realism into an examination of interiority usually associated with modernism. George's fantasy – that he wills Kate from her house by the force of his imagination – ironically mirrors how Kate and others write stories onto George.

Its experimentation with what remains unspoken between characters distinguishes *Winesburg* from earlier cycles, establishing an increased emphasis on alienation and disjunction. For instance, the stories are replete with moments and relationships that lack connection. Scenes of failed communication and missed moments together create a composite view of life in the town, but the stories themselves lack such comparisons and cross-references. For example, 'Mother', 'Paper Pills', and 'Death' constitute a divided trilogy, depicting the trajectory of Elizabeth Willard's life. Given this composite view, pride and regret, intimated in the earlier stories, eventually lead Elizabeth to remain silent with her son in the final scene of 'Death', causing her money, kept secret from her husband and her son, to remain buried in the house after her death. This burial comports with Elizabeth's many buried desires and with the cycle's treatment of a generalised inability to communicate. For instance, George tells his mother, 'I suppose I can't make you understand, but, oh, I wish I could' (Anderson 1999: 30). Touched by her son's attempt at disclosure, Elizabeth 'wanted to cry out with joy because of the words that had come from the lips of her son, but the expression of joy had become impossible to her' (30). Anderson depicts the almost, but never fully, realised use of language in his emphasis on the characters 'wishing' and 'crying' but never actually 'saying'. The cycle's use of passive voice and muted verbs reflects the impossibility of communication between the characters and their lack of agency. The image of words on the verge of spilling out recurs in the book, and each occurrence layers onto previous moments of buried expression constituting a cyclicality of words unspoken. Treated as discrete moments, these admissions would seem simply anomalous personal inadequacies; in their repetition, *Winesburg* constructs a metanarrative about the very problems of narration.

The autonomy of the individual stories in the Elizabeth Willard sequence and their separation within the text contributes to the disjunctive quality of the cycle. In a letter dated 15 January 1917, Anderson indicated to Waldo Frank his intentions about the placement of the Elizabeth Willard stories: 'The other story concerning the death of George Willard's mother should not, I believe, be published too closely on the heels of the first story about her' (Anderson 1917). While 'Death' is separate, closed, and autonomous as a single story, alongside 'Mother' and 'Paper Pills' it is integrated, opened, and interconnected. The genre 'is an open work consisting of closed stories. Having finished one of the stories, the reader's sense is often one of closure; having read the whole composite, his or her final impression is one of openness' (Lundén 1999: 60). On a larger level, the trilogy of stories set Elizabeth's experience alongside so many others in the town, and her individual experience resonates with previous stories. For instance, Elizabeth's death comports with a revelation had by another character, in a story in which Elizabeth does not appear. Despite a deep desire to be loved, Alice Hindman, a clerk in the Dry Goods Store, realises at the end of 'Adventure' that she and 'many people must live and die alone, even in Winesburg' (Anderson 1999: 92). Elizabeth's death fulfils this revelation. Despite these parallel moments and insights, the stories do not indicate that the characters share – or, are aware of – their common experiences.

The fissures and gaps between the stories suggest that cycles, ostensibly united by community, often rewrite the very notion of the term itself. As early as April 1918, Anderson was calling his stories *Winesburg*, to reinforce their interconnections (Curry 1980: 239). Anderson's depiction of Winesburg's geography is, however, ambiguous, reinforcing the stories' scepticism about the town generating a sense of *gemeinschaft* and complicating any unity that may be found in place alone. Specific locations, such as Winney's Dry Goods Store, recur but are not universally or consistently featured. The stories list street names, but their proximity to one another remains unclear. In the case of Winesburg, 'Anderson's Ohio village remains indistinct. In fact, the town map included in the 1960 edition of *Winesburg* reveals that only eight specific locations are identified' (Dunn and Morris 1995: 53). The illusion of the map suggests a desire to stabilise and read place. The illustrators completed the landscape with anonymous houses, churches, storefronts, and streets, mitigating the appearance of the cycle's intentional ambiguity. The uncertainty of the geographical markers within Winesburg is so extreme that 'one is never able to visualize the town's geography' despite the mapmaker's attempt to stabilise the town's dimensions (Mann 1989: 52). The resistance to easily recognisable, legible mapping reflects a concern with disrupting any sense of geographically based *gemeinschaft*. The geography of the place remains important in modernism – in the vein of Kirkland's desire to describe 'mud-holes' – but the emphasis shifts to a more deliberately tenuous sense of locality.

Locating Modernism in Place

Anderson saw *Winesburg* as wholly new, wholly modern, but his comments on *Winesburg*'s unity and inspiration often contradicted each other. For instance, he claimed on different occasions that the cycle was inspired by his hometown of Clyde and his tenement in Chicago. In a letter to Frank of November 1916, Anderson wrote, 'I made last year a series of intensive studies of people of my home town, Clyde, Ohio. In the book I called the town Winesburg, Ohio' (1984: 4). Some twenty years later, he would write that 'Winesburg was of course no particular town. It was a mythical town. It was people. I had got the characters of the book everywhere about me, in towns in which I have lived, in the army, in factories and offices' (Anderson 1942: 295). The place of inspiration matters in so much as it helps trouble a narrative of an exclusively urban modernism. His comments indicate the richly interconnected forces of the small town and city on modernist production, which the cycle so powerfully dramatises. As seen in the epigraph to this chapter, he would claim it as a novel and as distinctly not a novel.

Partly, problems of memory and typical modernist bombast account for these contradictions, but I think there is something deeper at work: the work itself contains contradictions. It is both like a novel and not. It is both new and not. Anderson's comments after *Winesburg* illuminate these paradoxes. He worked for years on a book, 'Mary Cochran', that would never be published. He voiced his frustrations in letters to his publisher Ben Huebsch in 1919:

> One of these days I shall be able to give you the Mary Cochran book. It has tantalized me a good deal but is coming clear now. In its final form it will be like *Winesburg*, a group of tales about the life of one person but each tale will be longer and more closely related to the development of the central character. It can be published in fact as a novel if you wish.
>
> It seems to me that in this form I have worked out something that is very flexible and that is the right instrument for me . . . No one I know has used the form as I see it and as I hope to develop it in several books. (Anderson 1919)

His comments on this new book illuminate his somewhat paradoxical conception of *Winesburg*. He distinguishes this new volume as having more unity around the central character, suggesting that the displacement of George Willard lends *Winesburg* less than novelistic unity. That 'Mary Cochran' can be published as a novel, even if it not one exactly, underscores the flexibility of *Winesburg*.[2] Anderson's turn away from plot to articulate instead dramatic yet fleeting moments of character revelation and the rendering of subjectivity shaped the short story for the next century, but his mode was not wholly unique.

Several individual texts influenced Anderson. The poetic cycle *Spoon River Anthology* by Edgar Lee Masters, with its emphasis on submerged voices in a small Midwestern town, reads almost like a blueprint for *Winesburg*. Indeed, Anderson read Masters's poetic cycle in a single evening (Love 1999: x). In his correspondence with Stein and in public statements, Anderson writes with great admiration for *Three Lives*, indicating that he read it well before he began writing *Winesburg*. He singles out 'Melanctha' as an exemplary model of short story form in a letter to Stein in 1924: 'Well enough I remember the first thing of yours I read – in the *Three Lives* – about the nigger woman. Why it hasn't been included in some of the lists of great short stories I don't know' (White 1972: 39). After the release of *Winesburg*, Anderson's letters indicate that Turgenev's *Sportsman Sketches* left a significant impression on him as well (Ingram 1971: 148). But it is the affinities between *Dubliners* and *Winesburg* that are most striking, especially as they set the stage for modernism in their respective contexts. According to Martha Curry, Anderson had no knowledge of *Dubliners* during the composition, citing Anderson's reading of *Ulysses* in 1920 at Frank's suggestions as his first exposure to Joyce and tracing the authors' first meeting to 1921. She concludes that 'independently of each other, James Joyce in Dublin and Trieste between 1904 and 1907 and Sherwood Anderson in Chicago between 1915 and 1916 were writing books remarkably similar in structure, narrative technique, and theme' (Curry 1980: 240).

What I find so interesting is the cycle's ongoing sense of newness: Anderson had not read Joyce yet they both produced volumes that seemed unlike what came before; Toomer, Hemingway, and Faulkner identified something uncommonly new in *Winesburg*; and titans of early twentieth-century criticism praise its innovations across many volumes. All of these pieces suggest that there were expansive changes to the literary landscape that the cycle tapped into and expressed. The structure of the cycle contributes to the sea changes in short stories that emphasise psychological complexity and round characterisation over plot and action. It paved the way for the fracturing of perspective in longer forms, such as the novel. Cycles suspend individual moments, letting them hang to develop motive and meaning, and then layer such moments one on top of another, creating meaning from accretion rather than development. Anderson's case reveals not so much the truth or definition of the genre but its power in capturing what seemed to be new experiences and ideas about storytelling.

Anderson's *Winesburg* typifies the modernist blockbusters that we most often associate with the cycle. The sheer abundance of place-centred cycles in US modernism testifies to the influence of limited locality. The three narratives of Stein's *Three Lives* are all set in a town called Bridgeport. Faulkner's Yoknapatawpha County serves as the setting for several of his cycles, including *The Unvanquished* (1938) and *Go Down, Moses*, as well as many of his works that straddle the line between novel and cycle. The small Mississippi town of Morgana provides the setting for Eudora Welty's *The Golden Apples* (1949). Steinbeck returns again and again to Californian towns in his four cycles: *Pastures of Heaven* (1932), *The Red Pony* (1933), *Tortilla Flat* (1935), and *Cannery Row* (1945). In addition to these, there are also those works that employ some level of limited locality on the borders of the cycle, such as Toomer's *Cane* (1923) and Langston Hughes's *The Ways of White Folks* (1934). Cycles set in urban centres tend to focus on a single area, as in Waldo Frank's *City Block* (1922). Although such cycles are set in urban spaces, they stake out a similarly limited geography within the cities, and the characteristics common to village narratives remain.

Susan Hegeman observes that a preoccupation with place denotes a particularly national form of US modernism. Given

> the geographic context of the cultural great divide, we may now ... see how often its interesting producers addressed, in similarly geographic terms, the paradoxes and unevenness of America's progress toward modernization. Willa Cather, W. E. B. Du Bois, William Faulkner, Zora Neale Hurston, William Carlos Williams, and many others may be said to have followed Pound's injunction to 'make it new' *within* the context of what might be described as the provincial, and the geographically and culturally marginal. (Hegeman 1999: 23)

Of the authors Hegeman lists, the works that concern the aforementioned geographic locales tend to be in cyclical forms, if not short story cycles exactly. For instance, Cather's *My Ántonia* (1918), although more highly integrated than a short story cycle, consists of a framed narrative and five stories that create a composite view of the Nebraska frontier. In blending of essay, history, anthropology, and story, Du Bois's *The Souls of Black Folk* (1903) descends from the sketch tradition. Likewise, Hurston's *Eatonville Anthology* (1926) consists of anecdotes and character descriptions of the small Florida town. Williams's poetic cycle, *Paterson*, stands as one of the most prominent locality-based modernist texts. Composed of a mix of prose, poetry, history, and drama, the cyclical texts to which Hegeman refers contain distinct parts, which, when taken together, constitute a whorl with place at the centre.

The sense of alienation that characterises *Winesburg* and its modernist cohort parallels the earliest cycles' depiction of the struggle between the narrator and his or her community. The emphasis on place and shared experiences evokes questions about the possibilities for sympathy and community. The stories emphasise the promise of being on the inside in such localities even as they treat how much more keenly felt and dramatic exclusion can be in such tight settings. These tensions are not unique to either regionalism or modernism but are indeed central to both. Scott Herring argues that 'when scholars consider the role of regionalism in modern twentieth-century literatures' they 'stereotypically relegate it to singular case studies' (2009: 3). This emphasis on singularity results from a general debasement of regionalism, often advocated by the modernists themselves. This brand of modernism 'likes to think that it has uprooted itself from provincialism as a way of life and the provincial as a geographic entity when it leaves any pretty how town behind' (Herring 2009: 2–3).

The preponderance of locality among modernist cycles makes clear that far from leaving the province, these localities are central to their modernist practices. Although some modernist texts positioned their innovation as a revolt from such places, they did so in the very terms and preoccupations of the earlier period. Short story cycles linked by a common setting express a deep ambivalence about the possibility of locality forging a sense of positive community. Cycles suggest that this anxiety about loss of community begins at the moment of settlement. After all, establishing something, such as a neighbourhood, a town, or a nation, necessitates knowing that it is impermanent. Even if doing so is futile, the sheer attempt to disentangle the web of lives and map these places is a critically nostalgic gesture, as it pays homage to and tarnishes localities such as Montacute, Dunnet Landing, and Winesburg.

Notes

1. For more on Hawthorne's early experiments in the form and his thoughts on literary reputation, see Melinda Ponder's *Hawthorne's Early Narrative Art* (1990) and Millicent Bell's introduction to *New Essays on Hawthorne's Major Tales* (1993).
2. For an extended treatment of Anderson's correspondence and composition in this period, see Martha Curry's 'Sherwood Anderson and James Joyce' (1980). For more on the Chicago connection, see chapter 9 of Tim Spears's *Chicago Dreaming: Midwesterners and the City, 1871–1919* (2005).

Chapter 2

The Persistence of Place

In 'Departure', the final story of *Winesburg, Ohio*, George Willard, the aspiring young writer, leaves his hometown for the city, which remains – significantly – nameless. The town matters, not the city. In the moments before his train departs, George does not 'think of anything very big or dramatic' but instead ponders 'little things – Turk Smollet wheeling boards through the main street of his town in the morning . . . Butch Wheeler the lamp lighter of Winesburg hurrying through the streets on a summer evening' (Anderson 1999: 138). The cycle ends with attention to small details, all connected to the physical spaces of Winesburg. The town itself serves as background, and touchstones such as the *Winesburg Eagle*, Winney's Dry Goods Store, and Main Street recur in the stories. The newspaper and these places are particular to Winesburg but virtually interchangeable with any small town. Since its publication, writers have used *Winesburg* as a palimpsest to write their own stories of a place just as George envisions it as 'a background on which to paint the dreams of his manhood' (204). Anderson refined a generic model for revealing the complexity, banality, and desperation of humanity by focusing on the details of a singular place.

Even though *Winesburg* did not originate the genre, it caused a seismic shift in the literary landscape and has shaped work in the genre since its publication. Many writers credit *Winesburg* as transformative, radically new, even revelatory. Faulkner, Hemingway, Toomer, Steinbeck, and a host of contemporary writers all describe *Winesburg* as liberating. Anderson celebrated *Winesburg* for enabling 'a new looseness' in fiction; that sense of novelty and innovation – even if it is mere chimera – recurs in authors' statements on how reading *Winesburg* for the first time radically altered their sense of what was possible in form and feeling.

Anderson's cycle, depicting the submerged desires and frustrations of citizens in a small town, opened up new vistas in terms of setting, subject, and style. Building on correspondence, essays, and public statements, this chapter examines how Anderson shapes contemporary fiction. Drawing on authors who explicitly cite the influence of Anderson on their work establishes the enduring legacy of *Winesburg* and constructs a lineage of short story cycles that descends from Anderson. Progeny of this lineage include, among others, Russell Banks's *Trailerpark*, Cathy Day's *The Circus in Winter*, and Rebecca Barry's *Later, at the Bar*. These contemporary cycles evince the persistence and simultaneity of multiple aesthetic styles afforded by cycles linked by limited locality. Banks, Barry, and Day engage not only the linking device – and the consequent anxieties about community – of limited locality but also draw on and extend the construction of critical nostalgia in their depictions of the present through the prism of distant and not-so-distant pasts. These cycles expose how nostalgia often masks and distorts past injustices, relationships, and homes, while also acknowledging how nostalgia seeks to restore and correct.

Liberating Form, Forming Place

Contemporary writers continue to treat the depths of lives in marginalised spaces – from a New Hampshire trailer park to Hoosier circus grounds to a dive bar in the sticks of New York. The cycles narrow even within the small-town settings to focus on a particular population, such as Banks's depiction of the residents of the eponymous *Trailerpark*, Day's treatment of circus folk in the fictional Lima, Indiana in *The Circus in Winter*, or Barry's focus on bar regulars in *Later, At the Bar*. In all of these works, a treatment of a certain economic underbelly specific to these localities persists.

In Banks's cycle, the town of Cantamount 'has been dying for a half-century'; it is a town 'where the poor are not only always with you but where annually they seem to increase in geometric proportion to the rich' (Banks 1996: 133). Banks does not sentimentalise poverty – the characters' lives are shaped and destroyed by lack of money and opportunity – and yet he shows how the economic decline of the place occurs simultaneous to the construction of a community in which one enjoys the 'comfort of living among people whose names and family histories you knew' and the 'security of living in a community that still honoured the old-fashioned virtues of thrift, honesty, independence and respect for the independence of one's neighbors, love of God, love of country, and love of family' (134). The decline of *gesellschaft*, in other words, ushers in the return of *gemeinschaft*, at least for the character who narrates this scene. The creation of community in the place is closely linked to 'the beauty of the landscape, the lakes and forests, the rivers and mountains, the flowers and wildlife' (133), which parallels Kirkland's celebration of the interconnections of community, nation, and landscape. Significantly, this treatment of poverty, community, and landscape comes from Doctor Wickshaw, whose rare, privileged class position and constant but never fully integrated role in the locality makes him both a part of and apart from Catamount similar to George Willard. Thus, *Winesburg* and its heirs epitomise the extent to which constricted geographic settings continue to highlight both the production and denial of affiliation.

The use of a common, bounded geographical setting, which links the stories without insisting on unity, proved exactly the kind of structure Banks needed in constructing *Trailerpark*. In an interview, he explains,

> *Trailerpark*, for instance, is very closely – not modeled after *Winesburg, Ohio* – but took that as an example. I said, gee, you can do this. You can write a cycle of stories that are located – that are connected – by place, and where minor characters become major characters in another story and vice-versa, and you don't have to adhere to the unities of time, because you've got such a strong unity of place. And the voice is consistent enough that ties them together and you get something that's not a novel in a conventional sense, but it's a narrative, a long narrative. (Banks 2003)

In *Trailerpark*, Banks accomplishes exactly what he set out to do: place connects stories that do not rely on novelistic conventions of temporality and characterisation. The opening and closing stories resemble novellas in their scope and action, and the stories in the middle are akin to vignettes or close character studies. The stories narrate the lives of residents of the 'Granite State Trailerpark out at Skitter Lake' (Banks 1996: 59). Granite State Trailerpark is miles from the already small town of Catamount. Twelve trailers, and their sometimes shifting but largely constant occupants, reside on the edge of the lake.

The trailerpark starkly symbolises the rootedness and transience of the characters' lives in this very limited locality. Their homes are mobile, but the economic and intimate conditions of their lives keep them stationed at the edge of the remote lake. Individual stories, often set years and decades apart, clarify and contextualise the events in other stories to a high degree, achieving interconnection in place and character but not time, as Banks's comments suggest. As in *Winesburg*, *Trailerpark* refers to specific places with the kind of brevity that assumes familiarity. Hayward's Hardware and Sporting Goods Store, Hawthorne House, Old Road, and Main Street recur throughout the stories; such places balance being both particular and interchangeable. For Luscher, 'this multi-dimensional spatiotemporal architecture suggested by the map – not the erratic bildungsroman – is the more significant component of *Winesburg*' (2013: 195). Luscher shows how the stories force our minds to create a map more complete than the one the book often gives. The maps readers create expose how place both 'consign[s] many to a liminal space and to atomized existences' and generates the shared 'sympathetic narrative sensibilities'; this tension 'replicates the imaginative assembly of the stories themselves' (Luscher 2013: 198). Luscher argues that this co-construction of space and story is Anderson's most meaningful legacy and the element of the book that most greatly influenced later writers.

As Banks describes, the protagonist in one story becomes a peripheral character in subsequent tales. The characters rise and recede just as the image of the cycle implies. The central character of the opening story, 'The Guinea Pig Lady', moves from being a figure at the centre of the locality to an extremely marginalised figure by the end of the cycle. As the title indicates, she is stripped of her name, Flora Pease, because of her disconcerting hobby of breeding guinea pigs in her trailer. As they increase in number and her control slips, Flora burns the trailer and builds a shanty just outside of the park. Thus, her nickname and physical position mirror her marginalisation within this already extremely limited locality. All of the characters gain some kind of limited access to Flora's actions and motivations; Banks's experimentation with the balance between what the characters do and do not know resonates with Anderson's treatment of geographic proximity and emotional isolation. So too, the other characters in Banks's cycle offer both insight and misinterpretation in regards to Flora.

At the centre of the story, Banks actualises the community of voices – one might even say gossips – by dedicating a paragraph to each character's opinion. This passage resembles a cycle in microcosm. Each character voices his or her perception of Flora's motivations and future, but there is little compassion and understanding. These opinions both vary and overlap, representing the range of experiences and voices in the park. This diversity of experiences in the context of close geographic proximity and shared experience is a central feature of cycles linked by locality. Resident Nancy Hubner attributes the proliferation of guinea pigs to loneliness: 'Obviously they are Flora's substitutes for a family and friends. She's trying to tell us something and we're not listening' (Banks 1996: 54). Although Nancy proves only partly right, this moment distils the alienation and the lack of communication common to these cycles.

By placing the characters in near-claustrophobic proximity, these books amplify the pervasiveness of such misunderstandings and misinterpretations. In the final story, 'The Fisherman', the second-person narrator confesses,

> It's true of trailerparks that the people who live there are generally alone at the center of their lives. They are widows and widowers, divorcées and bachelors and retired army officers, a black man in a white society, a black woman there too, a drug dealer, a solitary child of a broken home, a drunk, a homosexual in a heterosexual society – all of them, man and woman, adult and child, basically alone in the world. (Banks 1996: 260)

The trailerpark offers a refuge for the cast-offs of the larger society. In rural New England in the mid-twentieth century, Banks's cycle suggests that those who live outside of economic, racial, and sexual norms create a community with those that have fled or lost intimate family connections.

The problems – exclusion, expectations, and problems of expression – that led to them coming to the Granite State Trailerpark reappear in their place of sanctuary. In 'Dis Bwoy, Him Gwan', the sole African American man in the trailerpark is 'lonely' because 'everyone else in town either feared him or disliked him for being black' (109). He 'had no one he could talk to, no one he could gossip or grumble with, no one he could think of as a friend. When you are a long way from where you think you belong, you will attach yourself to people you would otherwise ignore or even dislike' (109). In the character's estimation – and in Banks's cycle as a whole – the typical problems of geographically based community attend these hamlets. Indeed, the condensed proximity, isolation, and small populace of the park cause or exacerbate the characters' loneliness. For instance, in 'Comfort', Buddy, who has not a friend in the world, is an outsider among outsiders, totally unlike his peers: '"Those other guys were made in Catamount, New Hampshire, to stay in Catamount, New Hampshire, and eventually to die in Catamount, New Hampshire. It was stamped all over their faces, all over their bulky muscles, all of the way they talked and laughed and punched each other around"' (126). The repetition of the place's name connotes the claustrophobia of the place where only a certain type and personality are accepted. Buddy, as an out-of-place character, resembles Enoch and Seth in *Winesburg, Ohio*. Banks extends Anderson's treatment of the individual's exclusion and the consequent feeling of aimlessness.

As in *Winesburg*, the characters' alienation stems from thwarted expression. The characters routinely attempt and fail to express their anxieties, passions, and appreciation. Contemporary cycles continue what *Winesburg* and other modernist cycles initiated: the inner lives of individuals cannot be expressed. Subjectivity continues to be incommunicable – always to others and often internally. In 'Comfort', the narrator links the ubiquitous drinking in the trailerpark to problems of expression, in this case of naming desire:

> he had been drinking with the Captain in the Captain's trailer for several hours, so he was slightly drunk, or he probably would not have tried to tell it at all. It's not so much that you will say things when drunk that you'd never say sober, as much as you will try to say things you'd ordinarily know simply could not be said. It's your judgment about the sayable that goes, not your inhibitions. (Banks 1996: 124)

Desires and fears exceed words, and the characters' alienation originates within the self and becomes exaggerated in relation to others in a close communal space. In this way, Banks's statements about the impossibility of expressing what is most true about one's self extends a modernist obsession with unsayable interiority. Its experimentation with what remains unspoken between characters distinguishes *Winesburg* from earlier cycles and established a shifted emphasis on alienation and disjunction within short story cycles since modernism. Banks's indebtedness to the form of *Winesburg* derives not just from the 'strong unity of place' but also from the ways place illuminates the stunted expression of subjectivity.

The cycle tempers this bleak outlook with moments of compassion and connection; repeatedly, moments of sympathy emerge from destruction and violence. In the opening story, Flora's few, tenuous relationships develop most strongly after fire has destroyed her home and she has been pushed to the margins of the locality. The nostalgia with which Doctor Wickshaw views the town remains unavailable to Flora, but she has brief moments of connection, as in her friendship with Merle, who visits her because 'you got a different perspective on the trailerpark from out there, practically the same perspective he said he got in winter from the lake when he was in his ice-house' (79). Occupying an outsider's position to the locality, if even for a few moments, dramatises the construction and vulnerability of the community they have formed. The scenes of tentative friendship formed from loss at the end of 'The Guinea Pig Lady' foreshadow later interconnections of community and alienation.

The second story, 'Cleaving, and Other Needs', builds on this theme when two distant cousins marry but fail to meaningfully connect. Their frustrated sexual desire and anxieties about infidelity erupt in gun violence, when 'Buck pulled the trigger and the hammer fell' as Doreen 'clamped her hand onto the barrel of the gun and pressed it as tightly as she could against the exact center of her chest' (92). This moment of near-fatal violence precipitates a violent sexual connection that produces their only child. The moment may offer catharsis and production but its effects are momentary as they remain unhappily married – with continued infidelities and violence – for four more years. The story concludes, 'Doreen and Buck never forgot that snowy night and the shotgun, however, and in later years, alone, they would wish they could speak of it to each other, but they never did speak of it to each other, not even the night that it happened' (93). That the night persists in their memories suggests its extraordinariness; they are able to finally say the things they think about one another. But the final passage, with its insistence of the unspeakable, confirms the absolute exceptionalism of this night. Silence and resentment define the rest of their lives together. The violence in this intimate relationship connects to the cycle's continued engagement with the alienation present in the closest relationships.

Nostalgias Past and Present

Of cycles linked by place, Banks (2003) said that one need not 'adhere to the unities of time', because they adhere to 'such a strong unity of place'. Loose uses of time and strict limits in place shape how Barry and Day construct temporality and nostalgia in *Later, at the Bar* and *The Circus in Winter*, respectively. All three cycles eschew clarity and consistency in chronology. That the stories do not appear in chronological sequence does not substantively matter; rather, the sense of recurrence matters most, as in the unexpressed commonality that is found between stories even though the events of the stories take place many years apart. The cycle's looseness of chronology makes it a generative genre for contemporary fiction. For instance, in a 2007 review of Rebecca Barry's *Later, at the Bar: A Novel in Stories*, Danielle Trussoni begins:

> The novel in stories is the Rube Goldberg contraption of the literary world, fiction that works in wondrous and roundabout ways. While the short story pauses to explore an illuminated moment, and the novel chugs toward a grand conclusion, the novel in stories moves in spirals and loops, a corkscrewing joy ride. Read the chapters in any order, and the overall narrative experience often remains virtually the same. For this reason alone, the novel in stories may be the most tuned-in form of contemporary storytelling. Nothing is lost in setting one's reading on shuffle. (Trussoni 2007)

The metaphors Trussoni employs of 'setting one's reading on shuffle' and the dizzying effects of a 'corkscrewing joy ride' resonate with very contemporary technological images.

Trussoni describes that the rollercoaster, Goldberg-esque style, makes elaborate rotations to express things that seem deceptively simple in *Later, at the Bar*: a lost moment between two people; a desire for home; the pulls of friendship and love; and the connections made possible by a seat at the bar. Outsiders – divorcees, obsolete farmers, the working-class unemployed and underemployed, and those marginalised by sexuality – populate Barry's stories. Independently, these stories describe drunken joy rides, the death of the bar's owner, and desire between patrons; collectively, the stories function like a census of the community. They document the existence of people, track marriages and divorces, list children, and note property; the stories also document those things that resist verification – the one-night stands, the minor slights and major resentments, the deaths that are done alone and without witness, and the quiet loves that go unrecognised and unrecorded. And it is this balance between what is said and what is unsaid as the stories narrate a specific place that renders the genre 'tuned-in' to contemporary experience. The genre's episodic, non-chronological narratives reflect the disoriented moments of insight that accompany modernity. As the rollercoaster metaphor implies, while the cycle affords spins and thrills, it remains grounded.

To these authors, the genre maintains that sense of novelty and invention, particularly upon reading Anderson. They repeatedly claim, as Banks does, that they circled around a set of stories featuring the same characters and/or setting, but reading Anderson's cycle liberated them to write in the form. Barry, for example, refers to the way in which one of her recurring characters, Harlin Wilder, kept creeping into her efforts in a writing workshop in graduate school. Returning to this character again and again became a frustration until she read *Winesburg*: 'My initial inspiration was *Winesburg, Ohio* . . . I read it and thought, "Hooray! Look at this. This guy is horrible at plot, too, and he wrote a wonderful book!"' (Barry 2008: 100). Barry identifies how cycles make it possible to subordinate plot to setting, character, and mood.

A preference for vignettes and stories over the sustained narrative of the novel recurs in Barry's interviews. She acknowledges, 'I am much more comfortable with vignettes, which in terms of form are my favorite type of thing to write. What I really wanted to do was capture these moments, these sort of beautiful pieces of time where a character's world changes or where they have a bit of clarity that then may or may not fade' (Barry 2008: 100). Here she articulates exactly that sense of what is both shared and lost in tight settings, which *Winesburg* captures. Her experiences living in a small town inspired the particular site of Lucy's Bar. She claims she was drinking a lot at the time; however, she reflects that she was 'more addicted to going to the bar than to drinking' (Barry 2008: 100). The social setting of the bar, with its enclosed space, fosters intimacy, within which the regulars share stories and experiences. Barry uses the repetition of snowstorms, a fact of life in upstate New York, to force the characters to experience prolonged and intensified proximity. Yet, as in Banks's cycle, the characters bring a sense of alienation and loneliness to the bar, which, despite bacchanalian drinking binges and long nights commiserating, fails to offer more than momentary connections.

Banks's story suggests that drinking loosens an internal censor on what can be said and understood; the promise of alcohol to break through the barriers of self and others drowns the characters in *Later, at the Bar*. One regular at Lucy's is Linda Hartley, who writes an advice column centred on love. As a newspaper writer and insider/outsider, Linda resembles George Willard and earlier central figures. In 'Love Him, Petaluma', she traces her own attempts at and failures in love, concluding that 'We only get pieces of love ... Sometimes that's the best we can do' (Barry 2007: 99). In Barry's cycle the unsustainability of love merges with the inability to get a story straight; the bar becomes the perfect site to meditate on and extend the search for both love and expression. As in Banks's 'Comfort', alcohol fuels desperate attempts to connect, which originate from a deep, but perpetually thwarted, desire for connection. In 'Not Much Is New Here', Linda 'drank some more and missed the way she'd been when she hadn't been in love with anyone' (135), but she laments that '"No one tells women how much better it is to be single than attached to someone"' (135). The ambivalence with which Linda treats romantic intimacies – longing for them, realising they are fleeting, acknowledging that she is happier without them – does not get expressed in her columns. Instead, they privilege light, airy advice. Partly, this is mercenary, as '"Procter and Gamble would pull all their ads"' (136), but mostly it derives from her desire to be read. Her longing for readers and expression surpasses her impulse to tell the truth: 'Without her readers, she wondered if she would even exist' (136). This anxiety of existence – of knowing one matters to a place and its people – permeates the cycle. Linda's string of love affairs and her advice column all originate in a desire to acknowledge her existence.

The bar's limited locality offers the basis for identity and belonging. Lucy's was established because its namesake 'loved live music and dancing and understood people who liked longing more than they did love' so that 'it became the center of the community' (3). Music represents just one form of expression that finds a home at the bar. To prefer longing to love reflects Linda's casting of the desires for love and happiness at odds with each other. Implicit throughout the cycle is that Lucy's becomes 'the center of the community' because the community is dying, economically and physically. Jobs are scarce, farms are abandoned, and most drink and die in the place.

As in Anderson's 'The Book of the Grotesque', the cycle begins with an ostensibly ancient figure who holds a privileged view of the town. Lucy is an artist who is both at the centre of and outside of the life of the town. 'To her,' the opening story describes, 'the bar was like a good wedding, where love, sex, hope, and grief were just in the air' (5). In *Winesburg*, the story likens the grotesques to apples. Barry also offers a botanical simile: 'Her once nimble feet grew arthritic and gnarled as the roots of the poplars that lined the streets in the center of town' (6). Body parts as synecdoche of the individual and geographical features of the locality extend the connection between this and earlier cycles, including also Jewett's and Kirkland's. They all also feed into the larger treatment of the rough and beautiful ways to carry loneliness. In the part-epistolary story, 'Not Much Is New Here', Linda writes to a distant boyfriend about the familiar sights and sounds of the bar, concluding, '*I sat there remembering what it is that I love about a small-town bar, the way it's like a perfect family, always there if you need it, but if you need to leave it for a while and get away, you can*' (153). The comingling of life's joys and disappointments places *Later, at the Bar* in the tradition of cycles that trouble the romantic view of *gemeinschaft*.

Cycles of limited locality dramatise how loneliness and a desire for connection give nostalgia its form and function. In Barry's cycle, the characters express a deep nostalgia for a near past that was never very good. When Harlin listens to an old message from his on- and off-again wife, he invites her to the bar, but the story makes clear that the nostalgia is, at least, misguided or even false, as violence, infidelity, and emotional distance marred their relationship. This small moment of personal nostalgia mirrors the denial implicit in communal nostalgia. Communal nostalgia is again tied to the landscape, as Harlin, his brother, and his brother's ex-wife travel across and out of the county:

> They passed old, tired-looking houses with peeling paint, and farmers worrying about their livestock. Some people said this part of the state was depressing, but Harlin liked the fading majesty of the old farmhouses, and the way just past Chemung County the landscape broke free and stretched out for miles of rolling hills and wild creeks. Once he'd asked Grace why she moved back here from North Carolina, and she didn't answer right away, He'd wondered if she didn't know or wished she'd stayed down south. Finally, she said, 'I love the land.' She lifted her shoulders helplessly. 'That's what it is. It moves me, this part of the world.'. . . he knew what she meant and liked her for saying it. (Barry 2007: 26–7)

Harlin imbues the landscape with regal beauty, ignoring the signs of economic depression. The land becomes a shifting, fluid metaphor for their own lives: the open country reflects a desire to break free, the houses with chipped paint signal a lost past and forgotten potential, and yet the possibility for connection across the openness and even wreckage remains. The landscape becomes a romantic repository for what this small town once was, but the stories also suggest that it was never particularly thriving. The few businesses were small and are now shuttered. The farms, revealed in the story 'Instructions for a Substitute Bus Driver', have always struggled against deprivation and personal trauma. From the town, Harlin conceives of the farm country as a prelapsarian idyll, but the stories pollute that landscape. Barry suggests that nostalgia masks and even incites a kind of fatalistic desire to ignore the present. The same tensions exist in *Winesburg* as the denizens of town construct themselves in contrast to the surrounding farms, but glimpses into the farm life as in 'Godliness' and 'The Untold Lie' reveal that the same problems of loneliness and frustrated expression occur at the farm too.

The most extended and bittersweet treatment of nostalgia happens in the final story, 'Eye. Arm. Leg. Heart.' The conclusion narrates, through his ex-wife Grace's experiences, the funeral of Harlin Wilder, one of the central recurring characters in the stories. 'The sudden burst of loneliness Grace Meyers felt' when she hears that Harlin has died of liver failure 'caught her off guard' (195). The temporal setting has moved years into the future. Grace's on and off relationship with Harlin ended years ago, Linda Hartley moved to Hawaii, and many of the other regulars had moved on or quit drinking. Only the bartender Rita and the long-suffering members of Harlin's friends and families attend. His death precipitates immediate nostalgia for Harlin and the old days of hard drinking, fighting, and reconciling with perpetual optimism. His lawyer grieves, '"They don't make them like Harlin anymore"' (195), and tells a story of how Harlin – in the midst of a binge – spent all of another wife's money on fencing and animal supplies to open a petting zoo on his father's old homestead.

Grace's nostalgia on hearing of his passing becomes a communal emotion at Harlin's wake. The remaining denizens of Lucy's Bar – and the policemen who corral them – come together at the Elks' Lodge over Budweisers and scalloped potatoes. The potluck, the paper plates, and the general sense of desperation once again highlight the relative poverty with which the characters live, which fuels and undermines the constant belief that the right idea might bring prosperity, emblematised in Harlin's failed petting zoo scheme. Harlin's 'relentless hope' made him perpetually nostalgic, which now invests his memory with sentimental longing: '[hope] was what kept him from being a bad man, and part of what made him a stupid one'

(223). The night of his wake 'was an early fall night, the kind Harlin had always loved, when there was a bite to the air that stirred things up – people, livestock, the wind and the leaves' (222). The sense of autumn – that is both perpetual and rare – links this cycle to American literature invested in regional landscapes. The autumn night, the Budweisers, and memory lead Grace to call up Harlin's lawyer for 'sloppy, drunken sex' (224), which is the cycle's final scene. Grace dives into her nostalgia and surfaces with a desire for connection. This final moment cements a very Winesburg-esque theme that the cycle returns to repeatedly: nostalgia becomes a repository for the failures of the past and possibilities of the future while fatalistically destroying the present. Barry's cycle engages this romantic rendering of the past, which critically turns on itself as alternately false, incomplete, or unsatisfying. Yet, the community offered by the bar – however limited and flawed it might be – offers a reprieve from the loneliness with which the characters struggle, as Linda articulates: *'It's such a comfort to be a regular at a bar, especially when you live alone. I mean that in the least pathetic, nicest possible way. I saw almost everyone I wanted to see and got caught up on some gossip'* (152–3). Linda's affinity for the bar, which she writes of in a letter to her long-distance boyfriend, expresses simultaneously her loneliness and her sense of connection.

In the final story of Day's *The Circus in Winter*, Jenny Perdido, a writer and professor, who has long since moved away from her hometown, returns to attend a funeral in January. The narrator describes that 'everything north of Indianapolis is so flat that sometimes, especially in winter, it is difficult to tell the difference between the earth and the sky. My mother once told me that if she had to draw a picture of loneliness and despair, it would be Indiana in winter: a wash of gray, a stand of naked trees, and line of electric poles disappearing into infinity' (Day 2004: 246). Symbolising dormancy and repetition in the lives of its inhabitants, the unchanging monotony of the landscape imprisons the narrator's mother and, for a time, the narrator. Jenny Perdido is a writerly figure, in the vein of George Willard; she is the great-grandchild of the Circus's founder. Unlike George Willard, who recurs throughout, Jenny Perdido only appears in two of the stories. Jenny chooses to leave her hometown, go to a big state school, and pursue a life of travel and learning to 'melt into a throng, and become whomever I wanted to be' (251). In her small Indiana town, too many people know her past disappointments – both those that have been inflicted upon her and those that she inflicted. That judgement makes her feel isolated. And yet, when she returns, she realises that 'What felt claustrophobic at eighteen feels strangely comforting at thirty-two' (251). She feels '*known*, really known' (251). Like Banks and Barry, Day infuses the landscape with sadness and loss but also a specificity that generates nostalgia. Jenny's experience echoes that of those in limited localities: the passage of time collides with regret and experience to generate a powerful but ultimately unsatisfying nostalgia.

Set in Lima, Indiana, the interrelated stories of Day's *The Circus in Winter* offer independent narratives that are linked through place, character, structural motifs, and theme. Lima is a fictionalised recreation of Peru, Indiana, the author's hometown, which used to house the Hagenback-Wallace Circus during its off-season. Day adopts many of the motifs of the circus to enhance the interconnections between the stories; for instance, she places photographs which reflect someone or something from the stories in front of each. Under the 'Programme of Displays', she lists each short story title as a display. Within the volume, the stories carry titles like 'Jennie Dixianna – or The Secret to the Spin of Death' and 'The Circus House – or The Prettiest Little Thing in the Whole Goddamn Place'. These titles evoke the sideshow descriptions given under the performer's name. Spanning from the 1700s to the present, the stories narrate the lives spent in a small town in Indiana and trace genealogies, sometimes hidden, of the town's circus people and their progeny. Although *Winesburg* focuses on the 1890s, in the choice of setting, structure, and theme, much in Day's cycle is reminiscent of *Winesburg* as the cycle recovers lost stories or lost elements of stories.

The people who populate the stories during the days of the circus include a promiscuous trapeze artist, an artist without a canvas who paints the walls of a house, an eccentric and abusive elephant keeper, and a toilet bowl cleaner. The people who inhabit Lima after the circus days have passed are no less oddities: a baseball phenomenon (and, more shockingly for this small town, the recipient of a college scholarship) and a clown turned dry cleaner. *The Circus in Winter* depicts a community of people marginalised within other social groups. If Anderson's cycle depicts grotesques – people hardened by believing in one truth for too long – Day's cycle seeks to make those who seem grotesque human. These characters do not falter so much because they believe too much in one thing but because they have trouble believing anything at all.

The buried lives in her stories are often circus performers of colour and women, because, while there have been museums erected to the great white men of the midway, little attention has been paid to and few records kept of these submerged groups within even this marginalised community. For instance, 'The Jungle Goolah Boy' began as an attempt to recover the life of someone unknown, a black man sitting atop an elephant in a photograph Day saw and for whom there was no record at any circus museum. This story creates a paper trail for a person for whom no record exists and is comprised of fictionalised newspaper articles, as well as the logs, letters, wills, and journals of the Grimm family who first owned and employed the ancestors of the man billed as 'The Jungle Goolah Boy'. These documents date from 1725 until 1888. From here, there is a break until 1900, when the sixteen-year-old boy, named Sugar Church, appears in the letters and chronicles of Wallace Porter, the proprietor of the circus. The route book of the circus chronicles his life until the circus closes in 1939 and an article about him appears in a 1940 edition of *Life*, replete with nostalgia for the circus. The article exposes the ways in which the circus capitalised on fear and racism but also celebrates how much Sugar could make working for the circus. The story ends with a Works Progress Administration[1] report from 1938, given by Sugar's long-estranged brother, Marvin, who once saw his brother perform 'wearing leather britches and a necklace of bones' (156). In its form, this short story borrows from epistolary modes and an archivist's resources. In the absence of a record, Day creates one. However, as the lack of continuity between the documents suggests and the gaps in time prove, the story remains incomplete. This story refracts Day's larger treatment of the inadequacy of stories but the unstoppable impulse to tell them.

As in Barry's and Banks's cycles, Day's stories reveal that the impulse for narrative connection manifests itself in sexual desire and physical intimacy. Wallace Porter, who will one day own and run the circus at the centre of the tales, initiates a courtship with future wife Irene by attempting to tell her the story of his lost regiment, the Eleventh Indiana. 'Almost twenty years had gone by,' he thinks, 'but he could still see the land rolling like an ocean into the blue sky. He tried not to remember other images: a barn in Alabama full of stinking, rotting, wailing men. His regiment lost 13 in battle, 161 to disease' (5). Wallace Porter's identity is trapped in the trauma of the past, and like *Winesburg*, the aftermath of the Civil War hangs heavily over the cycle's opening. These thoughts remain unexpressed, though, and Wallace instead sublimates his desire to speak honestly of the past in his attraction to Irene, which represents a future with wife, children, and home. But his narrative of the future is at odds with hers. Irene wants to leave behind the practices and traditions of the East and alight West in the tradition of Kirkland; Indiana represents possibility, newness, and choice. The power of Wallace's narrative – of giving his wife a stable, large home – overwhelms her. Instead of giving voice to her frustrated desire to travel, she internalises her frustrations, which becomes symbolically and literally cancerous. A tumour that 'had been a pea on their wedding day' grows to 'an apple'. He thinks, '*Instead of a baby, I planted this in my wife's womb, this beast which fed on her blood*' (22). The story literalises the idea that disappointment grows like a cancer unchecked. It is a violent, toxic image, and, the story suggests, an apt one for describing the effects of unexpressed desire. For both Irene and Wallace, nostalgia becomes a means to express a desire that never was.

Nostalgia is, according to Day's cycle, flexible: it can, as it does for Jenny Perdido, complicate and salvage what was once a too damning sense of the past; it can, as it is in 'The Jungle Goolah Boy', be an insidious, false mask that covers historical injustices; or, it can be a motivation for recovering or recreating a time, relationship, or possibility that was both hopeful and false. These cycles suggest all three possibilities in various moments. They show the real, but wholly imagined, power of nostalgia. In fact, they suggest that nostalgia is so powerful because of its ability to shape a sense of the present through a filtered vision of the past and an optimistic dream of the future. Nostalgia continues to shape Wallace's life after Irene's death, manifesting again in a physical desire for connection. Jennie Dixianna, a beautiful performer of the aptly named Spin of Death, identifies in Wallace Porter a possibility for advancement and privilege when he buys the circus to fill the void left by his wife and never-born children. She realises that what Wallace wants is 'a ghost' (30). She can play the part of his beloved and disappointed Irene, and their relationship suggests that desire stems from this longing for a past that never was. Jennie 'walked through the halls of his mansion as if she'd always lived there with him, and for that evening he allowed himself to believe that Irene had never died at all . . . that this was just another night in their long and happy marriage' (34). This scene shows the influence of nostalgia, as Irene never lived in nor wanted the house and their marriage was mostly unhappy and definitely short. The story does not chastise Wallace Porter – rather, it sympathises with him – but it does intimate the destructive force of unchecked nostalgia. Jennie has played such a part before – for her father who molests her for years following her mother's death. Day locates the origin of his violent, abusive acts in unabated longing for his dead wife.

Jennie's backstory, with its violence and incest, sharply dramatises the inverted social order that nostalgia threatens to enact, further symbolised in her father's reverence for the confederacy and its flag. Jennie's name is both homage and rejection of this past; she uses the advice of Sister, an ex-slave conjure woman, to ultimately kill her father. She modifies his beloved confederate flag to fashion her first circus costume. She exploits nostalgia for the confederacy for personal gain and fame, but the cost of the performance of the Spin of Death reminds that sentimentality over personal and collective histories often masks the uglier truths of those pasts. Jennie, in both public and private, 'become[s] a walking phantom, the living receptacle of unlived lives' (33). Jennie Dixianna carves out of a professional and personal life by trading on nostalgia. The cycle's depiction of her tragic end – trapped between her bed and wall, with liquor bottles littering her shabby abode, when a flood arrives – symbolises the futility of her small gains in the face of ambivalent nature.

A generalised sense of ultimate indifference (be it nature's, God's, or humanity's) to the fates of individuals is the source of nostalgia's power, because nostalgia seeks to give meaning and purpose to a life, even if that life has not turned out well. Those characters most afflicted with nostalgia – Wallace Porter, Jennie Dixianna, Linda Hartley, Grace Meyers, Harlin Wilder, Doctor Wickshaw – are those whose present circumstances are most at odds with their expectations. Nostalgia allows these characters to escape the hard work of reshaping the present, and, in this, the cycles criticise the numbing effects of nostalgia. Yet, the cycles also do so much to voice the complexity of the characters' lives – to show how they are caught up in structural and personal limitations about which the characters fathom only slightly. In this way, the cycles dramatise the ways larger forces, such as national divisions, economic collapses, natural disasters, and gendered and ethnic inequities, limit the possibilities for prosperity and connection in the characters' lives. The very structure of the genre, with its recursive treatment of character and theme, further deconstructs the sense of purpose and meaning that motivate and destroy the characters. The stories lack finality and resolution, signalling that the very drive to culminate life's meaning into one moment might be a dangerous chimera.

The landscape registers the blend of beauty and loneliness embedded in nostalgia, as in Jenny Perdido's description of the vast monotony of Indiana's sky and land. It is another transplant, the wife of a Civil War colonel, who sees that the landscape is both a disappointment and promise:

> This is why they call it the heartland:
> In the summer, the fields on either side of the Colonel's house glowed a brilliant green, rippling in the wind. The air stretched above like miles of blue canvas... Sometimes as she sat on her front porch in the evenings, Mrs. Colonel felt her heart swelling up as big as the horizon. Only then could she say that Indiana was almost as beautiful as her Virginia. During these lonely months, Mrs. Colonel fancied herself shipwrecked and stranded. Outside her windows was a green ocean dotted by islands of trees, and on each island stood a farmhouse, sheltered from the sun and the prairie winds by those blessedly spared shade trees. Each island looked remarkably the same, and sometimes she thought about walking off the porch, diving into the ocean and swimming to the next strand of trees. Maybe there, she'd find another woman waiting for her men to return, a woman as heartsick as herself. (90–1)

The most important part of the passage remains unstated: Mrs. Colonel does not swim out to another island. She persists in her isolation, even as she knows how it destroys her. She imagines her loneliness in geographic metaphors. The visible, immediate landscape signifies beauty and growth, gesturing to her girlhood and the one-time promise of productivity. Having lived her life in railcars and in a relatively loveless marriage, her new Indiana home presents at least the possibility of love and stability. Yet, the metaphor of islands, marked by monotony and distance, undercuts that possibility. She imagines that others' lives are lonely and broken – and the rest of the cycle confirms it – yet she lacks the will or power to seek out a connection. Instead, as the cycles repeatedly depict, she sublimates her desire to be understood into sexual desire, as she spends her winters lusting after a young painter, who does large-scale murals of the circus in her home's interior. Her inner life is, to her frustration, not lived inside her house either with the Colonel or the painter but here on the porch in the liminal space between the public and private worlds.

The contrast of winter in Jenny's mother's description and summer in Mrs. Colonel's rendering mirror the duality of the landscape: the locality is both claustrophobic and welcoming. The cycle ends on two points that show its connections to *Winesburg*. First, the penultimate story depicts the ways in which the railroad changed the town. In Anderson's cycle, the railroad metonymically stands in for how modernity transformed the lives of small-town residents. The railroad signifies the rise of *gesellschaft* and the collapse of a town's autonomy. In *The Circus in Winter*, it is the vanishing of the railroads in the 1980s that promises to undo any remaining *gemeinschaft* and interconnectedness. Earl Richards, for one, 'loved the railroad itself, the idea of it, at least . . . He liked to go down there and imagine rocking in with the beat of the train, waking up each morning in a different town' (190). Although Earl's reality is that he never leaves Lima, the railroad represents the possibility that he could. That he works for the railroad for decades without getting to ride the rails frustrates him endlessly. However, the threat of the railroad's upheaval out of Lima illuminates just how few possible economic and personal opportunities are available in the town – much like the depressed economic landscapes of Barry's and Banks's cycles. If the emergence of the railroad signalled a sea change for the small town of Winesburg, its departure symbolises the demise of Lima. The characters cannot get nostalgic about a return to *gemeinschaft* because the agrarian economic structure no longer exists for such a town and their alienation from each other thwarts new modes of economic or social progress. It is the railroad that takes George out of Winesburg, suggesting that the youth will leave such places behind.

The need to leave a place and return to it in stories marks the final narrative moments of *The Circus in Winter* much as it does in *Winesburg*. This concluding theme gains geographic specificity in the context of the circus town. In this moment and elsewhere, *Winesburg* provides a general model but not an exact blueprint. Jenny Perdido relates that her mother categorised everybody into competing types: 'town people and circus people' (269). Those who leave and make lives elsewhere are circus people. Jenny explains that being a circus person is both a gift and threat:

> It's a fire that burns hot and bright, and I know if I let it get out of control, I'll turn into flecks of scorched paper and blow away. But that fire also gave me the courage to leave Lima and make the life I wanted, for which I'm thankful.
>
> At the college where I teach, I'm surrounded by circus people. We aren't tightrope walkers or acrobats. We don't breathe fire or swallow swords. We're gypsies, moving wherever there's work to be found . . . No place is home. Every place is home. Home is our stuff . . . It's taken me a long time to figure out one very simple

thing: The world is made up of hometowns. It's just as hard to leave a city block in Brooklyn or a suburb in Chicago as it is to leave a small town in Indiana. And just because it was hard to leave Linden Avenue in Flatbush or the Naperville city limits or Lima doesn't mean you can't ever go back. (Day 2004: 270–1)

Being a circus person is marked by an ability to be transient and find meaning in each new place, which is the allure of the circus even to those who remained in Lima. The cycle's end suggests that a desire to leave a place, likened to a fire, threatens just as much as the stagnation of staying. Jenny's attitude suggests that where one lives is less important than how one lives, although so much in culture communicates the opposite. The cycle concludes with a radio signal – again, once a sign of modern communication, now a near-relic of the past – that allows us to 'hear our hometowns talking softly to us in the back of our dreams' (271). The end calls back to the final moments of *Winesburg*. Day's ending even makes mention of the idea that one should marry one's self, cementing that, in the short story cycle as a genre, growing up is not symbolised by marriage but by claiming an individual identity and place in the larger world. In both, a writer expresses how indebted he or she is to the hometown and how necessary leaving is. Both writers are haunted by the details and specificity of the place, even as the passages register the universality of the experience, noted here by the reference to city, suburb, and rural spaces. Even so, it is striking how often writers engage limited localities, especially small towns, to portray the competing senses of claustrophobia and intimacy that mark modern experience.

Problems of Form and Periodisation

One reason that the short story cycle as a genre gets obscured in critical accounts is that it defies the narratives of periodisation to which other genres more easily subscribe. *Winesburg* blends realism and the newest avant-garde practices to show modernism's arrival to the American small town, which continues in the short story cycles by Banks, Day, and Barry. Casting the processes and crises in terms of a mode of literary expression invested in both realism and the avant-garde, *Winesburg* engages a practice of modernism that is neither divorced from earlier forms nor resistant to Pound's famous injunction to 'make it new'. Rita Barnard argues that 'The "revolution" of modernity, as Anderson calls it, was not the exclusive experience of urban sophisticates: it extended unevenly and inexorably across the nation – even into the country store and into the minds of the folks who still gathered around the woodstove to chat' (2005: 40). The very themes that *Winesburg* brings to the fore – alienation, the inability to communicate, the depth of individual lives – often appear to be the particular province of modernism.

That they persist in contemporary short story cycles questions where and when such distinctions begin and end. It is this question of where that Barnard takes up: Anderson effectively opened up modernism beyond the city. Although others engaged rural spaces in modernist texts before him, Anderson became the key figure for many in rendering modernist techniques, which Barnard characterises as 'dislocation, repetition, and poetic figuration' (2005: 45), rural. As they present latter-day Winesburgs, the cycles by Banks, Barry, and Day also challenge the very parameters and meaning of modernism. The commonality of form, setting, and subject among these works, as well as the authors' explicit acknowledgements of *Winesburg* as forebear, ultimately position Anderson's cycle as a pioneer in exploring the malleability of both genre and literary style.

Day credits *Winesburg* as inspiration for *The Circus in Winter* precisely because it engages non-linear narrative:

> *Winesburg, Ohio* made an indelible impact on me and many other writers. For that, it's a great book. Then there's this: So often, linear novels get more credit in terms of 'greatness' than story cycles or story collections. Why? The story cycle form, the collage, is incredibly difficult to master. Actually, I think that our postmodern narrative sensibility is more informed by collage than chronology. (Day 2008)

The Circus in Winter has a postmodern textual self-consciousness. Day compares the cycle to the collage, attributing innovation and mastery in terms of structure to Anderson. Postmodernism here is best understood – as Madhu Dubey conceptualises it – not so much as an 'epochal shift' but 'as a moment of perceived crisis within the modern' with the understanding that 'aesthetic modernism more often than not sets itself at odds with many of the modern categories' such as 'progressive notion of time and history' and the possibility of 'centered and stable identity' (2003: 18). Thus understood, literary realism, modernism, and postmodernism represent shifts in emphases rather than whole-scale reinvestments and reinventions. As postmodernist as Day's cycle is, the preoccupation with grotesques, nostalgia, and alienation indicate that the cycle is not entirely distinct from earlier cycles.

The vignettes and individual stories in these cycles are like the print cousins to oral forms of storytelling. As writers attempt to recreate an American vernacular in print, the short story cycle lends itself to shorter stories that could be repeated and to making speech a primary means of constructing characterisation. Many of these cycles replicate the intonation, slang, and word choice of the region they describe. Day's work emblematises the ways in which contemporary storytellers translate oral stories to written text. In her work, she draws from stories passed down to her, but she fictionalises them to make them her own. For instance, 'Winnesaw – or Nothing Ever Stops Happening When It's Over' is based on a story told by her great-grandparents about a flood of the Mississinewa River in Peru, according to the author in a telephone interview (C. Day, personal communication, 2 March 2008). The basis for 'The Lone Star Cowboy – or Don't Fence Me In' is a story about twin brothers, one of whom shot the other; however, the house in the story was not painted with murals of circus acts but natural landscapes, such as waterfalls. 'Boss Man – or The Gypsies and Appear and Poof! They're Gone' is partly based on her own experience of having lived on a campground. However, as Day points out, basing stories on oral accounts and even on one's own experiences can be tricky, as truth and fiction intermingle. For instance, Day thought she had made up the clairvoyant woman who appears in 'Jennie Dixianna' after reading *Stars Fell on Alabama* (1934) by Carl Carmer at the age of twenty-four. Upon reading her book, however, Day's mother and grandmother reminded her that they had told her about the verse years before. Even though distinguishing truth from fiction is vexed, ultimately a writing style like Day's reinstates orality's communal impact.

Winesburg, Granite State Trailerpark, Lucy's Tavern, and Lima become the sites and repositories for the expression of alienation, dislocation, and repetition so often associated with modernism. Their stories acknowledge realism's commitment to pluralistic truth and the value of the individual, as well as postmodernism's scepticism of the all-consuming narrative. The short story cycle proves to be a form that yields new crops with each aesthetic development. These books are just a few of the cycles indebted to *Winesburg*; I might also have included Donald Ray Pollock's *Knockemstiff* (2008) and Stuart Dybek's *I Sailed with Magellan* (2003), among others. The reason for this proliferation is simple: place continues to make meaningful the paradoxes of community, namely the connections between individuals and the individual's insuperable solitude. This paradox transcends periodisation.

Note

1. The Works Progress Administration was a major economic stimulus programme that, among other initiatives, employed writers and intellectuals to record American history and folk culture during the Great Depression.

Chapter 3

Writing Time in Metaphors

Three years before Ray Bradbury began writing the stories that would become *The Martian Chronicles* (1950), he read Sherwood Anderson's *Winesburg, Ohio*. In the introduction to the revised 1997 edition, Bradbury claims that 'It was Sherwood Anderson's *Winesburg, Ohio* that set me free. Sometime in my twenty-fourth year, I was stunned by its dozen characters living their lives on half-lit porches and in sunless attics of that always autumn town. "Oh, Lord," I cried. "If I could write a book half as fine as this, but set it on Mars, how incredible that would be!"' (1997: viii).[1] Anderson's inspiration is felt in the stories' common setting and the pervasive sense of nostalgia that promises – but never delivers – to relieve the toxic effects of progress. Here, though, he takes aim not at urbanisation but at so-called technological improvements like nuclear proliferation and automatised labour. The subject shifts; critical nostalgia remains.

Bradbury's stories, unlike Anderson's, feature characters that, for the most part, do not recur, and there is no central figure to connect the stories. He had published many of the stories previous to their inclusion in the volume under different names and with different details. Bradbury calls the form a 'book-of-stories-pretending-to-be-a-novel' and lists his *Dandelion Wine* (1957) as following in the same tradition (1997: x). Bradbury admits that his stories evince little direct influence from *Winesburg*:

> Will you find blood traces of Sherwood Anderson here? No. His stunning influence has long since dissolved into my ganglion. . . . Anderson's grotesques were gargoyles off the town roofs; mine are mostly collie dogs, old maids lost in soda fountains, and a boy super-sensitive to dead trolley cars, lost chums, and Civil War Colonels drowned in time or drunk on remembrance. The only gargoyles on

Mars are Martians disguised as my Green Town relatives, hiding out until comeuppance. (Bradbury 1997: x)

The grotesque force of nostalgia links these figures and books. *Winesburg* influenced *The Martian Chronicles* in its design and the stories' emphasis on limited locality, which shifts from a small town to a planet. Some of the stories are set on Earth, but most concern travel to and settlement of Mars. Despite this difference in scale, the limited locality functions in much the same way.

Limited locality stabilises place but opens up time to be fluid and recursive as Bradbury's inspiration and tales suggest. Critical nostalgia is invested in how ideas of the past shape the present and future in inescapable and, often, destructive ways. The short story cycle renders and collapses the divisions made between past, present, and future. That the short story emerged simultaneous to what James Wood calls the 'new and unique project in literature' (2008: 87) – of portraying multiple temporalities and the passage of time – intimates its important place in literary history. Novelists translated the cycle's techniques for evoking multiple, individual times and simultaneous public history; these borrowings blur generic distinctions. Thus, writers as diverse as Gustave Flaubert, Ray Bradbury, and Amy Tan work in and poach from both genres. Ultimately, however, the novel necessitates a conclusion, while the cycle revels in the anti-ending, the ellipsis, the new beginning; consequently, the short story cycle often portrays perpetual temporality.

This perpetual temporality connects with the genre's treatment of identity as in process. Cycles dismiss unities of time in favour of exploring the way time expands, contracts, and shifts in relation to perspective. Questioning the meaning attached to any single moment, cycles linked by temporal markers bring characters' linguistic, cultural, familial, and ethnic identities into moments of coherence that simultaneously resist totalising. Short story cycles' deployment of temporal metaphors shows how subjective and objective times coexist and how such metaphors bridge the perceived divide between personal and public times. Temporal markers dramatise how the progression and flux of time construct provisional personal and communal identities.

These cycles, although radically different in subject matter and style, represent the dominant modes of using time to make cycles cohere. Bradbury's *The Martian Chronicles* follows a linear chronology and describes the exploration, conquest, and repopulation of Mars by humans. Conversely, in Erdrich's *Love Medicine* the stories jump back and forth across time to narrate the lives of interconnected families in the western United States.[2] Bradbury's cycle invokes a confluence of historical forces – time as value-laden, work as a calling, and travel as necessitating standardised time – and contextualises them in relation to anxieties about the space race. Erdrich's cycle invokes broader, oppositional conceptions of time – as recursive and arbitrary and as causal and meaningful – to depict time as implicated in an entire system of measurement that made possible the destruction, exploitation, and forced removal of the Chippewa people. As they treat time in relation to space exploration and the reservation, they meditate on the ways in which particular kinds of (supra)national spaces force competing conceptions of temporality to coexist. Both volumes understand the United States to be preoccupied with imperialist impulses that ignore how the nation's actions in the present and future recreate the past. Even as they critique such projects, they also point to the irreversibility of this course, the complicated connections between time and narrative that arise from such projects, and the tenacity with which individuals encounter these systems.

A common thread in Erdrich's and Bradbury's cycles is the treatment of time in relation to two or more cultures. In *Love Medicine*, Chippewa ideas of time conflict with the standardisation and measurement of time in the mainstream United States. Erdrich focuses on the experiences of Chippewa and white characters whose lives are intertwined on the reservation, a space that exists both within and on the margins of the United States. In the *Chronicles*, Bradbury represents the Martians' cultural conception of time as being at odds with human conceptions. The Martians' situation – facing extinction – mirrors the threats to Native people during and after the exploration of the New World. The cycles' multiple cultural constructions of temporality engage with time in ways that resonate with what Gloria Anzaldúa calls a 'Borderland', which 'is a vague and undetermined place created by the emotional residue of an unnatural boundary. It is in a constant state of transition' (1999: 25). Such Borderlands develop 'wherever two or more cultures edge each other' (Anzaldúa 1999: 19). Borderlands are physical, linguistic, and cultural, but they also have a temporal dimension in that the 'state of transition' initiates its own time based on the movement from one way of perceiving reality to another. In this creation of a transitional temporality, the cycles are also akin to Mary Louise Pratt's idea of the 'contact zone', which 'refer[s] to social spaces where cultures meet, clash, and grapple with each other, often in contexts of highly asymmetrical relations of power, such as colonialism, slavery, or their aftermaths as they are lived out in many parts of the world today' (1991: 34). Both *Love Medicine* and the *Chronicles* enact the conditions of the Borderland and contact zone as they depict cultures meeting, clashing, and coexisting. The stories render the uneasy negotiations of multiple temporalities through sensory perception and metaphor. The cycles' disjointed but interconnected structures, with their emphasis on what I call 'interstitial temporalities', reflect the experience of time at a crossroads, whether that is between two or more languages, cultures, or spaces.

From Railroads to Rocket Ships: Progress and Time in *The Martian Chronicles*

Bradbury's *Chronicles* adapts one of the most linear of forms of narrative: the diary. Each story, identified by the month and date of its happening, documents the exploration, invasion, and conquest of the fourth planet by the United States. Narrated in the third-person past tense, the *Chronicles* features important episodes in human history on Mars that appear to move toward a final end-point. Some of the entries consist of full stories; others are mere sketches. There are gaps in time between the stories, and the duration of these gaps varies widely. Most often, months pass between episodes; however, sometimes a series of stories will take place on the same day or occasionally years will pass between stories. Despite the uneven passage of time, the stories progress chronologically and are almost uniformly identified by month and year.[3] Noting the journal-like nature of the volume, Walter J. Mucher contends that 'His narrative represents the temporality of Martianness . . . it represents the space in which Martianness may be made attainable' (2002: 172). Thus, the stories actively record a development of Martian consciousness based on temporality.

In its form and content, Bradbury's cycle is reminiscent of the journals kept by explorers as they travelled and mapped the New World (as well as the village sketch narratives of Chapter 1). Bradbury collapses the entire history of New World exploration and colonisation into twenty-seven years. As they show the progression of human life on Mars, the sequence of the stories is largely teleological. The narrative structure appears to indicate that each entry or story moves the narrative toward a final culmination of Martianness, which Mucher attributes to the fact that Bradbury wrote the last story, 'The Million-Year Picnic', first (2002: 180). Although the *Chronicles* engages the relationship of time to technology and standardisation to record exploration, an undercurrent of scepticism about linear, segmented time recurs throughout the *Chronicles*. The stories often imply – and sometimes explicitly describe – scepticism about the possibility of forging a single Martian identity and humanity's right to claim one. While the cycle follows a chronological order, the multiple narrative voices and the cyclicality of the narrative events, both within the cycle and larger historical patterns, undermine this teleology. The standardisation of time, and the ability to measure, know, and record history by it, is ultimately dubious in the *Chronicles*. The volume's many attempts to understand time through metaphor reveal the intensity of this scepticism.

Bradbury's particular deployment of time replicates the development of standardised, measured time, which was initiated and intensified under early capitalism. According to E. P. Thompson, during the stages of 'nascent industrial capitalism', the idea of time underwent radical transformation (1967: 80). The spread of industrialised labour required a rigorous measuring and regulation of time. Thompson characterises this shift as moving from a 'task-oriented' sense of time wherein '"natural" work-rhythms' determine the course and scope of labour to a sense of time as a commodity wherein labour is measured by time (1967: 60). In the earlier model, social life and work intermingle, whereas social life and work are distinct under industrial capitalism. Emerging modes of manufacturing required a 'greater synchronization of labour and a greater exactitude in time-routines', and the power of these changes to people's work lives translated into their leisure and personal time (Thompson 1967: 80).

In the context of the United States, Max Weber connects this intensified insistence on the value of time to a Protestant ethos of work and belief in every individual having a calling or purpose. Although the initial religious connotations of these ideas have faded, he argues that Protestant beliefs in the brevity of life and necessity of purpose inspired Western nations – and the United States in particular – to view time as having intrinsic value. Weber lists a number of Ben Franklin's maxims that centre on the notion that 'time is money' as evidence for a particular national attitude toward time and work (1998: 48–51). Time, work, money, and virtue became so interdependent in the United States that Weber concludes that the 'Waste of time is thus the first and in principle the deadliest of sins . . . Loss of time through sociability, idle talk, luxury . . . is worthy of absolute moral condemnation' (1998: 157–8). The logic of individual perfectibility, originating in religious belief but transferring to economic and social spheres, transformed the way people lived. Many of the characters in Bradbury's cycle express a belief that they were chosen and destined to settle Mars. They treat the exploration of space in almost the exact same terms as Franklin's maxims and Weber's observations. The entire project of Martian exploration originates from the promise of future perfectibility.

Bradbury's cycle adheres to the division and regulation of time initiated under nascent capitalism and extended during industrialisation. Railroads were instrumental in these changes; where once a passenger might wait a whole afternoon for a train, efforts to standardise time sought to guarantee that trains arrived and departed at specific times. More than the lone, sad passenger waiting on the train, the money lost to inefficient travel compelled railroad companies to unite. The reliance on varied local times hindered consistent, reliable transportation, and most industrialised companies adopted standard local times in the 1880s and 1890s. In 1884, the International Meridian Conference convened in Washington, DC; the participants 'divided the world into twenty-four time zones, established Greenwich as the zero meridian, and set the exact length of a day', thus standardising time at regional, national, and international levels (Doane 2002: 5). The cycle's adherence to standardised time connects to expansion and movement: namely, the development of technologies to expand humanity's presence in space. In place of the railroads, space travel becomes the impetus for the proliferation of standardised time in Bradbury's cycle. Compounding this industrial impulse to explore and expand is the urgency with which the United States wishes to claim and settle Mars in this cycle. The US military does not wish to waste a moment of time in its quest to find a new home and resources for its citizens, who face many external threats.

In expanding the actual space wherein humans operate, Bradbury magnifies the reach of standardised time. The every-man astronauts of the Martian spaceships must learn to better account for time in their travels. It takes the travellers one month to travel from Earth to Mars. On the first expeditions, the men – and they are all men initially – have little control or knowledge over where they land. By the fourth expedition, the men are able to select the place and time of their landing. Despite this adaptation, the men are incapable of acclimatising to a different sense of time on Mars, revealing the extent to which they hold fast to time's Earthly standardisation. Although days, months, and years no longer mean what they did on Earth, they insist on measuring everything in Earth days, months, and years, from the time they work on projects to the time they spend travelling through space. Their adherence depicts time as a human invention that can continue when the natural environment no longer supports it.

This reliance on temporal markings exposes the travellers' desire to find earth-like objects and places on Mars; both signal their desire for familiarity in the foreign environment. The astronauts rebuild Mars in Earth's image – as much as they are able. The American astronauts move through apparently abandoned Martian cities to construct small towns in rural spaces that mirror a sentimental idea of their lives back home. For example, they bring 'Oregon lumber' to build 'the nicest little villages you ever saw' such as 'Green City', which is located right off of the 'Illinois Highway' (Bradbury 1950: 108). The future of Mars – the very apotheosis of progress and perfectibility – eerily resembles a Norman Rockwell portrait, which, the stories intimate, was largely chimera, as the landscape and native Martian inhabitants resist such colonial effacement. When the Martians attack, they do so by taking aim at the military-astronauts' nostalgia and adherence to Earthly time.

In 'The Third Expedition', the sixth story in the cycle, the indigenous Martians use 'Telepathy, hypnosis, memory, and imagination' to recreate a small town, Green Bluff, Illinois from 1926 (64). Green Bluff seems a surrogate for Bradbury's own hometown of Waukegon, Illinois, which he often fictionalises. Each of the men sees his own hometown in this place, even though they come from different parts of the United States and are born decades apart. The town becomes whatever the men want it to be; it symbolises their desire for home, cast here as an idealised American small town. The town's architecture includes leaded-glass windows, cupolas, porch swings, and Victorian houses complete with dunce-cap roofs, scrolls, and rococo (50). The nostalgic rendering of place mirrors Anderson's cycle, as *Winesburg* is set in the 1890s, and sentimentality for the near-past permeates the stories. Nostalgia is a collective fantasy, what Boym calls 'a historical emotion' that 'is coeval with modernity itself. Nostalgia and progress are like Jekyll and Hyde: alter egos' (2001: xvi). Bradbury dramatises the destructive force of nostalgia, imbuing all of those details – that would seem to provide solace – with toxicity to signal the costs of this interplanetary progress, especially Earthly conceptions of time.

Writing Time in Metaphors 67

When the men from the expedition approach a woman from the town, they attempt to use space and time to resolve their confusion:

> 'Everyone knows,' she said, 'this town was built in 1868. Is this a game?'
> 'No, not a game!' cried the captain. 'We're from Earth.'
> 'Out of the ground, do you mean?' she wondered.
> 'No, we came from the third planet, Earth, in a ship. And we've landed here on the fourth planet, Mars – '
> 'This,' explained the woman, as if she were addressing a child, 'is Green Bluff, Illinois, on the continent of America, surrounded by the Atlantic and Pacific oceans, on a place called the world, or, sometimes, the Earth. Go away now. Good-by.' (Bradbury 1950: 55)

The way in which the woman moves from the local to the global mirrors and satirises the astronauts' ethno- and planetary-centricity. The astronauts are looking for stability and knowledge, and by creating this space, the Martians lull the astronauts into trust. They affirm this trust by populating the town with the men's dead loved ones. Grandparents, brothers, and even children greet the men, and they spend a luxurious day basking in the familial glow of a bygone era. The sight and familiarity of those long lost deepen the men's feelings of comfort – they do not want to know that this is not reality and that their loved ones are not real. The desire to remain oblivious signals the men's deep sense of alienation from each other and from their lives on Earth. As the men attempt to explain the odd place where they have landed, they all develop different hypotheses, but no one listens to anyone else. The Martians exploit the men's feelings of alienation and their inability to communicate; isolating them in their homes that same evening, the Martians kill the men of the third expedition.

This slaughter represents the symbolic endpoint of such nostalgic renderings of place and an inability to embrace an interstitial temporality. The malevolence hiding behind leaded windows renders the Winesburg-like setting grotesque. Even as the story builds sympathy for the complicated lives of the astronauts and the Martians, Bradbury implies that such sentimentality invites insidious results. Anderson's cycle also contains an implicit critique of such sentimentality, as it destabilises the myth of a pastoral American Eden ruined by modernisation and industrialisation. Bradbury cites this story as one of the few that bears a direct imprint of Anderson's cycle.[4] Bradbury revises Anderson's trope of 'the grotesque', which is the 'notion that the moment one of the people took one of the truths to himself, called it his truth, and tried to live his life by it, he became a grotesque and the truth he embraced became a falsehood' (Anderson 1999: 9). In this story, the 'truth . . . embraced' is twofold: human supremacy and nostalgia. The astronauts' obstinate faith in their own innate claim to Mars and in their idyllic rendering of the past prove to be their undoing. The Martians in human drag reflect the astronauts' grotesque adventure and attitudes. This story emphatically embraces central themes of *Winesburg*, casting them in the setting of the idealised space of the small town on Mars.

Despite getting their 'comeuppance' in this story, subsequent stories portray the astronauts as ultimately victorious in recreating Mars in Earth's image, and they replicate the very kind of towns represented through hypnosis. The recurrence of such elements lends the volume a cyclical quality, even as individual stories remain independent. As in this example, the revelations of one story do not get communicated or impact the actions or sensibilities in another. In Bradbury's cycle, this disjunction parallels the lack of communication between the various expeditions and among the settlers. The cycle's diary-like structure, with the assignation of a date to each story, reflects the depth of the astronauts' insistence on Earthly standardisation. Because the stories depict, for the most part, characters that adhere to the logic of exploration and the connected demands of imperialism, capitalism, and masculinity, the humans mostly maintain and even extend many established attitudes toward time.

Imagining the Future of Time

Bradbury's *Chronicles* represents most of the explorers and settlers as adhering to objectified, standardised time; however, the stories repeatedly zoom in on individual characters who challenge the primacy of such an understanding of time by embracing interstitial temporality. Bradbury's most explicit statements on a different relationship to experiencing time appear in 'Night Meeting'. Set in August of 2002 in the midst of human settlement on Mars, the main action of the story concerns the meeting of a Martian and a human on a deserted highway. The man, Tomás Gomez, believes that Martians have become extinct from an epidemic of chicken pox that swept the planet after the third expedition; this meeting understandably unsettles him. Tomás Gomez is one of a few characters in the cycle whose name marks him as an ethnic minority in the United States. Bradbury paints these characters as sympathetic to the conditions of Martian extinction, which resonates with the effect of smallpox on Native Americans. However, these characters remain complicit in colonisation.

In Tomás Gomez's story, a conflict arises over the question of time on the red planet. Bradbury foreshadows the story's discussion of time in an encounter Tomás has with an old man, who explains to him, 'If you can't take Mars for what she is, you might as well go back to Earth. Everything's crazy up here, the soil, the air, the canals, the natives (I never saw any yet, but I hear they're around), the clocks. Even my clocks act funny. Even *time* is crazy up here' (Bradbury 1950: 103). Many of the settlers try to remake Mars in Earth's image, evidenced in the purpose of Tomás's travelling, which is to christen 'Green City' off of the 'Illinois Highway'. The man advocates letting Mars remain what it is. For him, time represents the absolute limit of what they cannot recreate and reminds them of the superficiality of their control over the landscape. Their renaming of the towns and their adherence to Earthly time prove futile.

Tomás's own observations on time reveal a sense of temporality for which linearity cannot account. As he drives alone, Tomás perceives time as sensory:

> There was a smell of Time in the air tonight. He smiled and turned the fancy in his mind. There was a thought. What did Time smell like? Like dust and clocks and people. And if you wondered what Time sounded like it sounded like water running in a dark cave and voices crying and dirt dropping upon hollow box lids, and rain. And, going further, what did Time *look* like? Time looked like snow dropping silently into a black room or it looked like a silent film in an ancient theater, one hundred billion faces falling like those New Year balloons, down and down into nothing. That was how Time smelled and looked and sounded. And tonight – Tomás shoved a hand into the wind outside the truck – tonight you could almost *touch* Time. (Bradbury 1950: 103–4)

Linear time depends upon an objectivity, in which time can be measured, used, wasted, and controlled; however, this scene proposes that time is subjective. The scene represents that how we experience time determines what it is, rather than it having some quality outside of our experience. Tomás perceives time as sensory; a sense that he can smell it introduces a series of questions about how we sense time. Even as Tomás seeks to understand time through his senses, he can do so only through analogy to Earthly objects. Time smells like the tangible objects used to measure it. After this analogy, however, the comparisons shift to the emptiness within tangible objects: the sounds of things falling in hollow places, the images of silent film and dark rooms, and air-filled balloons falling into nothing. In these analogies, time is the absent thing in an object. In the final statement, time gains spatial dimensions when Tomás reaches out to touch 'Time', naming the hills through which he drives 'Time'. The capitalisation of 'Time' throughout the story assigns it the designation usually reserved for proper nouns, so it gains the distinction of Mars, Earth, and other place names. This designation extends to other terms of time such as 'Past' and 'Future'. This scene asks whether it is possible to know what time is through our bodily experience of it.

While the above passage offers a tentative conception of time through sensory perception and metaphors, Tomás's subsequent meeting with a Martian further destabilises time and space, by challenging the belief that our bodies are dependable. When the Martian, who identifies himself as Muhe Ca, reaches out to take a cup of coffee offered by Tomás, the narrator explains, 'Their hands met and – like mist – fell through each other' (105). In this scene, sight gives an impression that touch denies, calling into question the reliability of any sense. They can see through each other, and yet each feels his own physicality:

> Tomás felt of his own body and, feeling the warmth, was reassured.
> *I am real*, he thought.
>   The Martian touched his own nose and lips. 'I have flesh,' he said, half aloud. '*I am alive*.' (Bradbury 1950: 106)

Tactility proves insufficient when they try to confirm their knowledge through sense. The emphasis on the italicised '*I*' reflects a desire to control their individual sense of what they know. The body loses its materiality, and this loss initiates a loss of control over time. Each is heading to places the other cannot see, and this leads them to question who is in the present and who is from the past.

Not knowing if either (or both) of them is actually in the present becomes the catalyst for questioning whether we can know or measure time. When Tomás tries to orient the stranger, he explains that it is 2002. Muhe Ca asks what that means to him, and Tomás concedes that it means nothing at all. Muhe Ca explains, '"It is as if I told you that it is the year 4462853 S.E.C. It is nothing and more than nothing! Where is the clock to show us where the stars stand?"' (109). Efforts to measure time become meaningless in the Martian environment. They must find a compromise that both grants their bodies some knowledge and accounts for their coexistence. Thus, Muhe Ca offers an explanation: 'My heart beats, my stomach hungers, my mouth thirsts. No, no, not dead, not alive, either of us. More alive than anything else. Caught between is more like it' (109). The interstitial state between alive and dead and past and future opens up the possibility of their coexistence without stripping them of all of their knowledge. Within this logic, there is an undercurrent of accepting the unknowable. The Martian argues, 'What does it matter who is Past or Future, if we are both alive, for what follows will follow, tomorrow or in ten thousand years. How do you know that these temples are not the temples of your own civilization one hundred centuries from now, tumbled and broken? You do not know. Then don't ask' (110). This scene establishes the power that linear time has on Tomás only to dismantle that belief through his sensory perception. Bradbury implies that the senses provide the best knowledge of time while also asking whether we can trust them. The Martian's final statement indicates that consciousness determines time's meaning.

The Martian teaches Tomás about the pitfalls of insisting on Earthly measures of time, advocating instead for an interstitial time, resonant with the borderland they inhabit. This lesson does not, however, get communicated to the other humans on Mars, and this story's revelations are isolated from the rest of the cycle. The scene indicts the general attitude while allowing for some flexibility and sympathy from Tomás. It shatters the insistence, present in several of the other stories, that Martians are now extinct. Their mutual positions as solitary, perceptive, and accepting generates solidarity between them. Alongside the sheer presence of the Martian, this solidarity destabilises any sense of who is in power and has control. That Tomás is ethnically marked suggests that there are points of connection among ethnic Americans and Martians, particularly in terms of experiencing temporality. Bradbury explicitly draws a connection between ethnicity and Martianness in an earlier scene. When asked about who he would side with, if there were Martians, a character named Cheroke says, 'I've got some Cherokee blood in me. My grandfather told me lots of things about Oklahoma territory.

If there's a Martian around, I'm all for him' (81). In the end, however, he does not side with the Martians and is killed. The Martians become the last in a long series of groups constructed as ethnic or racial in a US culture dominated by European whiteness. In this cycle, humanity on Mars is largely white, American, militarised males. The characters' epiphanies of the common experiences of Native Americans, Latinos, and Martians intimate possibilities for solidarity, but the stories' narratives of conquest and death ultimately remain pessimistic about the power and meaning of such affiliations. Tomás and Cheroke register the ambivalence with which ethnically marked US citizens participate in US imperialism. The 'Night Meeting' between this particular human and Martian confirms a sense of simultaneous reality for them, despite their sense that they may not share the same temporality. Whether they are meeting each other during the peak or in the aftermath of their civilisations becomes a meaningless distinction, because they share a present experience.

The Generic Production of Simultaneity

Short story cycles linked by temporal concerns – and the *Chronicles* in particular – explore simultaneity in all of its contradictions. Simultaneity invites the individual to participate in public time while also expanding the individual's sense of a personal time. It is, according to Andrew Hoskins, most simply understood as 'events at a distance witnessed in real-time by a global audience' (2004: 111). The project of nation-building (or, in Bradbury's volume, of planet-building), marked by a vested interest in expanding the nation's space through colonialism, is coeval with the emergence of simultaneity. The ability to travel to Mars, to colonise it and survive there, and to communicate between Martian towns and Earth opens up simultaneity even further. In this volume, worldwide simultaneity has expanded to interplanetary simultaneity. In Bradbury's world, technology allows humans to travel not only across oceans but across the whole of the solar system, and it empowers them to communicate across space. According to Lauren Kogen, simultaneity also refers to 'the notion that we are experiencing multiple temporalities at once' (2006: 45). Simultaneity fosters the proliferation of a subjective, personal time for 'thinking, feeling, knowing, communicating individuals' (Nowotny 1994: 28). As technology and communication open up an even greater scope of simultaneity, the stories represent individuals seeking an individual consciousness of time, just as Muhe Ca and Tomás do. Indeed, the very division of the stories and the predominance of non-recurring characters point to the proliferation of individual experiences of time.

Bradbury's tendency toward openness, evidenced in the stories' punctuation, represents an expansion of time. Although the cycle dates and sequences the stories chronologically, the inclusion of ellipses disrupts the consistent forward flow of time. Ellipses recur throughout the *Chronicles*, signalling an extension or blending of time. Bradbury employs ellipses to indicate that a piece of dialogue or a song continues, as when a 'voice-clock' chimes 'Time, time, time, time . . . ever so gently', or when a sequence of events continues, as when a native Martian fantasises that 'there would be a thunderclap, a boll of smoke, a silence, footsteps on the path, a rap on the crystalline door, and her running to answer . . .' (Bradbury 1950: 24). In these cases, ellipses indicate some action that persists and blends into another. Here, time loses its ability to separate one thing from another. Ellipses – recurring in the cycle – point to events, dialogue, and moods that bleed from one moment to the next.

The most striking use of ellipses occurs at the ends of stories. Of the twenty-six stories in the original edition, eleven end in ellipses, including the final story of the volume. Many of the concluding ellipses appear in those stories that might also be termed sketches, suggesting the stories' liminal status. However, several of the more substantial and fully developed stories also include ellipses at their conclusion. In both the sketches and longer stories, these ellipses extend the present by suspending the conclusion of the story and the volume as a whole. They indicate that one story, although marked as happening at a discrete time, leads into and informs the others. What then of the final story, which has no subsequent narrative? The story concludes: 'The Martians stared back up at them for a long, long silent time from the rippling water. . . .' (222). The Martians in this sentence refer to the final humans to escape Earth in 2026. The native Martians appear to be gone; the humans who look into the water are now the only Martians. The end punctuation of this closing sentence indicates a finality that the ellipsis denies. According to Mucher, 'leaving the ending suspended by an ellipsis' refers to the way that 'The future follows a text to its "conclusion," temporally, since it recycles itself' (2002: 185). In this reading, the ellipsis at the end cycles back to the events that led to this inevitability. Throughout the *Chronicles* and particularly in the conclusion, ellipses perforate the rigid distinctions of time upon which the structure of the cycle and most of the characters' beliefs depend. The cycle's repetitious use of ellipses questions the linear chronology of the stories and implies that it is possible for history to return onto itself so that events that seem disconnected and disparate are actually interconnected and simultaneous. Naming themselves Martians ironically replicates the removal of natives from the landscape in other acts of colonisation. The openness of the end punctuation resonates with the Martian's comment to Tomás that his ruined society could be contemporaneous with human settlement on Mars. The use of ellipses, coupled with the Martian's comments, constructs a fraught Martian identity based on interstitial temporality.

In the last third of the cycle, the near-destruction of the Earth becomes the final and ultimate act of simultaneity. The destruction of Earth, complete with SOS signals, becomes the tragedy around which people share a sense of time. A three-story sequence narrates the events leading up to and following the beginning of nuclear war on Earth. Set on the same day in November 2005, 'The Luggage Store', 'The Off Season', and 'The Watchers' constitute a sequence of highly integrated stories narrating the destruction. The form of 'The Luggage Store' and 'The Watchers' replicates the sketch form of many of the stories in the cycle. As the last title, 'The Watchers', indicates, the stories portray individuals who watch Earth's destruction from Mars. The act of watching Earth's destruction apart yet together represents a supreme moment of simultaneity; however, the multiple points of view of the trilogy reflect the limited truth of any single narrative.

The three stories move chronologically through the events of that night, until they reach the final moment of shared spectatorship. The first story begins, appropriately enough, with a communication from Earth to Mars about impending nuclear war: 'It was a very remote thing, when the luggage-store proprietor heard the news on the night radio, received all the way from Earth on a light-sound beam. The proprietor felt how remote it was' (Bradbury 1950: 164). Just as radio and the discovery of light and sound waves made the conditions for simultaneity possible, they are now communicating this important news to other planets. These technologies make Earth seem both immediate and inconceivably distant. The proprietor of the luggage store and a priest discuss the news, and the latter expresses his incredulity, 'It's so far away it's unbelievable. It's not here. You can't touch it. You can't even see it. All you see is a green light. Two billion people living on that light? Unbelievable! War? We don't hear the explosions' (164). For him, sight and touch lend credence to belief; his identity as a priest is suspended as he reconciles the news with his perception. 'The Luggage Store' depicts the night before the outbreak of war, and the characters remain incapable of fathoming what that will mean for either planet.

Whereas the priest and proprietor only hear news of the impending war, the characters in the next story see the explosions. As Sam Parkhill builds a hot-dog stand meant for the thousands of settlers destined for Mars, war breaks out on Earth. Sam and his wife look up, and

> Earth changed in the black sky.
> It caught fire.
> Part of it seemed to come apart in a million pieces, as if a gigantic jigsaw had exploded. It burned with an unholy dripping glare for a minute, three times normal size, then dwindled. (Bradbury 1950: 177)

The scope of the devastation seems just as impossible in this story as the reality of Earth seemed in 'The Luggage Store'. The narrator endeavours to make sense of it by describing it as a puzzle exploding. And yet, for all of their disbelief, Sam Parkhill, the owner of the luggage store, and the priest all know that Earth remains home to many of the would-be and current settlers.

'The Watchers', the final story in the trilogy, is a near-manifestation of simultaneity in story form. Told in the third-person plural (which contrasts the first-person narration of the first two stories), the final story narrates how an unnamed 'they' came out of their Martian homes to watch the destruction of Earth. Whatever different times it may have been in these disparate Martian towns, in watching this event they come to inhabit the same temporality: 'They all came out and looked at the sky that night. They left their suppers or their washing up or their dressing for the show and they came out upon their now-not-quite-as-new porches and watched the green star of Earth there. It was a move without conscious effort; they all did it, to help them understand the news they had heard on the radio' (179). Continuing to insist on an Earthly measure of the day, the people watch from nine in the evening until midnight when the

Earth finishes burning, and even then they continue watching. At two in the morning, a message comes across in Morse-code flashes of light, presumably because other means of communication have been blacked out. The message reads:

> AUSTRALIAN CONTINENT ATOMIZED IN PREMATURE EXPLOSION OF ATOMIC STOCKPILE. LOS ANGELES, LONDON BOMBED. WAR. COME HOME. COME HOME. COME HOME. (Bradbury 1950: 180)

The sentence structure and appearance on the page replicate the look of a telegram. The use of an obsolete technology implies the sheer devastation of Earth's infrastructure and resonates with the communication of personal and national tragedy via telegraph during the World Wars. With this replication, Bradbury transfers the connotation, of a recent but irreversible loss, of those wartime messages in this unfamiliar and unnerving setting. 'The Watchers' enacts global simultaneity on Mars. The anonymity of the speakers and actors in the story enhances the effect of sharing an experience with those unknown to us. They read the event together as it is happening, distinguishing this as an act of simultaneity of unparalleled scope.

And yet, the contradictions of simultaneity persist; the watchers feel both close to and very distant from Earth. Although they all watch together, each is also alone with the magnitude of what he or she witnesses. The story ends by returning to the scene of 'The Luggage Store', where the proprietor has anticipated a demand for suitcases. He suspects correctly, 'By dawn the luggage was gone from his shelves' and with it most of the people who came to Mars looking for a way out of Earth's problems (180). This final story in the trilogy heightens the importance of measured time, referring throughout to the particular hours. However, all of that is merely backdrop for Bradbury's final statement on time: witnessing loss clarifies the extent to which we are undeniably bound to one another and also desperately alone.

Written and published in the initial years of the Cold War, the cycle directly addresses the time of its production. In this cycle, the Mars of the future becomes a repository for the anxieties of the mid-century. Namely, the destruction of Earth in a nuclear war signals the extent to which Bradbury's is not so much a narrative of a distant future but a prophetic vision of a possibly all-too-close present.

Cold War anxieties of the need to claim extranational space and the development – and precariousness – of nuclear arms saturate the stories. The cycle presupposes a US victory in the space race, as all of the missions and settlers are from the United States. By making Mars a surrogate for contemporary national anxieties, Bradbury explores the place of the United States in history while offering an allegorical warning for the present and future. The loose structure of the cycle allows individual stories to explore each historical parallel and creates a damning metanarrative on historical repetition. Even the ending of the cycle, with its image of human-Martians looking at their reflections in the water, forecasts that life will continue on Mars as something repetitive and unique. The cycle's structure, based as it is on measured, linear time, mirrors the cycle's critique of how structures of power use and misuse time. However, recurrence within the stories and isolated bodily experiences of time challenge time's hegemony. Thus, the *Chronicles* depicts the nature of time by engaging the most powerful and polar metaphorical conceptions of it. The cycle derives its structure from calendric time and a highly linear form, the diary, and a conventionally linear narrative, exploration. In so doing, the cycle unhinges the very assumptions we make of time, genre, and story to explore how cyclicality creeps into even the narratives and endeavours we perceive to be the most linear, chronological, and teleological.

Simultaneity of the Personal: Indian Time(s)

In contrast to *The Martian Chronicles*, Erdrich's *Love Medicine*, which tells the stories of interconnected Chippewa families over a fifty-one-year span, abjures linear time in favour of a disjointed temporality. Whereas Bradbury embeds his scepticism of linear time in isolated scenes, Erdrich's characters openly and frequently express scepticism about standardised time. In 'The Good Tears', for instance, Lulu Lamartine voices a distrust of all measurements, including time: 'All through my life I never did believe in human measurement. Numbers, time, inches, feet. All are just ploys for cutting nature down to size. I know the grand scheme of the world is beyond our brains to fathom, so I don't try, just let it in' (Erdrich 2005: 282). Lulu's attitude of letting life in without the trappings of measurements articulates that time, like all of life, does not happen in a straightforward, easily divisible way. Within *Love Medicine*, time cannot be measured or contained. The characters routinely malign measurements and regulatory practices, including everything from the census to meal times to the distinctions between the past, present, and future. In the story 'Scales', for instance, the title refers to the scales used to weigh construction materials for a new highway. These scales represent a larger failure to account for the Native American presence in the state's infrastructure (Ferguson 1996: 548). Time is implicated in an entire system of measurement, which enabled the destruction and exploitation of Native Americans.

This repeated scepticism does not, however, mean that either the characters or the stories escape linear notions of time. Instead, the stories depict the characters adapting and even sometimes adopting linear time to construct interstitial temporalities that give their lives meaning. In these ways, the *Chronicles* and *Love Medicine* are not so far apart as they might initially appear to be. Linked as they both are by a temporal structure, they reveal a sense of history that blends linearity and cyclicality. The generic concern with autonomous yet interconnected stories enables the cycles to engage simultaneity as indefinitely expanding. *Love Medicine* centres on the ways that personal histories multiply; it offers a sustained development of simultaneity, which depends upon a personalised experience of time being brought into coherence with others' temporalities. Like the *Chronicles*, *Love Medicine* approaches questions of time through metaphors. Time is alternately a circle, a tangled knot, a river, and a pinball machine; as the characters struggle to grasp time, it becomes all and none of these things.

The tension between linear and cyclical temporalities surfaces in the organisation of *Love Medicine*. Each story lists the year of its major action; the designation of years divides the stories into separate units, while the consistency of the organisational principle highlights their interconnectedness. The year assigned to each story identifies when the main events of the story take place, locating the story in the larger chronology of the cycle. The first story is set in 1981, whereas the following story jumps back to 1934. Subsequent stories then move chronologically forward, until the last third of the cycle which picks up where the first story began. The final story takes place in 1985. Erdrich's inclusion of years and the development of a chronology adhere to the conception of time as progressive. The stories are also linked through a common geography and recurring interconnected families. The overlapping of temporality and kinship as structuring devices generates a sense of generational time that is both progressive and cyclical.

Even still, the cycle depicts a more cyclical sense of time than the dates and sequence indicate. The displacement of the opening story from its original chronology frames the subsequent stories so that earlier events are read through the lens of the later event. Thus, Erdrich immediately disrupts expectations of causality and resolution within the stories. Presenting the ending at the outset warns us not to expect or understand these lives to be teleological. The stories upset our expectations of causality by often moving from one storyline to an apparently unrelated one, only to return to the original plotline several stories later. Read together, the stories offer multiple causes, interpretations, and consequences for any single action or relationship. They remind us of the limited truth of any individual point of view.

Even though the stories assign a year to the action, that year does not always reflect the content of the narratives. The narrators jump back and forth across time, shifting tenses and scenes, sometimes within a single paragraph. Erdrich often labels sections by their narrators, whether they are in first or third person, but she does not always do so. Sometimes she assigns numbers to each part of a story or includes page breaks but does not do so universally. For instance, the opening story, 'The World's Greatest Fisherman', is divided into four parts, the first of which is told from the third-person limited perspective of June Kashpaw. The latter three parts are told in the first person by her niece Albertine Johnson, whose name appears above the second section. The first section of the story concerns a single night in 1981, and the rest of the story concerns events that happen a month later. However, time becomes slippery in Albertine's sections as the past invades the present. She remembers long scenes from her childhood and recounts stories that pre-date her birth. These digressions reveal Albertine's particular sense of time while also challenging the idea that the story happens in 1981.

The use of names and time distinctions to organise and label the stories reflects the overlap between individual subjectivities and their rendering of temporality. Erdrich's stories dramatise how the rise of shared, standardised time within industrialised societies also incited the expression of individualised time. Stephen Kern emphasises that 'The affirmation of private time radically interiorised the locus of experience. It eroded conventional views about the stability and objectivity of the material world and of the mind's ability to comprehend it' (1983: 314). As the earliest story's main action is set in 1934, Erdrich's stories describe industrialisation's effects on the reservation over the stories' fifty-year span. Compounding these competing notions of temporality is the cycle's investment in Ojibwe understandings of temporality, most powerfully rendered in 'The Island', the only undated story in the cycle.

'The Island' offers the most sustained treatment of characters upholding traditional Ojibwe customs. The story reveals the cycle's strongest exploration of an Ojibwe identity based on indigenous practices. Bookended by stories set in 1934 and 1948, 'The Island' takes place somewhere in that fourteen-year span, but the story fails to identify exactly when. The lack of exact dating resonates with the characters' experiences. Told in the first person by Lulu Lamartine, the story centres on a group of characters that exist outside of conventional time. The patriarch of the Kashpaw clan adopts Lulu against the will of his wife, Rushes Bear, after they have raised their children. From the outset, the relationships between these three deviate from the chronology of the rest of their lives. As she gets older and after experiencing rejection from the Kashpaws' biological son Nector, Lulu goes to live with her cousin Moses Pillager, who lives alone on an island and maintains many ancestral practices. His very existence defies time, as his mother tricked death by not speaking his name aloud when an epidemic overtook the reservation during his childhood. He lives the remainder of his days nameless and in the shadow of life. The title of the story references the place of the island, the isolation of his existence, and the alienation of Lulu's upbringing. Lulu eventually gives birth to two sons by Moses, one of whom, Gerry, inherits his father's tenacity, becoming a trickster existing outside the confines of the judicial system, which seeks to control his life by claiming his time.

'The Island' portrays these characters as creating bonds of kinship precisely because they share a different relationship to time than the other characters. The patriarch explains to Lulu that he retains Rushes Bear's love because he has a different sense of time than the other men in her life: 'No clocks. Those young boys who went to the bureau school, they run their life on white time. Not me, I go on Indian time. Stop in the middle for a bowl of soup. Go right back to it when I've got my strength. I've got nothing else to do, after all. I'm going to die soon' (Erdrich 2005: 71). He attributes their connection to a conception of time that is specifically Indian. That he resides on an island within the reservation, which is itself a kind of island within and distinct from the larger US and Ojibwe nations, compounds his sense of time. The story hints that Lulu goes to Moses for this same reason, and her particular favouritism of Gerry is a testament to the way Moses lived an Indian sense of time.

'The Island' – which lacks a date, spans several years, and features characters that maintain 'Indian time' – destabilises the chronology of the cycle as a whole. It invests the cycle with an explicit tension over linear, measured time that the volume then enacts. The story presents an idea of traditional Chippewa time, but Lulu and most of the other characters in the cycle cannot simply deny 'white time', and the story becomes one part of a larger commentary on the way interstitial temporalities operate in the characters' lives. Adopting and adapting both traditions, they create new temporalities within the contact zone.

Immanent Personal Histories in *Love Medicine*

While the sequence and dating of the stories do not always indicate connection, some stories are dated simultaneously and relate connected events – in much the same way 'The Luggage Store', 'The Off Season', and 'The Watchers' do in the *Chronicles*. The first trilogy is comprised of 'Lulu's Boys', 'The Plunge of the Brave', and 'Flesh and Blood', all set in 1957. The second trilogy of stories includes the title story, 'Resurrection', and 'The Good Tears' and describes events that take place between 1982 and 1983. Whereas the trilogy in the *Chronicles* depicts the simultaneity of an interplanetary public event, the trilogies in *Love Medicine* depict the simultaneity of localised personal events in the lives of three central characters: Lulu Lamartine, Nector Kashpaw, and Marie Lazarre. Each trilogy treats the same series of events from different characters' perspectives. Teaming the stories reveals the precarious understanding each character has of the events. Collectively, these stories comment on the nature of history and on the construction of communal experience.

'Lulu's Boys', 'The Plunge of the Brave', and 'Flesh and Blood' relate the concurrent experiences of Lulu, Nector, and Marie nearly twenty years after Nector chose to marry Marie over Lulu. Identified by the year 1957, these stories focus on the events leading up to Nector's decision to leave Marie for Lulu and the aftermath of that choice. These events appear to be somewhat isolated from the rest of the stories in the cycle, in that they take place nine years after the previous story and thirteen years before the next. However, the stories that precede and follow the 1957 stories ground the ongoing saga between these three figures. The overlapping of these with earlier and later stories insinuates that the passage of time matters little. The designation of 1957 cannot contain the range of the narratives, as even within the stories the narrators jump across time. The multiplicity of narrative points of view exacerbates the temporal disjunctions within the stories and comments on the sometimes fractured quality of simultaneity. While the overarching event of these three stories is Nector's attempt to leave Marie, the first and last stories disrupt the centrality of this dilemma by focusing on the submerged lives of the women. The extent to which personal traumas and dilemmas recur in Lulu's and Marie's lives destabilises the centrality of Nector's narrative. The first and last stories represent that simultaneity does not make the same event equally important to all of the individuals involved. The temporal slippages, compounded by the differences in narrative style, generate a simultaneity that is fissured and only partly realised.

As much as Nector is torn between Marie and Lulu, the more powerful stimulus for the events that connect these stories is his personal crisis over time. Erdrich's depiction of Nector's misgivings on time articulates his unease with adopting white time. Thoroughly entrenched in local and national government, Nector describes time as passing in a 'flash', until one day it stopped. He was 'sitting on the steps, wiring a pot of Marie's that had broken, when everything went still' (127). In this domestic scene, full of broken items and demanding children, Nector Kashpaw meditates on the passage of time:

In that stillness, I lifted my head and looked around.
What I saw was time passing, each minute collecting behind me before I had squeezed from it any life. It went so fast, is what I'm saying, that I myself sat still in the center of it. Time was rushing around me like water around a big wet rock. The only difference is, I was not so durable as stones. Very quickly I would be smoothed away. It was happening already. (Erdrich 2005: 127)

Time, imagined as a stream rushing past, exceeds Nector's control. The current shapes and erases him as rapids do rocks, except that his body registers the current of time much more quickly than stones do. The idea of himself as a rock quickly smoothed away reflects his inability to direct the current and determine its flow. The year of his revelation is 1952, just on the cusp of his affair with Lulu. The section ends, 'And here is where events loop around and tangle again' (128). Although he loves both women, Nector's decision to pursue Lulu and possibly leave Marie signifies a much larger conflict about the pressures of living with multiple conceptions of temporality. Nector's loss of control contrasts sharply with the certainty of his rival, Moses, in 'The Island'. His desire to leave Marie for Lulu results from a desire to leave the life that has caused time to move beyond his control. Nector attempts to recreate this sublime moment many times, suggesting the futility of trying to hold on to a moment. Nector's meditation, in particular the metaphor of water, raises questions about the nature of time that this short story cycle endeavours to grapple with, if not always answer. Is the stream Nector describes actual time or his recognition of it? Can the present expand indefinitely, as it does here for Nector so that it encompasses seventeen years? Or, is the present like the water rushing past in Nector's description: already gone just as one realises it is there?

In both *Love Medicine* and the *Chronicles*, and Nector's crisis echoes William James's notion of consciousness as a stream:

> When we take a rapid general view of the wonderful stream of our consciousness, what strikes us first is the different pace of its different portions. Our mental life, like a bird's life, seems to be made of an alternation of flights and perchings. The rhythm of language expresses this, where every thought is expressed in a sentence, and every sentence closed by a period. The resting-places are usually occupied by sensorial imaginations of some sort, whose peculiarity is that they can be held before the mind for an indefinite time, and contemplated without changing. (James 1884: 2–3)

In this scene, Nector is chasing the period; he is looking to perch for a moment, stop time, and examine his sensory perceptions. He desires to experience 'sensorial imaginations' over a long duration at will. In 'Night Meeting', Tomás's extended meditation on time as sensory actualises the perchings that James describes. 'Like water in a dark cave' resonates with Tomás's sense that time continues regardless of anyone's awareness of it. Although they write from radically different cultural perspectives, the recurring metaphor of water in Erdrich, Bradbury, and James illustrates a connection between time and consciousness, which can only be understood through metaphor.

The second trilogy of stories tentatively answers some of the questions that Nector's meditation inspires. The title story and 'Resurrection', both designated by the year 1982, as well as 'The Good Tears', marked as 1983, confront the cyclical nature of personal histories. The stories focus on the end of Nector's life and the reconciliation Lulu and Marie strike. 'Love Medicine', narrated by Lipsha Morrisey, the adopted (grand)son of Nector and

Marie, depicts Nector, at the end of his life, finally gaining control over time. Suffering from dementia, probably brought on as a complication of diabetes, Nector reverses and collapses time by entering into a 'second childhood'. Lipsha refuses to believe that Nector would reverse time 'from eating too much Milky Way' (Erdrich 2005: 232). Instead, he believes it when Nector says, '"I been chosen for it. I couldn't say no"' (232). Lipsha maintains that Nector 'was called to second childhood like anybody else gets a call for the priesthood or the army or whatever . . . No, he put second childhood on himself' (232). The language resonates with Weber's observations about the cultural power of the 'calling' in the United States. That the notion of vocation emerges not in the context of Protestant US work ethos but in the context of leisure for a Chippewa man reflects the extent to which the idea of a calling saturates contemporary culture. However, Nector's call to a second childhood reverses the expectations of vocation. Instead of perceiving time as intrinsically valuable or precious, he sinks into idle time and releases himself from the demands of work. In the context of his earlier crisis over time, it makes sense that Nector would claim this kind of control over time.

Nector's second childhood expands the present to include whatever time he wants. It is as if he is damming the stream that coursed over and eroded him for so long. He stops and redirects that stream to where he wishes his consciousness to go. In one scene, he thinks that he and Lulu are still in the midst of their affair, which resonates with the earlier sense that his affair grew out of a desire to stop time. When Nector finally dies, his life flashes before Lipsha (250). In this passage, time transforms from an image in nature to an object of pop-culture: 'Time was flashing back and forth like a pinball machine. Lights blinked and balls hopped and rubber bands chirped, until suddenly I realized the last ball had gone down the drain and there was nothing' (251). Although the image of the drain evokes water, Lipsha's metaphor draws from a very different source and reveals his personalised sense of time. Both metaphors imply that time is something that happens to us, not entirely within our control. Time places limits on how long we can play the game; either the last ball falls down the chute, or the water goes down the drain.

The story concludes that death might be the only constant in our personal histories and that death represents the supreme balance between the linear and cyclical. Lipsha reflects, 'It struck me how strong and reliable grief was, and death. Until the end of time, death would be our rock' (253). The titles of the final two stories in the series, 'Resurrection' and 'The Good Tears', indicate that death also makes rebirth possible. 'The Good Tears' ends with an image of the two women together. As Lulu recovers from eye surgery, Marie nurses her back to health:

> We did not talk about Nector. He was already there. Too much might start the floodgates flowing and our moment would be lost. . . . For the first time I saw exactly how another woman felt, and it gave me deep comfort, surprising. It gave me the knowledge that whatever happened the night before, and in the past, would finally be over once the bandages came off. (Erdrich 2005: 297)

By acknowledging how much their lives have looped around each other, becoming tangled again and again, they accept each other's friendship and move forward. Their reconciliation suggests that, although time moves circularly, there exists the possibility for movement beyond the inescapable recurrence that a circle implies. As the bandages come off, Lulu describes how 'The light was cloudy, but I could already see. She swayed down like a mountain, huge and blurred, the way a mother must look to her just-born child' (297). That birth and death coincide in this story points to the simultaneity of all of life; in death, they cycle back and are born again. This rebirth is not only a return; it is also a movement forward made possible by compassion. The negotiation of divergent perspectives, multiple metaphors, and interstitial temporalities renders *Love Medicine* a pliable, shifting product of the contact zone.

In the absence of an absolute understanding and experience of time, these cycles engage metaphors. Time is alternately a pinball, a stream, and the emptiness in an object. Time is material and immaterial, contemporary and ancient. These stories depict the ways in which time renders our connections real and reinforces our separation from one another. In these cycles, time flies, heals, and runs out. It can be wasted and made up. It is a test that something stands or fails to stand. Time can be stolen, borrowed, or lost. It is a force so infuriating and powerful that the characters constantly lament and harness it. These stories dramatise the expressions and idioms of time that abound; ultimately, time itself becomes a metaphor for the ineffable. Rendering temporality into metaphors is the best way, according to the cycles, to make sense of and gain a modicum of control over all that is 'beyond our brains to fathom' (282).

Notes

1. Unless noted, all references to *The Martian Chronicles* are to the 1950 edition.
2. Each author released revised and expanded versions; Erdrich did so in 1993 and then again in 2009, and Bradbury did so in 1997. *Love Medicine* is the first book in a tetralogy that includes *The Beet Queen* (1986), *Tracks* (1988), and *The Bingo Palace* (1994). For more on the relationships between Erdrich's original and revised publications, see Nagel 2001: 18–55.
3. The exception to this is the sketch 'The Naming of Names', which is listed as happening in '2004–2005'. Unlike the other stories, which focus on specific incidents, 'The Naming of Names' describes a process of naming places, which explains the variation in its dating.
4. The discrepancy between Bradbury's reference to Green Town in the introduction to the 1997 edition and the story's use of Green Bluff is because, I speculate, Green Town is the name of a town in *Dandelion Wine*.

Chapter 4

Tracing New Genealogies

Louise Erdrich's *Love Medicine* constructs the passage of time across generations; thus, Erdrich renders place, ethnicity, and nation familial. The cycle has experienced a resurgence since the 1970s, in which family occupies a central place in the structuring and linking of cycles.[1] This proliferation includes Maxine Hong Kingston's *The Woman Warrior: Memoirs of a Girlhood among Ghosts* (1975), Gloria Naylor's *The Women of Brewster Place* (1982), Jamaica Kincaid's *Annie John* (1985), Amy Tan's *The Joy Luck Club* (1989), Julia Alvarez's *How the García Girls Lost Their Accents* (1991), Christina García's *Dreaming in Cuban* (1992), and Jhumpa Lahiri's *Unaccustomed Earth* (2008). Engaging issues of identity and belonging simultaneous to a spiked interest in ethnicity and gender among academics and the public alike, these volumes have enjoyed a high degree of critical and popular attention. The number of awards given to them, the extent to which these texts are taught, and the fact that several of these cycles were adapted into television productions and films testify to their widespread appeal.[2] The proliferation of such volumes and the critical attention they generate reveal a preponderance of cycles that engage kinship as a central narrative concern and a dominant structural device.

The cycle's form allows for multiple points of view and defers closure, which aligns with its scepticism about the possibility of coherent wholeness, be it of a narrative or of a self. Karen Weekes argues that gender identity finds an outlet in the generic form: 'The structure of these cycles replicates the complex structure of women's identities: it reflects attempts to connect these fragments in a meaningful way' (2002: 3). The production of identity from fragments resonates with the genre's general preoccupations with the ongoing and contentious process of identity-making. Of cycles appearing in the 1980s, Margot Kelley asserts that '75 percent of the current writers [of the genre] are women, often women who live in positions of double marginality as members of visible minorities' (2000: 296). Tamara Sylvia Wagner argues that these cycles were part of a larger literary explosion in the last decades of the twentieth century that brought 'gender problematics to the fore. Almost routinely couched in either culture or generational conflicts (usually both), they let familial issues assume center stage' (2005: 160). These texts offer complicated, often ambivalent, responses to the interconnections among gender, ethnicity, family, and identity. They challenge the supposition that any one of these elements defines a character, text, or author, and yet the reception of these cycles – and to some extent the volumes themselves – replicates what Kate McCullough has called the 'gendered production of the ethnic', which refers to the ways in which writing exposes ethnic identity as a process that is both 'individually chosen' and 'culturally determined' and ultimately 'enacted through the gender or sexuality' of its female characters (1999: 251).

This chapter explores the production and reception of three recent cycles linked by family and written by ethnic American women writers: Tan's *The Joy Luck Club*, Alvarez's *How the García Girls Lost Their Accents*, and Lahiri's *Unaccustomed Earth*. Treating as they do Chinese and Chinese American, Dominican and Dominican American, and Bengali and Bengali American families, these volumes would seem to be worlds apart, but in their treatment of the triangulated relationship among kinship, gender, and ethnicity they are more like neighbours with good fences. These cycles exist on the margins of the genre; whereas Tan's and Alvarez's volumes straddle the border between cycle and novel, Lahiri's volume exists somewhere between collection and cycle. The volume's final three stories, entitled 'Part Two: Hema and Kaushik', constitute a cycle-within-a-collection.[3] The preoccupation with family as a fragmented and ongoing process gets reflected in the genre.

These cycles not only represent the experience of being a visible minority in the United States, but they also explore the extent to which the families' national identities hinge on migrations, particularly the experience of those who move back and forth across spaces relatively easily. This representation of migration reflects the historical moment and particular circumstances of the families; the stories reflect a period of ease and accessibility of air travel, reduced political tensions in the countries from which the families come, and the families' affluence. In their treatment of travel and citizenship, these cycles show in very practical terms the perforation of national boundaries, imagining modes of belonging that belie a single national identity. The female characters negotiate gender and sexual roles in plural environments, treating identity as multiple, and contingent. In these cycles, identity – and by extension gender and ethnic attachments – derives not only from biological relationships but also from what I term 'formative kinship', which originates in shared experiences that the characters choose to value. They model the ongoing and participatory nature of kinship, whether it originates in blood or choice.

On the Margins of Genres and Nations

Criticism on these volumes routinely addresses the connections between autobiography and ethnic identity. Scholars often focus on the extent to which Tan's recounting of a mother, Suyuan Woo, who leaves two children behind in China, aligns with Tan's own mother's experiences or the extent to which the Garcías' experiences match with the Alvarezes'. A strong autobiographical strain also runs through Lahiri's work, as she draws on familiar experiences of Bengali families living along the east coast of the United States. In 'A Note on the Loosely Autobiographical', Alvarez confirms that she draws on autobiography in her fiction but warns that the linkages can be deceiving: 'Memory is a composite of what we remember and what we are reminded to remember' (2000: 166).

Although many readers focus on the correlation of the cycle with autobiography, still others focus on the extent to which these cycles reflect ethnic sources. For instance, scholars examine the extent to which mah-jong, indicative of cultural identity, influenced the form of *The Joy Luck Club* (Nagel 2001: 190). In contrast, Marc Singer argues that that Tan's invocation of history and Chinese identity derives as much from 'occidental cliché' as from actual history (2001: 324). Frank Chin's (2005) invective against Tan and Kingston accuses both of misrepresenting and exploiting Chinese narratives and ethnic stereotypes to appeal to white audiences. Hirsh Sawhney (2008) accuses Lahiri of having too narrow a worldview and spoon-feeding white audiences a taste of cultural difference. Although these two ways of reading come to different conclusions, they originate from the same impulse and logic: these cycles fail or succeed in rendering ethnic American experiences in content and form. What is missing from these compelling analyses is the ways in which the volumes' cyclical form recurs across autobiographical and ethnic distinctions.

One explanation is that these authors draw inspiration from one another and the short story cycle allows for the combination of multiple cultural influences. In an interview Tan gave shortly after the release of *The Joy Luck Club*, Dorothy Wang, the interviewer, relates:

> [Tan] cites Bible stories, told by her late father, a Baptist minister, and 'tons of fairy tales, both Grimm and Chinese,' as influences. But in 1985 she read the novel that changed her life: Louise Erdrich's 'Love Medicine,' a set of interwoven stories told by different generations of a Native American family. Captivated by Erdrich's images and voice, Tan began writing stories. (Wang 1989)

All of the influences Tan cites are short narrative forms, and the particular identification with Erdrich suggests a formal model that focuses on family. As Tan's interview suggests, the short story cycle is so prominent among ethnic American writers of the period because it invites tensions between reality and fiction and between multiple traditions. This ambiguity in terms of form is not, however, favoured by publishers. The interactions between Tan and Putnam testify to the publishing industry's aversion to the short story form. Although Tan conceived of *The Joy Luck Club* as something closer to a collection of stories than to a novel, her publisher, Putnam, pushed for the volume to be treated as a novel. Eventually, Tan and Putnam compromised and the book was described as a 'first work of fiction' on the cover (Somogyi and Stanton 1991: 26). The ambiguity of this descriptor denotes a pervasive lack of recognition for the cycle.

These short story cycles borrow their structure and thematic content from the organisation and conflict of the family. Familial cycles typically include stories narrated from the perspectives of individual members, as in Jing-mei Woo's dominant narrative voice in the opening story of *The Joy Luck Club* or Yolanda's narration of the opening story of *How the García Girls Lost Their Accents*. These multiple narrative points of view construct a collage-like portrait of the family. This collective portrait both draws from and counteracts the picture produced by any individual story. These cycles routinely employ an ostensibly central figure whose experiences and narrative are deeply shaped by his or her family. For instance, the frequency of their narration and the centrality of their conflicts often position Jing-mei and Yolanda as protagonists of their respective cycles. Although they are central characters, many other points of view and narratives emerge that undermine the assumption of the traditional and total protagonist. The cycle's structure often brings multiple voices together, as in the final story of Tan's cycle, 'The Blood of the Conquistadores' in Alvarez's cycle, and 'Going Ashore' in Lahiri's sequence. In this trio, Hema and Kaushik function as dual protagonists. The alternating voices of the stories parallel collective experiences that are experienced individually. The characters' recognition of the simultaneity of experience becomes the basis for kinship among and between generations. Cycles linked by family focus on events or situations fundamental to kin relations: marriages, infidelities, parent–child conflicts, deaths, and sibling relationships. The conjunction of family as principle of organisation and as major theme often revises and reimagines what the family means in the context of migration and gender conflict.

Just as cycles of limited locality address the belief that geographic proximity can engender community, short story cycles linked by family address the possibilities and limitations of forming and sustaining kinship. The cycle mimics and meditates on the historical processes influencing ideas of kinship and identity. Short story cycles linked by family directly confront the assumption that family and kinship are natural, universal, and perpetually consistent, which results from a belief that family exists outside the bounds of history and individual experience. By entrenching these families in the larger historical context, cycles linked by family challenge this pervasive, universalised conception. This universality results, according to Anne McClintock (1995), from two pervasive conceptions of family: as metaphor and as institution. As metaphor, the family serves as an analogue for an understanding of history as hierarchical and deriving from a single source. New events or movements shoot off like a new branch on a family tree. Family as a metaphor for history collapses various, often contradictory, conceptions of history into a 'global genesis narrative'. At the same time, as an institution family 'was figured as existing, naturally, beyond the commodity market, beyond politics and beyond history proper. The family thus became both the antithesis of history and history's organizing figure' (McClintock 1995: 44). By taking a limited family circle as the point of reference and positioning that family in relation to historical events, these short story cycles work to particularise and complicate universalised notions of family.

On one level, historical specificity works as backdrop in the individual cycles and as a basis for the particular make-up of these families. In *How the García Girls Lost Their Accents*, the reason for the family's migration is to escape the dictatorial rule of Rafael Leónidas Trujillo Molina. The girls' father, Carlos García, fears for his and the family's safety because of his involvement with an anti-Trujillo group. Likewise, in *The Joy Luck Club*, Suyuan Woo flees her family home in China because of the Japanese invasion of Kweilin, and a few years later she moves to California with her second husband, Canning Woo. Although these events serve as historical backdrops and the catalysts for migration, Nagel (2001) and Singer (2001) point out that the chronology between historical fact and narrative do not always align. These inaccuracies comment on the ways in which memory distorts perceptions of the past and the way fiction rewrites history to its own devices.

These cycles illustrate how historical forces shape a family. The families' departures both divide the principal families from their extended families and also create closer kinship among the newly created families that structure the cycle. The memory of these events is always present, but it rises to the surface on certain occasions, as when Carlos sees a black Volkswagen, the car Trujillo's men drove, or when Suyuan and Jing-mei fight during the latter's teenage years. The stories show that the memory of the events emerges cyclically and that such memories are the basis of kinship. When memory of these events is lacking, as it is for Jing-mei and the youngest García, Sofia, the awareness of this lack causes alienation; however, depending upon another's memories brings these characters closer to their families. Thus, the events which made exodus necessary pave the way for novel kinship in their new homes.

These cycles are set in a period of dramatic changes to family and immigration law in the United States. Although the stories span many decades, the bulk of the second generations' childhoods and the parents' original migration takes place from the 1950s through the 1970s. This period saw widespread changes to immigration laws and trends, which contributed and responded to changing attitudes toward the family. The Immigration and Nationality Act of 1965, or the Hart–Celler Act, repealed the national origin quotas of the Immigration Act of 1924. In the new legislation, family reunification became the most determining factor in gaining entry.[4] Changes to immigration law reflect the belief that separation from the family is inhumane. Although the changes to legislation often replicated the discrimination of earlier eras and tended to homogenise family, these laws also ultimately reveal the premium put on family in the legal and cultural imaginary. In their representations of separated families, Tan, Alvarez, and Lahiri all address the pain caused by familial separation.

Although these cycles do not directly reference legislative changes to immigration law, they embed the effects of these changes in the very narrative conflict of the stories. For instance, although they flee slightly earlier, the Garcías' situation mirrors a larger migration from the Dominican Republic to the United States. According to Lucía M. Suárez, in the wake of Trujillo's assassination in 1961, the military invasion of the Dominican Republic triggered spikes in migration: 'Between 1961 and 1965, 35,372 Dominicans were legally admitted to the United States. During the 1966–70 post-invasion period, the number of legally admitted Dominicans increased to 58,744. In effect, the Dominican Republic (with a total population of less than 5 million people) has one of the highest rates of legal migration to the United States' (2004: 123). Although their migration preceded the influx after Trujillo's death, the Garcías' experience resonates with common experiences of migration from the Dominican Republic. However, the Garcías enjoy certain privileges because of their connections and means, such as the ability to send the girls to private schools when attacked with racial slurs and violence in a public school.

'Hema and Kaushik' also treats the ways in which class affects the experience of migration and how immigration laws shape the characters' lives. In 'Once in a Lifetime', the first story in 'Hema and Kaushik', the narrator notes that Kaushik's parents left India in 1962, 'before the laws welcoming foreign students changed' (Lahiri 2008: 224). Hema explains, 'While my father and the other men were still taking exams, your father already had a PhD, and he drove a car, a silver Saab with bucket seats, to his job at an engineering firm in Andover' (224). Rather than being a central conflict, legal issues primarily serve to contrast the relative comfort his family enjoys to Hema's. Whereas their class differences would have made them strangers in Calcutta, the loneliness of Cambridge brings first their mothers and then the families together (225). The mothers meet and become friends when Kaushik's mother recognises the familiar signs of pregnancy in Hema's mother. The shared experience of motherhood unites them and bolsters the sense that 'Those differences were irrelevant in Cambridge, where they were both equally alone' (226). This meeting highlights how kinship forms under such circumstances, making possible the sisterly connection between the two women and laying the foundation for the principal characters' affiliation later.

Because Kaushik's family returns to India and then again to New England, living in several cities, migration is not a permanent, insuperable barrier as it might have been in earlier periods or for those with less affluence. Similarly, in Alvarez's cycle, the García girls return every summer to the island, and the cycle shows the ability of the extended family to travel. In *The Joy Luck Club*, the characters have less regular access to travel to China, although the cycle ends with Jing-mei and Canning visiting their extended families, including Suyuan's daughters. Although migration does not imply permanence in these cycles, it does represent a powerful, often long-lasting, experience that forges new familial relations. The changes to immigration law and practice serve as historical backdrop for the families' new formations and movements, just as changes to domestic policy and cultural attitudes about the family also greatly affect their lives once in the United States.

US family law similarly underwent significant revisions in this period, reflecting shifts in attitudes about the role of the federal government in the personal lives of its citizens. The Supreme Court lifted bans on interracial marriage in the 1967 case *Loving v. Virginia*. Access to birth control increased, and abortion became legalised again. Fathers gained some power to sue for parental rights, and the courts introduced no-fault divorces. These sea changes ushered in a 'progressive withdrawal of official regulation of marriage formation, dissolution, and the conduct of family life, on the one hand, and by increased regulation of the economic and child-related consequences of formal or informal cohabitation on the other' (Glendon 1996: 2). What had been covert practices, such as a mutual desire for divorce, were now legally sanctioned. Lawrence M. Friedman argues that the new laws acknowledged the widely held belief that the happiness of the individual trumps the virtue of maintaining the family. Friedman notes that this view of marriage is a 'peculiarly modern conception of marriage' in that marriage is now viewed as an 'individual matter, a personal matter. It is a reflex of what has been called expressive individualism' (2004: 77), which maintains that every individual is unique and has the potential to fully realise his or her total self. The family, once defined by social obligations, represents now another site for this expressive individualism.

Within these cycles, intergenerational conflict registers the personal consequences of the sea changes to such conceptions of the family and the individual. Expressive individualism figures largely in the personalities and choices of the second generation in these cycles. Divorce is pervasive among the second generation, and the first struggles to understand why. In Alvarez's cycle, Yolanda divorces her husband, and Sofia marries her husband against the wishes of her family. In *The Joy Luck Club* three of the four daughters experience divorce, while one remains unmarried. In 'Hema and Kaushik', the main characters experience a number of relationships, many involving cohabitation, before Hema agrees to an arranged marriage. The repetition of divorce both within and across cycles indicates that family cycles draw from these changes. The frequency of divorce signals the extent to which kinship ties break and formalised family ties sever. Certainly, these patterns signal an increase in expressive individualism among the second generation. However, the cycles complicate the impulse to create easy oppositions between generations. Although they also prize individual expression and contentment, the parents manifest this desire differently. In *The Joy Luck Club*, Ying-Ying St. Claire has an abortion when she becomes pregnant by her abusive and cruel first husband. Ying-Ying, Lindo Jong, and An-Mei's mother all find ways out of unhappy marriages in China, either through manipulation, suicide, or separation. Thus, expressive individualism figures into their marriage choices but not with as much visibility as in their daughters' relationships.

The ambiguity between the sanctioned expression of personal choice and the practices of the family serves as the basis of conflict in Alvarez's 'A Regular Revolution'. In this story, the parents send their daughters to all-girls private school after a classmate introduces Sandra to tampons, which their parents see as a harbinger of promiscuity. At school, the girls become acquainted with hair removal cream, smoking, and a copy of *Our Bodies, Ourselves* (1973). All of these incidents trouble the parents because each seems connected to burgeoning sexuality and freedom they hope to control. These 'constant skirmishes' erupt into a 'regular revolution' when Sofia is discovered with marijuana (Alvarez 2005: 111). Their mother Laura is perplexed and feels ambushed by a new, unknown danger: 'And here she'd been, worried sick about protecting our virginity since we'd hit puberty in this land of wild and loose Americans' (114). Laura blames her daughters' experimentations on Americans and, in response, exiles Sofia to the island. There Sofia adopts the manners and behaviours of her cousins but in an exaggerated form. When her sisters notice that her island boyfriend is 'quite the tyrant, a mini Papi and Mami rolled into one' who instructs her not to wear trousers, talk to men, leave the house, or do anything without his permission, the sisters raise their own revolution, exposing Sofia and her boyfriend's sexual activity (120).

To save her from a life without choice, the sisters expose Sofia's greatest sin, in their parents' eyes. Paradoxically, by exposing her, they choose for her. They see this betrayal as serving the greater good of liberating Sofia. The responses to the outcome of Sofia's exile play out in miniature the conflict over personal choice that drives the stories in this cycle. The girls see personal choice – in terms of sex, school, and friends – as vital to life, while Laura wishes to protect them from the dangers of choice. However, the stories do not create such an easy mother/daughter split. Laura enacts her choice by not telling their father Carlos about Sofia's transgression, and the girls speculate that she 'had her own little revolution brewing' (116). Moreover, these experiences in choice generate kinship ties among various members of the family: the girls band together to deliver Sofia from danger, Sofia connects with her cousins, and the girls learn more about their mother. At the same time, their responses to the politics of personal choice drive a wedge into their familial connections: Sofia resents the girls' intervention and the girls alienate themselves from their cousins. In these short story cycles, the formalisation of personal choice in law and practice simultaneously strengthens and weakens familial ties.

As the women's experiences in *The Joy Luck Club* and 'A Regular Revolution' make clear, another historical factor proves meaningful to kinship in these cycles: the changing role of women as members of the family. The cycles are partly responding to a number of prominent studies that emerged in the 1970s on gender and family.[5] Within second-wave feminism, there was a surge of interest in interrogating maternal relationships, and these works take direct aim at the naturalness of maternal feeling and responsibility. In the formation of kinship in connection with changing gender identities, these cycles focus on mother–daughter narratives. Although these cycles appeared largely from the 1980s to the present, they represent earlier historical moments, so that the cycles track continuity and transformation across many decades. Not only do the characters live through and experience these changing gender roles, they also benefit and suffer from the after-effects. From greater career choices, to diversity in marriage and parenting, to higher rates of divorce and anorexia, to increased anxieties over achievement, the second generation models a range of responses to these shifts. This contrasts with the older generation of women who remain in their marriages and work mostly in the home.

Yet, the women in the older generation do create new meanings for themselves. Perhaps the clearest example of this is Laura García, who invents clever home devices, such as the rolling suitcase, and who stays with her husband but struggles with her daughters' divorces, unorthodox career paths, and mental breakdowns while remaining supportive and caring. She balances the unfamiliar attitudes and problems of her daughters with her sense of responsibility; her inventive streak signals that just as she creates new technologies for the home, she invents new relationships in the home. As Laura's narrative suggests, these cycles centrally depict women from both generations struggling and negotiating their roles as mothers, daughters, and sisters. Although they invoke family as structure and symbol, they destabilise expectations of universality. Moreover, they distinguish between family and kinship, depicting both as changeable.

Cycles linked by family theorise on the ways in which family generates and denies kinship. While family refers to a set of concrete relationships, kinship denotes a range of associations that connect two or more individuals. Kinship conveys a sense of affinity and common bonds. It suggests a biological relationship compounded by experience. Kinship then is flexible enough to be particular to a set of relations, such as a father and son, as well as a larger web of affinities, such as extended families and, in the case of these cycles, ethnic groups. Almost simultaneous to the legislative and social measures on immigration, family, and gender, several key studies on kinship emerged. In 1969, Claude Lévi-Strauss's opus on kinship, *The Elementary Structures of Kinship*, was translated into and published in English from the revised 1967 French edition. Originally published in 1949, Lévi-Strauss's anthropological study on the structures that determine kinship advances the idea that kinship is not based solely, or even primarily, on descent but on the act of joining two families through marriage. This model of kinship diverges from the idea that kinship follows a vertical model in favour of a horizontal model. Lévi-Strauss's findings advance a relatively novel theory: kinship stems from affinity rather than consanguinity. The confluence of legislative and judicial acts concerning family and the concurrent fascination with kinship in anthropology indicate a significant cultural interest in defining and understanding the family in this moment. These short story cycles draw from this interest as they invoke and explore the implications of kinship as symbol and choice.

Affinity, Dysfunction: Form and Family

The cycles' structures mirror the affinities and fissures of kinship they portray. In their loose coherence, the structures reflect the organisation of the family unit, brought together by circumstances, common bonds, and shared experiences. Some stories illuminate the extent to which commonality and understanding exist among characters. For instance, the stories in *The Joy Luck Club* concerning Ying-Ying and her daughter Lena create a long narrative, which illustrates the high degree of shared characteristics among the two women – including a certain level of stubbornness, an appreciation of prettiness, repressive marriages, and a desire to not have children – and the affinity that results from these commonalities. Ying-Ying has been pregnant three times, but it is only with Lena that she wants her child. Reflecting the kinship of their protagonists, a high degree of correspondence emerges among the stories, with the final two, 'Rice Husband' and 'Waiting Between the Trees', set on the same day. The relative continuity among their experiences and narratives mimics their affinity, as suggested by the repetition of water and wood imagery.

And yet, gaps emerge in their kinship. In 'Waiting Between the Trees', Ying-Ying describes their relationship: 'She and I have shared the same body. There is a part of her that is part of mine. But when she was born, she sprang from me like a slippery fish, and has been swimming away ever since. All her life, I have watched her as though from another shore' (Tan 1989: 274). The separation of the stories from each other mirrors the distance in the relationship and the disjunction inherent to the cycle. Ying-Ying's characterisation of watching each other from foreign shores resonates with other mother–daughter relationships in the cycle, and even with the relationships among the daughters. Although 'Waiting Between the Trees' and 'Rice Husband' take place on the same day, the shared event between them – the collapse of a pretty but poorly constructed end table – portends the affinities and gaps of the cycle as a whole. In its frailty, the end table resembles both of their marriages, a theme that recurs. However, in the first story, Lena only hears the crash of the table from the guest bedroom, not knowing that her mother has broken it to provoke her daughter into actively getting rid of the worthless things in her life, including her marriage. Gaps abound in the communication between the mother and daughter, within the marriage, and between the stories, and yet a desire to bridge the shores remains present.

Within cycles linked by family, gaps and disjunction signify breaches in kinship. In the example above, Ying-Ying and Lena reach a momentary identification with each other that the gaps between their stories and their lack of mutual understanding undermine. Temporal gaps perhaps most comprehensively crack the narrative unity of the stories. Shifts within and among stories destabilise unity within a section and within the cycle. In 'Hema and Kaushik', for instance, white space and significant paragraph breaks signal gaps in time, as in the opening story 'Once in a Lifetime', wherein years pass between the first and second sections and time severs earlier kinship ties. Lahiri emphasises the relationship between temporality and kinship in two of the stories' titles: 'Once in a Lifetime' and 'Year's End'.

Temporal markers separate the three sections of Alvarez's cycle: 1989–1972, 1970–1960, 1960–1956. Alvarez's cycle narrates, in reverse chronological order, the migration of the García family from the Dominican Republic to the United States. The stories follow the transition of the four daughters from privileged descendants of Europeans in the Dominican Republic to political exiles and middle-class Americans. The chronological inversion upsets the expectation of cause and effect; moreover, the gap in years between the first and second sections reflects that what is presented is selected and not all-inclusive. This gap starkly illustrates that total fluidity cannot be assumed. Stephanie Lovelady asserts that the 'gaps and loops' of the volume's temporal disjunction reflect 'the fractures and messy overlaps in their narrators' attempts to make sense of the crossing between childhood and adulthood and between one country and another, either their own or someone else's' (2005: 32). The stories move further and further into the past but are not comprehensive. Time is at the mercy of memory to the extent that by the end of the cycle, as she recounts how she caused the separation of a mother cat from its kitten, Yolanda breaks voice and asks, 'You understand I am collapsing all time now so that it fits in the hollow of my story?' (Alvarez 2005: 289). William Luis notes that right before and after this moment time moves forward quickly and the perspective shifts dramatically from the little girl Yolanda to the narrator of 1989, signalling another temporal crack (2000: 847–8). That the story violates the cycle's own rules of time and the narrative voice breaks into the second person when describing the violation of the cat's family self-consciously signal the mutual gaps in kinship and narrative.

The Production of Formative Kinship

These cycles imagine that kinship is created and chosen. While biology and circumstance determine the conditions of kinship, these cycles also establish that experience and preference play a vital role. 'A Regular Revolution', for instance, describes how the García family's resolution to remain in New York bolsters feelings of kinship among the girls. The girls' father resigns himself to the idea that 'It is no hope for the Island' and pledges, 'I will become *un dominican-york*' (Alvarez 2005: 107). His revision of what it means to be both Dominican and New Yorker finds expression in this pledge. Carlos's announcement incites a unified response from the girls:

> You can believe we sisters wailed and paled, whining to go home. We didn't feel we had the best the United States had to offer. We only had second-hand stuff, rental houses in one red-neck Catholic neighborhood after another, clothes at Round Robin, a black and white TV afflicted with wavy lines. Cooped up in those little suburban houses, the rules were as strict as for Island girls, but there was no island to make up the difference. (Alvarez 2005: 107)

This moment, when the family realises they will never permanently return to the island, dramatises the conflicts that threaten the family: the girls' lack of choice; the loss of wealth and specialness; the loss of extended family and space of the Dominican Republic; the feeling of isolation and hopelessness to improve the island under Trujillo's regime; and the sense of being torn from one's home, not yet at home in the new one. The girls' wailing and whining contrasts with Carlos's straightforward, unemotional statement. The plural 'we' and the shared emotional response reflect kinship among the girls. That the sisters collectively narrate the story, as designated by the assignation of 'Carla, Sandi, Yoyo, Fifi' before the story, reinforces the shared response. In the context of exile, the scene portends the volume's treatment of the fissures and fusions within the family. The kinship among the sisters, in particular, arises from consanguinity but is made real by shared formative experiences.

The depiction of the García family dramatises how the loss of home and family serves as a catalyst for the creation of new or strengthened kinship. Although critical discussions of these cycles emphasise the significance of intergenerational relationships, short story cycles linked by family are replete with moments of intragenerational kinship based on shared formative experiences. In Alvarez's cycle, for instance, those moments when the García girls stand up for one another solidify their kinship in ways that biology alone cannot. These cycles develop a pattern of kinship that opposes a purely biological or inherited definition. Formative kinship enables modes of connection that have important implications for relationships based on shared experiences such as the family, community, and nation. These short story cycles suggest that multiple forms of kinship coexist. These cycles represent kinship as ongoing, participatory, and chosen.

In these cycles, the loss of family from migration or death is a formative experience that initiates new modes of kinship for the characters. At the symbolic level, in a cycle explicitly linked by family, the death of a family member signals an ultimate gap in the family's structure. In *The Joy Luck Club*, the death of Suyuan Woo functions as a felt absence in the stories. Not only has Jing-mei lost her mother at the outset of the cycle, but An-Mei, Lindo, and Ying-Ying have all also lost a woman who has been like a sister to them. The loss of their families from migration spurs them to create a surrogate family of women, and the cycle intimates that the bonds of this kinship circle are unbreakable, even by death. The initial shared grief over their lost families and lives in China provokes a sense of kinship among the women, reinforced by the raising of children, shared experiences at the mah-jong table, and their camaraderie. Not only do the mothers choose each other as family, but they become aunts to one another's daughters and, for better or worse, sibling relationships develop among their daughters.

The final story, 'A Pair of Tickets', crystallises in both form and content how loss creates and supports kinship. The story actually contains two stories. The first, which centres on Jing-mei and her father Canning's visit to Shenzhen and Shanghai, frames the full story, alluded to throughout the cycle, of how Suyuan came to abandon her twin daughters on the roadside. The double stories, narrated by Jing-mei and Canning, mirror Suyuan's absence; these are Suyuan's stories told and experienced by others. Hearing of her mother's loss second-hand brings Jing-mei closer to her parents because her grief allows her to better understand theirs. In a cycle dominated by the kinship among women, Canning's first-person narration is vital. His centrality to this story mitigates the exclusivity of kinship to women, although the gendered production of kinship remains prominent. He represents the necessary intermediary in bringing the women together, as evidenced in how he navigates the complicated relationships among the women in the joy luck club, strategically deferring to them in matters of communication with Suyuan's lost daughters. That the sisters have been essentially lost to one another – and have all lost their mother – adds poignancy to their reunion. Jing-mei reflects on the meaning of loss and leaving as she departs from her father's family and prepares to meet her sisters:

> And now at the airport, after shaking hands with everybody, waving good-bye, I think about all the different ways we leave people in this world. Cheerily waving good-bye to some at airports, knowing we'll never see each other again. Leaving others on the side of the road, hoping we will. Finding my mother in my father's story and saying good-bye before I have a chance to know her better. (Tan 1989: 330)

As she ruminates on farewells, Jing-mei expresses a vision of kinship and connection that depends as much upon departures as it does on togetherness. The scene, set in the liminal space of an airport, articulates the tensions inherent in being close with someone. Kinship is the knowledge of being both apart from and a part of another. Transcendent moments such as this are momentary, although they recur in memory. The ability to capture and release these transcendent moments makes the cycle an apt form for expressing the contingency of connection.

The final images of 'A Pair of Tickets' evoke the conditional form kinship often takes. As she approaches her sisters, Jing-mei sees their mother. She sees the same short hair, but also knows that 'it's not my mother, yet it is the same look she had when I was five and had disappeared all afternoon, for such a long time, that she was convinced I was dead' (331). Memory is cyclical; the act of reunion brings up a moment when she was lost from her mother. Now, in the context of reunion and her mother's death, Jing-mei understands her mother's feelings in the moment she thought her daughter dead. As the sisters embrace, Canning takes a photo: 'The flash of the Polaroid goes off and my father hands me the snapshot. My sisters and I watch quietly together, eager to see what develops' (331). The Polaroid captures the moment and reproduces it immediately, mirroring the ephemeral nature of this meeting. As they watch the picture develop, Jing-mei relates that 'together we look like our mother. Her same eyes, her same mouth, open in surprise to see, at last, her long-cherished wish' (332). In death, their mother brings together her daughters; she gets her long-cherished wish, the meaning of Suyuan's name (322–3). The Polaroid, the confusion, and the clarity in this scene all indicate that the formative experience of shared loss forges this moment of heightened kinship. It is ultimately a moment; the larger logic of the short story cycle implies that, though this memory will recur like the one from Jing-mei's childhood, this level of transcendence cannot be maintained. Death dramatises the contingency and production of kinship.

In 'Hema and Kaushik', Lahiri isolates the long process by which formative experiences of loss bring the title characters into a transient kinship. These three linked stories follow the characters' emergent kinship from childhood acquaintances in the northeastern United States to adulthoods spent around the world. They share memories and events, but that is true of many people in their lives who do not mean as much to them. Their relationship suggests that kinship forms from the residual memories of one's life and through a series of ongoing choices. In the opening story, 'Once in a Lifetime', when Kaushik's family returns to the United States, the now teenage Kaushik leads Hema through a snow-filled field to a family burial plot in the woods behind her house. Death has lived close to her, but she was unaware. Realising that Kaushik is digging the snow away from a tombstone, she explains, 'You uncovered a row of them, flat on the ground. I began to help you, unburying the dead, using my mittened hands at first, then my whole arm. They belong to people named Simonds, a family of six. "They're all here together," you said. "Mother, father, four children"' (Lahiri 2008: 249). The last Simonds buried is Emma in 1923; the likeness to her own name and lapsed time unsettle Hema. That the family maintained kinship in death troubles Kaushik. Looking at the uncovered family's plot, Kaushik confesses, 'It makes me wish we weren't Hindu, so that my mother could be buried somewhere. But she made us promise we'll scatter her ashes into the Atlantic' (249). His mother is dying of breast cancer, and they return to New England to distance themselves from well-meaning but intrusive extended family. Death has been living even closer than Hema imagined. During this time, his family stays with hers, but the families remain disconnected. The separation of his mother from her body and her body from him denies what little comfort there might have been in their separation because of death. Hema breaks into tears and then hysterics, but his admission sparks feelings of mutual understanding and caring that neither understands until much later.

Kaushik's mother's death is the formative experience that initiates their kinship, but it develops through a series of choices and actions. The stories allude to many other individuals who might have become significant to either character but do not. In the second story, 'Year's End', Kaushik is drawn to his stepsisters, Rupa and Piu, from his father's second marriage; they too have lost a parent. For a time, he acts like a big brother to them – taking them for doughnuts, introducing them to places in their new home, and joking with them. In the end, though, when he finds them with pictures of his mother, he severs these ties by shocking the girls. He hurts them in the most stinging way, as he yells, 'Well, you've seen it for yourselves, how beautiful my mother was. How much prettier and more sophisticated than yours. Your mother is nothing in comparison. Just a servant to wash my father's clothes and cook his meals. That's the only reason she's here, the only reason both of you are here' (287). In this scene, the absence left by death causes him to say things that 'harmed and terrified them' (289). The stepsisters represent a kinship tie that Kaushik does not elect, and he never repairs the relationships. Leaving his father's house, he drives north up the Atlantic and buries his mother's pictures, giving her the resting place that he longed for in 'Once in a Lifetime'.

Kaushik tells Hema this story in 'Year's End', because he knows that she is the only person who will understand why he has done these things. A new passage, not included in the original version published in *The New Yorker*,[6] reveals the extent of his feelings of kinship with Hema:

> You would have been in college by then, on Christmas vacation as I was. But I remembered you not much older than Rupa, and I remembered a day after a snowstorm, when something I'd said caused you, like Rupa and Piu, to cry. I had hated every day I spent under your parents' roof, but now I thought back to that time with nostalgia. Though we didn't belong there, it was the last place that had felt like a home. In pretending that my mother wasn't sick and being around people who didn't know, a small part of me was able to believe that it was true, that she would go on living just as your mother had. (Lahiri 2008: 291)

The conflation of Rupa and Hema and their homes reflects how formative and aligned these experiences are. He cannot recover the kinship lost with Rupa and Piu, but he can communicate the significance of that day in the snow-filled field with Hema. Telling Hema about how cruelly he treated the little girls brings them closer. That he felt most at home at her house is significant not only for what it says about the way his father moved on but also about his nomadic career and life, which fully comes out only in the final story. 'Year's End', a bridge story, comments on the cyclicality of memory and the construction of kinships; in it, Kaushik acknowledges the ways in which death both brings him closer to and drives him away from kinship.

The full cyclicality of 'Hema and Kaushik' and its implications for kinship do not emerge until the final story, 'Going Ashore'. The story describes how both Hema and Kaushik have had many people with whom they could have formed kin ties – cousins, friends, lovers – but the residue of the events in 'Once in a Lifetime' connects her to him uniquely. The story recounts three weeks spent in Rome and the deep connection they enjoy during this time, before Hema travels to India to marry. Kaushik moved here for a woman and visited it with his mother and father before their return to New England. Hema has been here with Julian, her long-time, married lover. Thus, the city signifies the range of relationships both have enjoyed. Although they have had other, longer relationships, it is not until they meet again as adults that they really experience attachment. When they meet in Rome, something compels them to one another. A nearly forgotten memory – the earlier scene from 'Once in a Lifetime' – triggers a connection. As they begin to undress,

> Hema remembered that it was Kaushik's mother who had first paid her that compliment [of being beautiful], in a fitting room shopping for bras, and she told this to Kaushik. It was the first mention, between them, of his mother, and yet it did not cause them to grow awkward. If anything it bound them closer together, and Hema knew, without having to be told, that she was the first person he'd ever slept with who'd known his mother, who was able to remember as he did. (313)

This ability to remember his mother, and the intimacy it engenders, suggests that having shared this seminal moment allows them a level of access to another that they long avoided.

The cycle ends with another loss, which clears space for the construction of new affinities. Kaushik asks Hema not to go to India and not to marry, but instead to go with him, 'but he had not asked her to marry him, and she knew it was not a fair trade' (323). Shortly after they separate, Kaushik dies off the coast of Thailand during the tsunami of 2004; he is the same age as his mother was at her death in the opening story. His watery burial realises his earlier dream of being buried alongside his mother. His death also cements and reflects Hema's continued sense of kinship. When a small obituary runs, Hema confesses, 'By then I needed no proof of your absence from the world; I felt it as plainly and implacably as the cells that were gathering and shaping themselves in my body' (333). Hema experiences the loss and creation of new kinship bodily, as she is expecting a child. His absence registers on her body just as the new, chosen kinship she feels toward her child does. The loss is raw, but she sees its productive potential. Having refused to follow him and give up her impending marriage, Hema knows that Kaushik has left nothing behind save her memories of him.

That Hema marries and has a child with Navin confirms the stories' sense of kinship: based on formative experience, kinship builds on biology and circumstance, but it requires choice. When her parents return to Calcutta, the loss of her parents inspires Hema to create new ties: 'It was her inability, ultimately, to approach middle age without a husband, without children, with her parents living now on the other side of the world . . . it was her unwillingness to abide that life indefinitely that led her to Navin' (298). The narrator asserts that choosing kinship is bold. Hema's desire to marry Navin corresponds with one of Lévi-Strauss's assertions that choice in marriage contributes more to kinship than genealogy. She expects that over time experience will compound choice and they will love each other, and, in fact, this has already begun. Hema and Navin's nascent relationship shows that choice generates affinity. Earlier in 'Going Ashore', the narrator explains that as long as they like and choose each other, they will certainly get married, and 'Hema found this certainty, an attitude to love she had scorned in the past, liberating, with the power to seduce her' (298). The ending of the story and Kaushik's death somewhat paradoxically affirm this optimism. The stories express a view of kinship as a relation over which one has control. Her pregnancy is a very literal sign of the way in which loss can engender familial belonging. The ability of Hema and Kaushik to connect and have meaning to each other outside of formalised kinship reflects the cycle's many ideas of what family means. In this emphasis on choice, kinship bears the imprint of twentieth-century debates on what constitutes a family.

Tracing a Genealogy of the Contemporary Family Cycle

By imagining kinship as flexible and contingent on circumstance and choice, these cycles envision new modes of connection. The extent to which they confront stereotypes is evident in the inclusion of actual genealogical trees within the paratextual materials. In *The Joy Luck Club*, the 'tree' is pared down to a two-column list of the mother–daughter relationships, with the overarching title 'The Joy Luck Club', which names this unconventional family. Even in this simple listing, Tan suggests that kinship proves to be both biological and chosen. In *How the García Girls Lost Their Accents*, the family tree sprawls across two pages. What and how Alvarez labels the various branches of the tree reveals how the cycle revises the meaning of kinship within the stories. On one level, such trees orient the reader and stabilise the stories, which initially seem disconnected. On another, the tree serves to cement the relationships between characters and to determine origins. Trees that preface cycles often also become part of the play with kinship enacted within the stories. The inclusion of trees is often ironic. Short story cycles linked by family are centrally concerned with what a list or tree cannot capture; the stories make ambiguous the relationships that the trees initially appear to firmly establish.

The use of genealogical trees in fiction, and in short story cycles in particular, both subscribes to and subverts typical uses of genealogical trees, which privilege consanguinity as the organising principle of clans and arrange a family into neat, definable, and hierarchical relationships. The most significant revision these trees make is to disrupt what McClintock calls the 'trope of the organic family' by pointing attention to how stylised the tree is (1995: 45). First, they place women and children at the centre of family life, challenging the 'natural' hierarchy suggested by the tree itself and disrupting the expectation that a patriarch sits atop the tree. In Alvarez's cycle, the star at the top of the tree is not a patriarch or even a couple but is instead 'The Conquistadores'. The tree depends on the girls' understanding of their family history, and Alvarez plays with the symbolism of the tree to show which ideas of family, ancestry, and respectability the girls have internalised. In a cycle treating the 'gendered production of the ethnic', this label ironically comments on the extent to which the family internalises the racism of upper-crust Dominican society, as the tree shows the girls' maternal family, 'the de la Torre Family', as the direct and sole descendants of the

Conquistadores. It also suggests that Alvarez is upsetting gender hierarchies in a milieu in which machismo is rampant and a constant source of tension. The name of the family appears in bold, as do The Conquistadores, the girls' parents, and the girls themselves. The tree relegates everyone else to normal type and thus lesser importance. A dashed line and question marks link their paternal family, the Garcías, to The Conquistadores, making them a renegade branch of the tree. The use of the girls' language and humour furthers the tree's connection to the stories. For instance, maternal cousins are represented only as 'The hair-and-nails cousins.' These cousins espouse the family's traditional notions of femininity and domesticity, and the García girls embrace synecdoche to distance themselves. Generations of maternal ancestors are omitted from the tree, save one 'great-great-grandfather who married a Swedish girl', who stands as the only link between the 'de la Torre Family' and the girls' own Papito and Mamita.

Although the tree sprawls, such vacancies show how history and attitudes privilege certain relatives over others. Many relations go unnamed or are lumped together: 'The hair-and-nails cousins', '33 other known Garcías', 'an American' who married and divorced Tía Isa, and an unnamed uncle who married Tía Mimí 'finally'. The phrase 'known Garcías' acknowledges the many illegitimate García children, while the missing relatives and questionable links indicate a shadowy past best forgotten. On the other hand, the tree assigns some relatives multiple names, with the third daughter receiving four: 'Yolanda, Yo, Yoyo, or, in the States, Joe'. Affection, as much as disdain, is evident in the tree. All of the details in Alvarez's tree point to the extremely constructed nature of family. The de la Torre family, in particular, prizes its ancestry but overlooks much. With the tree, Alvarez pokes fun at the notion of being able to name and place boundaries around a family.

Although this particular vision of kinship as both fixed and pliable proliferates among cycles of the late twentieth and early twenty-first centuries, it extends from a longer tradition of cycles and novels that draw on the family unit in their structures. For instance, these cycles draw from modernist texts that employ a family of voices competing for authorial legitimacy. Kennedy notes that short story cycles linked by family, or what he calls '"genealogical" novels', unfurl 'as separate yet intertwined short narratives about different family members' (1995: x). He cites Faulkner's *The Sound and the Fury*, Virginia Woolf's *To the Lighthouse*, and John Dos Passos's trilogy *U.S.A.* as examples. These texts repudiate 'the organizing authority of the omniscient narrator, asserting instead a variety of voices or perspectives reflective of the radical subjectivity of modern experience' (Kennedy 1995: x). I would add to Kennedy's list Eudora Welty's *The Golden Apples* (1949), which circulates around a group of families in Morgana. Welty includes a list of the 'Main Families in Morgana, Mississippi' before the stories commence, which is strikingly similar to Tan's list. Welty's depiction of the family is prescient of kinship in the contemporary cycle: 'Welty begins with the affirmation that of course love is possible; family is the bedrock fact that defines most people's lives, whether they are in it or out. But she goes profoundly further to face the reality that the very fact that we can and do love is precisely the cause of most of our everyday problems' (Polk 2008: 137). The duality of the affinity and dysfunction of family is a theme that recurs throughout Welty, Faulkner, Woolf, and Dos Passos.

Perhaps the most radical example of the family as context for the exploration of multiple voices is Faulkner's *As I Lay Dying* (1930) (Faulkner 1990a), wherein a family member narrates each chapter of the larger story of the burial of the mother, Addie Bundren. *As I Lay Dying* blurs the line between genealogical novel and cycle. Kennedy argues that this form has become so ubiquitous that the novel has been 'veering toward the story sequence as a decentered mode of narrative representation' (1995: x). Cycles and novels linked by family proliferate precisely because they challenge the authority of individual experience. With its assignation of names to chapters and its construction of essentially a family tree in its structure, the form of *As I Lay Dying* aligns with many of these cycles. Most significantly, Faulkner's volume and the cycles it influenced participate in a dialogue about the institution of the family and its relationship to the individual.

In so doing, these contemporary cycles and their modernist forerunners descend from earlier cycles, largely by and about women, which link otherwise loosely connected stories by their interest in family. Judith Fetterly and Marjorie Pryce (1992), Kate McCullough (1999), D. K. Meisenheimer (1997), and Cindy Weinstein (2004) argue that many women writers working in the form from around the turn of the last century, such as Jewett, Alice Dunbar Nelson, Sui Sin Far, and Zitkála-Šá, initiated a line of formal and thematic descent that has as its heirs the modernist and contemporary cycles linked by family. Far's cycle *Mrs. Spring Fragrance* (1912) illuminates the complexity of these earlier treatments of kinship. In her stories, there resides no single vision of family, ethnicity, or national belonging. Instead, she depicts a variety of familial affinities and conflicts that centre primarily on differences of opinion about the proper way of being Chinese in America; characters' responses include assimilation to and rejection of Anglo-American culture, as well as many who strike balances. Far's cycle offers no neat narrative on which characters get rewarded or punished for their choices, and, in this way, the cycle resists any kind of singular story of immigration. Characters engage in nostalgia for lost traditions, but Far exposes how complicated life was in China too. The cycle's form, composed of vignettes and stories, with the occasional but not constant appearance of the title character, reinforces the multiplicity of the communities she portrays. She disrupts a simple China-to-San Francisco narrative by depicting characters who reverse direction, live in Seattle, and cross the border to Canada and back. In a time when nativism defined attitudes toward immigration, Far's cycle refuses to make stories of immigration singular and stereotyped.

Conflict within families arises in these stories largely because of differences of opinion about cultural traditions. The title story's central conflict concerns the pull between arranged and so-called love marriages. The prospective bride's parents have long ago arranged a marriage to a scholar, but she has fallen in love with a businessman. Mrs. Spring Fragrance deftly manages everyone's expectations by arranging for the scholar to marry the woman he loves, freeing the prospective bride to marry her love and saving the families from embarrassment. The characters realise that, though tradition venerates scholarship, American capitalism might make the businessman a better match. The story contains meditations on the value and problems of each model of value and marriage; the characters' lives prove that there can be happiness in both, as Mrs. and Mr. Spring Fragrance are deeply in love and had an arranged marriage. Far suggests that demonising the old and new does no good but that each person must figure out what is best. Much of the conflict in these stories centres on marriage, because it is the basis of new forms of kinship, especially when extended families live an ocean away. In this, the stories dramatise Lévi-Strauss's theories on kinship.

Mrs. Spring Fragrance exemplifies the ability to bring together the old and new, and Far plays with her as a twist on the 'participant/observer' archetype, as she too wishes to write a book of stories on her observations on mainstream American culture. In so doing, Far reverses the conventions of the genre at the turn of the twentieth century, when so many sketchbooks and cycles portrayed narrators going into foreign and exotic locales and translating them for East Coast audiences. Far herself, born to a father of English descent and a mother of Chinese descent raised by English missionaries, lived in England, Montreal, and both the East and West Coasts of the United States. Her biography belies a singularity in national identity, similar to Tan, Alvarez, and Lahiri. So too her stories belie essentialising about the meaning and substance of America, Canada, or China. She depicts no singular Chinese culture, and she dramatises the complexity of American culture, which assumes a stable Anglo tradition that does not account for the nation's complex make-up.

This and other early cycles illustrate how the triangulated production of family, gender, and ethnicity has been present long before the recent proliferation of such cycles. Identity – be it national, ethnic, or gendered – has long been contested ground, and the cycle's disjunction and multiplicity reflects the multiple formulations this triangulation takes. The cycle's form comments on the ways in which kinship and identity can be pinned down for a transcendent moment but then get undermined, extended, and revised. An emphasis on women and family becomes the code by which these cycles address issues of inclusion and exclusion. Like their forerunners, contemporary short story cycles linked by family simultaneously treat the immense pull of consanguinity, critique its implicit and often explicit paternalism, and generate new models of family based on choice and experience (Weinstein 2004: 9). The filial short story cycle undermines the dominance with which blood determines kinship and instead shows how choice too determines who counts as family.

Notes

1. Notable examples of cycles linked by family in the mid-twentieth century include Erskine Caldwell's *Georgia Boy* (1943), Evan S. Connell's *Mrs. Bridge* (1959) and *Mr. Bridge* (1969), and John Updike's *Too Far to Go: The Maples Stories* (1979).
2. This group has received considerable acclaim, including the National Book Critics Circle Award for Kingston and Erdrich. Tan and García were nominated for the National Book Award. Naylor's cycle won a National Book Award and was adapted into a miniseries and television show, and Tan's cycle was made into a popular movie. In addition to winning the Frank O'Connor International Short Story Award, Lahiri's volume had the distinction of landing atop bestsellers lists upon its release, a rare feat for short stories.
3. Similar volumes include Junot Díaz's *Drown* (1996) and *This Is How You Lose Her* (2012) and Amy Bloom's *A Blind Man Can See How Much I Love You* (2000).

4. For more on immigration law reform, see Lawrence M. Friedman's *Private Lives: Families, Individuals, and the Law* (2004) and Mary Ann Glendon's *The Transformation of Family Law: State, Law, and Family in the United States and Western Europe* (1996).
5. In addition to *Our Bodies, Ourselves*, there was Adrienne Rich's *Of Woman Born* (1976), Dorothy Dinnerstein's *The Mermaid and the Minotaur* (1976), Nancy Friday's *My Mother/My Self* (1977), and Nancy Chodorow's *The Reproduction of Mothering* (1978) (Bostrom 2007: 45).
6. 'Year's End' and 'Once in a Lifetime' originally appeared in *The New Yorker* in the 24 December 2007 and 8 May 2006 issues, respectively.

Chapter 5

Resisting Identity

In 1945, Malcolm Cowley edited and introduced *The Portable Faulkner*. Appearing at a time when much of his work was out of print, this volume initiated a renewed interest in Faulkner, which culminated in his 1949 Nobel Prize in literature. Cowley's introduction clamoured for a re-examination of Faulkner's achievements: 'All his books in the Yoknapatawpha cycle are part of the same living pattern ... each novel, each long or short story, seems to reveal more than it states explicitly and to have a subject bigger than itself. All the separate works are like blocks of marble from the same quarry: they show the veins and faults of the mother rock' (1967: xv). Cowley identifies the interconnectedness of Faulkner's oeuvre as its most distinguishing feature and its highest accomplishment. In regard to specific texts, Cowley describes many as a 'cycle of stories' or alternatively as a 'series of episodes resembling beads on a string' (1967: 584, xxv). The loose but not wholly unified quality that Cowley identifies in both the collected works and in individual volumes indicates narrative cyclicality, derived from the 'mother rock' of authorial vision. As a public intellectual and respected editor and critic, Cowley was a tastemaker, and the release of the portable edition and the influence of his introduction with its claims to unity shaped Faulkner studies for decades.[1]

Faulkner's fiction constructs and relies on a commonality of locality, kinship, and temporal structures. As Cowley, and nearly every critic, notes, Yoknapatawpha County serves as the setting for much of Faulkner's work. Experimentations with temporality are an obsession and structure the volumes' connections and fissures. Genealogical connections come to the fore in the interconnected Sartoris, Compson, McCaslin, Snopes, and Sutpen families. Linked as they are by setting, interconnected families, and temporal structures, *The Unvanquished*, *Go Down, Moses*, and *Knight's Gambit* are all short story cycles proper. Many others, such as *As I Lay Dying* and *The Wild Palms* (1939), test the generic boundaries of genre and borrow from the narrative techniques pioneered in the short story cycle. His novels, in particular, deploy the narrative techniques forged in the cycle in ways that challenge the insuperability of any generic category. Thus, the best way to grasp his oeuvre is through the paradigm of the short story cycle.

With its privileging of multiple, competing narratives and openness, the cycle is ideally suited to articulating the crises of history and identities that Faulkner dramatises. The genre is particularly essential to understanding Faulkner's treatment of race and identity, reaching an apex in *Go Down, Moses*, which is his most sustained treatment of black–white relations. The stories in *Go Down, Moses* recount various events in the history of the McCaslin family from before the US Civil War to World War II. The stories illustrate the ways in which the white and black branches of the McCaslin, Beauchamps, and Edmonds family tree are entangled; yet, the colour line divides the family. *Go Down, Moses* explores both the sustained and heightened moments of interracial intimacies, which include every possible kinship relation. The crises of identities that the stories most sharply narrate tend toward the white McCaslin line grappling with their unacknowledged kinship with the black Beauchamp line. Although the stories collectively – and often individually – encompass a broad temporality, the stories also focus on moments or a series of moments. Thus, the cycle offers an analogue to the production of identity, particularly racial and ethnic identity, in that such identities resist rigid distinctions, essential characteristics, or defined origins.

Go Down, Moses shows how deeply imbricated black–white relations are in the McCaslin clan and then highlights the multiple and varied responses to these intimacies by both the black and white characters. The treatment of black and white relations, marked by a crisis of interpretation, aligns with the cycle's statements on the very possibility of reading – be it a ledger, a narrative, or a person. The short story cycle engages crises of interpretation in its very form, which engenders the volume's primary concern with interracial relationships that are hidden, disavowed, and erased from public and private memory. In Faulkner's work, and especially in *Go Down, Moses*, there is, as Édouard Glissant puts it, 'an upheaval of the unitary conceptions of being, a deferral of the absolutes of identity, and a vertigo of the word' (1999: 105). *Go Down, Moses* represents a fictional treatment of what Toni Morrison calls for in *Playing in the*

Dark: 'to examine the impact of notions of racial hierarchy, racial exclusion, and racial vulnerability and availability on nonblacks who held, resisted, explored, or altered those notions' (1993: 11). From the patriarch's unabashed exploitation of Tomasina and Eunice to his possible remorse and even love, to Buck and Buddy's homegrown abolitionism, to Ike's repudiation of the land, to generations of exploited labour and Roth's continued indifference, *Go Down, Moses* interrogates the possible identities carved out by the white McCaslins in response to interracial intimacy and their denials of it. It also charts the responses from the descendants of the patriarch's relationship with Eunice: from Lucas's whiskey stills and attempts on Zack's life to Fonsiba Beauchamp's desire to flee the scene. The stories depict the characters resisting the expected models of identity available to them.

Containing both independent and interconnected stories, the cycle reflects the family history of the McCaslins, particularly in the tension between autonomy and belonging and in the construction of provisional identities. The first section of this chapter establishes the place of the cycle in Faulkner's body of work, considers the extent to which Faulkner revises an established tradition, and tracks his innovations to the form. Subsequent sections treat the depiction of limited locality, formative kinship, and interstitial temporalities in *Go Down, Moses*. The cycle shows place, family, and time to be the products of fiction. Their fictive origins do not diminish their power; rather, fictions chart places, produce kinship, and mark time. The stories comment on the fictions necessary to the production of larger collectivities, whether they be based on locality, nation, race, kinship, or time.

A Form without a Name

Faulkner made conflicting statements on the genre of *Go Down, Moses*. In a letter to Robert K. Haas dated 1 June 1940, he terms *Go Down, Moses* 'a connected book-length mss. from material written as short stories' (Blotner 1976: 126). In 1947, in an address at the University of Mississippi, he stated that the volume should be read as a collection of short stories (Evans 2008: 201). Originally published as *Go Down, Moses and Other Stories* in 1942, when the stories were reissued in 1949 Faulkner wrote to Robert K. Haas that he would rather the title be printed as *Go Down, Moses*. Stating that 'Moses is indeed a novel', he held that the suffixed phrase was unnecessary

(Blotner 1976: 284). However, he did not see any purpose in adding chapter numbers or omitting the story titles in the 1949 edition. In this letter, he compares the titling and form to both *The Unvanquished* and *The Wild Palms*. These comparisons and his insistence that the story titles and section divisions remain indicate something distinctive about these works.² Faulkner's disparate statements on the generic form of *Go Down, Moses* reflect a lack of language adequate to describe them.

Although doing so would seem to be evidence of authorial foresight, attempts to construct a single unifying narrative line fall short. Whenever one attempts to trace a figure or theme as the connecting thread, the tapestry unravels. Attempts to prove the unity of *Go Down, Moses* focus on Isaac McCaslin, the theme of black–white relations, or the significance of the McCaslin clan. Reading Ike as the unifying figure fails because he is absent in over half the stories. The treatment of black–white relations as the central unifying theme renders the wilderness and hunting stories anomalous. The McCaslins may seem to connect the stories, but 'Pantaloon in Black' fails to adhere to the familial motif (Skei 1985: 242). All of these elements are connective tissues, but they do not result in unity. The disjunction inherent to the volume's form reflects the stories' open-endedness, abjuring resolution in Ike's development, the depiction of race, and the notion of McCaslin kinship.

Such contradictions and discrepancies have narrative power; they produce new insights about the characters, events, and even the interconnections among the texts. Faulkner deeply distrusted and disavowed facts, and this belief informs his characterisation of the gaps and inconsistencies in his fiction (Blotner 1976: 222). Because every act of interpretation and every statement is contingent, contradiction represents a possibility for creative production. Cowley and his critical heirs cite contradictions and uneven thematic elements as weaknesses, but the author's own view, confirmed in the texts, celebrates how the contradictions and seemingly incongruous themes inform one another. Faulkner's composition process and revision practices further resist the critical tendency to read only unity and harmony in his canon. A story is never finished, never complete. Composition is deeply imbricated with revision.

Revisions to the stories in *Go Down, Moses* confirm the general sense that the volumes are open and alive and part of a larger cycle of works. Faulkner's belief in the dynamic nature of his writing shapes the writing and revision of *Go Down, Moses*, particularly in terms of inconsistency and change. Originally published in outlets such as

Harper's, Colliers, and *The Atlantic*, the stories varied in tone, character, and characterisation from their later incarnations in the volume. For instance, although not published until the book's release, Bayard Sartoris served as the original narrator of an early version of 'Was' rather than the third-person narration of Cass Edmonds. The jovial tone and emphasis on the impish child narrator of the original story resembles that of *The Unvanquished* (Faulkner 1991), which also features a view of black–white relations but almost exclusively through the perspective of Bayard Sartoris. The change in narrators and the addition of the first section did not come until the inclusion of 'Was' to the cycle. These four paragraphs introduce Isaac McCaslin and his repudiation of the McCaslin land. Although Ike does not appear again for nearly half the volume, this section operates like an overture. Just as an overture establishes major themes and melodies in a symphony or musical, this section establishes the major themes, characters, and events in the cycle. The opening identifies Ike as a major character and his repudiation as an important event. This section forecasts the slippage of time with its shifting verb tenses, and it initiates confusion over familial ties. Although it enhances the interconnections in the volume, this opening section disrupts the autonomy of 'Was' as an individual story. Experimentation with genre recurs throughout *Go Down, Moses*. For instance, because of their length and potential autonomy both 'The Bear' and 'The Fire and the Hearth' can stand alone as either long short stories or novellas. Although they have been excerpted and anthologised, they gain meaning and depth from their inclusion in the cycle. 'The Bear' and 'The Fire and the Hearth' stretch the limits of stories but are short stories nonetheless. This generic instability aligns with a narrative instability within the stories.

Faulkner's own sense of the stories' interconnections changed as he wrote and revised them. For example, it was not until the composition of the title story that Faulkner began to conceive of the complex family entanglements that would shape his revisions for the stories' inclusion in the cycle (Early 1972: 15). Although not originally conceived as such, many of the stories focus on the McCaslin family. This change is evident in the switch from Bayard Sartoris to Cass Edmonds in 'Was', and also in the switch from Quentin Compson as the young boy to Isaac and from Jimbo to Tennie's Jim in 'The Old People' (Skei 1999: 20; Early 1972: 71–2). 'The Fire and the Hearth' fleshes out the details of the Beauchamps' connection to the white branch of the McCaslin family; these connections are missing from the original introduction of Lucas and Molly in an early version of the narrative titled 'Gold Is Not Always' (Early 1972: 7–9). Faulkner revised this previously published story and combined it with another published story, 'A Point of Law', and a previously unpublished story; together, these three stories became the three chapters in 'The Fire and the Hearth' (Skei 1999: 19). In addition to the familial and formal elements added to the stories, Faulkner included new description and anecdotes in his revisions (Skei 1985: 236).

Although Faulkner incorporated new material to connect the stories, the additions do not result in unity between the stories or between this volume and his other works. Reading across his stories, novels, and cycles exposes what Faulkner terms 'inconsistencies' that were not always resolved in individual texts. In *Go Down, Moses*, these inconsistencies consist of discrepancies in the timeline of events, gaps in genealogy, and uneven characterisation. This instability is significant because it demonstrates Faulkner's sense, evidenced in his letters, that the text is alive and that fiction may distort fact to get at truth. The discrepancies between stories generate tension in that one must suspend and negotiate the 'facts' of one story against those of another. One example of this is the ancestry of Sam Fathers, of which multiple accounts are given in earlier and the final versions of 'The Old People', 'Lion', 'The Bear', and 'A Justice' (Early 1972: 13).

In *Go Down, Moses* the conditions leading to the eventual marriage of Buck McCaslin to Sophonsiba Beauchamp, the parents of Isaac, remain a mystery. This absence is strongly felt as the opening story centres on Buck's close rescue from a marriage to Sophonsiba, a marriage unwanted by Buck but desired by her and her brother. Cleanth Brooks describes having questioned Faulkner about this very gap:

> I asked Mr. Faulkner once how it came about that Uncle Buck and Miss Sophonsiba subsequently did get married and produce a child, Isaac McCaslin, in view of Uncle Buck's having been rescued from Miss Sophonsiba's clutches. Surely after this narrow escape Uncle Buck would have become even more wary, more gun-shy. Faulkner explained that he never got around to writing about how Uncle Buck was finally run to earth. (Brooks 1983: 133)

We might dismiss this explanation as simply the product of authorial whim, and whim might account partially for this omission. However, this gap also illustrates an inability to definitively know one's origins. With the never-ending sentences and tangents, Faulkner's fiction lends itself to assumptions of comprehensiveness. The absence of description of such an important kinship relation, one that would produce the last legitimate male McCaslin, signifies that all of the kin relations are uncertain and open to interpretation, which is a central theme and crisis in *Go Down, Moses*. The gap in this history of Ike's parentage resonates with so many others, and these inconsistencies produce the textual sense of contingency in relation to identity and origins.

The incongruence relates to – perhaps even results from – Faulkner's experimentation with point of view. Individual stories (or sections within a novel) often register the viewpoint of a single character, most clearly exemplified in *The Sound and the Fury* and *As I Lay Dying*. A single character's perspective may butt up against his or her telling in a later story, as is the case with Quentin Compson in *Absalom, Absalom!* Nearly every novel and short story cycle treats the multiplicity of experience; in telling the causes and effects of any single event, multiple narrators offer their own points of view on the events. Although the novel is most often associated with an expanded interest in perspective, the short story cycle's form enables a radical challenge to the very nature of the point of view. These multiple narrative voices lobby so much for authority that David H. Evans claims that 'Faulkner's richest works, like *Absalom, Absalom!* and *Go Down, Moses* are less like verbal mosaics than rhetorical battlefields, in which virtually every character is fiercely concerned to present a narrative that will displace its competitors, gain the assent of its audience, and become the authorized version' (2008: 19). Every voice attempts to author a version of his or her life story and that of the place, time, or family. The very interrogation of what we know, how we know it, and what that means energises Faulkner's fiction and underpins his deployment of the linking devices.

Just as the multiple points of view vie for authority, repetition at the level of language, names, events, and imagery unsettle the nature of truth. In the particular case of *Go Down, Moses*, repetition exposes truth as conditional, temporary, and constructed by the circumstances of the teller. For instance, in 'The Bear', the third-person narrative voice repeats the line: 'So he should have hated and feared Lion' (Faulkner 1990b: 201, 204, 216). This line, the meaning and referent of which is deferred until the third section of the story, signals a progression forward in the action of the story while also revealing that the story is being told retrospectively. The slippages between past and past perfect in the story endow the story with a feeling of inevitability, and the statement portends that Isaac subverts expectations, foreshadowing his sedition in the fourth section of 'The Bear'.

Repetition at the level of naming similarly undercuts any sense of progression or personal agency. Many of the descendants of the McCaslin patriarch, Lucius Quintus Carothers McCaslin, bear all or part of his name. This naming both reveals and obfuscates genealogy and characterisation. In 'Delta Autumn', the diminutive 'Roth' parallels the weakness Isaac sees in the patriarch's descendant. Although weaker in character, his actions parallel those of his namesake. The events of the past repeat, but they repeat with a difference. When Roth abandons his child by an unnamed woman, who is Lucius's great-great-granddaughter by his own daughter Tomey, Roth effectively repeats the actions of the patriarch. He resists identifying with his biracial child and partner. Repetition and proliferating perspectives effectively challenge the truth of the very structures which seem to link the narratives and give meaning to the characters' lives: community, kinship, and time. The repetition also establishes the provisional nature of any given identity.

Hunting Story and Tracking Localities

Go Down, Moses sets the drama of the McCaslin clan on their family farm, its environs, and the surrounding county. The limited locality intimates Anderson's influence on Faulkner. Anderson and Faulkner met in 1925 through Eleanor Anderson. Faulkner stayed at the couple's apartment in New Orleans and spent many of his afternoons with Anderson. In 'Sherwood Anderson, 1925' Faulkner appreciates the simplicity of form and sympathy of tone in *Winesburg*. For him, the form fit the substance. 'Had the book been done as a full-length novel', he argues, the sympathy 'would have been mawkish' (Faulkner 2004b: 247). In 'A Note on Sherwood Anderson, 1953', Faulkner articulated his indebtedness to Anderson:

> I learned that to be a writer, one has first got to be what he is, what he was born; that to be an American and a writer one does not necessarily have to pay lip-service to any conventional American image such as his and Dreiser's own aching Indiana and Ohio or Iowa corn or Sandburg's stockyards or Mark Twain's frog. You had only to remember what you were. 'You have to have somewhere to start from: then you begin to learn' he told me, 'It don't [sic] matter where it was, just so you remember it and aint [sic] ashamed of it. Because

one place to start from is just as important as any other place. You're a country boy; all you know is that little patch up there in Mississippi where you started from. But that's all right too.' (Faulkner 2004a: 8)

Faulkner credits Anderson for encouraging him to write about Mississippi and allowing locality to permeate his writing. The advice Anderson gave Faulkner, as well as language within the essay, reveals an anxiety over the connection between region and nation.

This statement suggests the extent to which Anderson and Faulkner saw themselves as writing within and building a national literature. In Faulkner's statement, the region contains within it the possibility of being both separate from and a synecdoche for the nation. In parroting Anderson's colloquial language, Faulkner substantiates his choice of place and aligns himself with a tradition of writers whose interest in place defined their work without rendering them merely regional. The exactness of the speech seems somewhat dubious as a quarter century has passed, but it makes clear Faulkner's indebtedness to Anderson. Their conception of American literature 'suggests a collection of centres that are simultaneously peripheries' (Hagood 2008: 19). Faulkner's construction and defence of a national literature emerges in another essay on Anderson, in which he bristles at the comparison of Anderson to Russian and French writers: 'I can not [sic] understand our passion in America for giving our own productions some remote geographical significance' (2004b: 253). As he defends Anderson against charges of being an '"American" Tolstoi', there is by extension a defence of himself against being read in anything other than local and universal terms. The connections between Anderson and Faulkner reveal the extent to which the conventions of limited locality remain couched in attempts at national integration.

In Yoknapatawpha County, Faulkner constructs the ultimate limited locality. His depiction of this bound, geographic place both supports and undoes the belief that geographic proximity necessarily fosters affiliation. 'Faulkner's enduring success', according to Evans, 'was to make the mechanics by which communities are imagined into the substance of his own creative oeuvre' (2008: 27). In *Go Down, Moses*, that locality is even more limited, as the action of the stories circulates on or around the McCaslin farm, located seventeen miles outside of the county seat, Jefferson. The stories recount a century of family histories on the place; on the surface, the McCaslin land serves as a heightened form of limited locality, with the farm creating an autonomous population within the larger county. While the farm grounds and connects the stories, the locality proves more porous than it initially appears.

The characters and actions exceed the locality's bounds. In the title story, the opening is set in Chicago, where Molly and Lucas's grandson faces execution. According to Molly, getting kicked off the plantation initiates his ultimate end in Chicago. In her estimation, leaving the farm unleashes the course of events that take his life and that the distance from the McCaslin place to Jefferson is greater than the distance from Jefferson to Chicago. Other stories in the cycle confirm the porous nature of the micro-locality. The most significant example of the openness of the ostensibly limited locality is the hunting camp and grounds, which shift and recede over time. The hunting camp serves as the dominant setting in the trio of stories centred on Isaac McCaslin: 'The Old People', 'The Bear', and 'Delta Autumn'. The collective effect of these alternative settings unsettles the notion that the McCaslin place offers a coherent centre to the stories.

In *Go Down, Moses*, setting is like a series of concentric circles that become entangled because of an embattled construction of Southern identity. The inner circle is the McCaslin farm, which the county envelops. The South, in turn, circles Yoknapatawpha. The South is then encircled by and embroiled with the nation. Glissant characterises Faulkner's setting as powerful and exclusionary: 'Into this fictional county Faulkner put his whole native land of Mississippi, and the entire South as well (one emphatically says "the South," with a capital "S," as though it represents an absolute, as though we other people of the south, to the south of this capitalised South, never existed)' (1999: 30). The inclusion of an article and capitalisation of 'the South' suggest its symbolic power and exclusion of other kinds of southern localities. The county comes to stand for an entire geopolitical region and gets treated as its own identity, akin to a regional ethnicity. The institutionalisation of this framework aligns Southern literature with ethnic literature as being both part of and separate from a national literature. This sense of regional ethnicity stems from the legacy of slavery. *Go Down, Moses* dramatises the often-denied relationships among black and white southerners and the cost of this denial.

The plantation setting of *Go Down, Moses* ostensibly invites a nostalgic rendering of the South. The one-time plantation bears the generic qualities of such a depiction: the restored big house, the long family lineage, and the sharecroppers and renters who are the descendants of former slaves. Faulkner's comments on Anderson betray sentimentality for place as the starting point for artistry. And yet, *Go Down, Moses* undercuts this nostalgia to complicate and criticise any romanticised sense of place. In this, the use of locality resonates with cycles connected by limited locality: what appears as nostalgia often exposes criticism for romanticising the past. The stories concerning the later McCaslin generations depict the characters' invocation of sentimentality for the past. They extol the virtues of the untouched Big Woods and the fecundity of the McCaslin patriarch, both of which depended on slavery. The stories set in Buck and Buddy's time undercut this wistful simplification by showing the ambivalence Buck and Buddy feel toward their father and by highlighting that industrialisation was already well under way in the Big Woods. They resist identifying with the metanarrative of superiority that envelops their father.

Most of all, by depicting the complicated, entangled web of relations among the McCaslins, the stories unmask the nostalgia that celebrates antebellum race dynamics. In contrast to what is often perceived as 'Faulkner's nostalgia', Evans argues that 'the past as it appears in his novels is almost invariably presented in the form of a process of ongoing degradation, its moral stability a dubious and delusive mirage' (2008: 12). *Go Down, Moses* engages this nostalgia in 'Was', the main action of which is the earliest chronological event in the cycle. In this story, the slaves are commanded to stay on the plantation; however, when Tomey's Turl runs away to the Beauchamp plantation, the story reveals that Tomey's Turl is able to usurp the boundaries of the plantation. His ability to navigate beyond his sanctioned geography critiques the nostalgia that later stories express as characters lament the supposed loss of the clear divisions and control practised under slavery.

Although this story has a playful tone and Terrel functions as a trickster in various scenes, the implications are quite serious. Buck and Buddy are would-be abolitionists, slowly freeing their father's slaves, moving the slaves into the still unfinished house, and turning a blind eye to the slaves' night-time roving. At the same time, they do not emancipate all of the slaves as they see themselves as necessary midwives to freedom. Ambivalence permeates this era of the McCaslin saga. The actions of the McCaslin twins are in conflict with their beliefs; their ethical code is idiosyncratic. The days of their father are often treated as halcyon, with later generations constantly establishing their ties to him, but his sons' reactions to his authority and legacy reveal scepticism for the merits of their father. The past, although often evoked as such by the characters, hardly seems free of degradation. The cycle begins by establishing that patrilineal descent – the basis for nostalgia, inheritance, identity, and land – is itself a deeply troubled relic of the past. The cycle shows the destructive power of assigning all possessions to a single son – ironic in the case of twins – of the family line.

One character who continuously struggles with the legacy of the McCaslin past is Ike; the plantation is the source and site of his battle. Locality is a metonym for the patriarchal slaveholding culture to which he is heir. In three of seven stories of the cycle, his development over eighty years takes centre stage. As most critics view 'The Bear' as the moral centre of the book, Ike plays a key role in establishing the interconnections of the cycle and coming to any resolution for the volume. Ike's experiences highlight the conflict of the individual and community but also show the arbitrary nature of selecting an individual to stand out from the community. Ike is a classic example of a protagonist that could easily have been someone else; indeed, he could have been many other people. Although he is recognised as the *de facto* heir to the McCaslin property and prestige, by virtue of his being descended from Lucius Quintus Carothers McCaslin through white males, the stories present several alternative protagonists for the McCaslin family saga, either because they act as heirs to the property or spirit of the patriarch. The Edmonds line, which includes Cass, Zack, and Roth, all represent the practical heirs. The penultimate story suggests that the future of the line remains open and embodied in the unnamed son of Roth and James's granddaughter.

However, it is Lucas who best mirrors the entrepreneurial spirit of their shared paternity, and he is at the centre of the other long story in the volume, 'The Fire and the Hearth'. Although very different from 'The Bear', the former story also treats accountability and self as Lucas hunts for the buried treasure of Buck and Buddy. According to the logic of the superiority of male descent, Lucas represents as likely a candidate as Ike as he descended from the male line of McCaslins. Lucas, whose biracial descent discredits any claims he might make to McCaslin privilege, highlights the contradictory logic of the colour line and patriarchy. Ultimately, he gives up the hunt for treasure to restore stability to his marriage. He chooses a lateral kinship with his wife over linear kinship, emblematised by a buried treasure. His presence disrupts the logic of a protagonist, or, in other words, a single heir to the narrative inheritance. Although many read Ike as the sole protagonist of the volume, the cycle actually deploys multiple protagonists. Peripheral protagonists such as

Rider in 'Pantaloon in Black' and Gavin Stevens in the title story further erode any foundation for reading Ike as solely central.

The primacy that critics such as Brooks and Cowley place on the sequence of stories depicting Ike reveals an impulse toward teleology. The trio of stories provides the most extended treatment of any character in the volume and aligns with the formal conventions of the *bildungsroman*. The activity that occupies his coming of age, hunting, parallels the teleology of Ike's development. However, acts of deferral mark the hunting experience, much like Ike's development. When resolution is achieved, either in the killing of the bear or the act of repudiating his inheritance, the end is unsatisfying. It is the ritual of hunting which is to be enjoyed and not the kill. Similarly, it is the conflict of Ike's position that is interesting, not the abdication of it. In all of these narrative events, the third-person narration engages a retrospective tone, which is heightened in 'The Bear'. Although hunting would seem to be an act predicated on surprise and a lack of foreknowledge, the story suggests otherwise:

> So he should have hated and feared Lion. Yet he did not. It seemed to him that something, he didn't know what, was beginning; had already begun. It was like the last act on a set stage. It was the beginning of the end of something, he didn't know what except that he would not grieve. He would be humble and proud that he had been found worthy to be part of it too or even just to see it too. (Faulkner 1990b: 216–17)

The retrospective tone and the sense that the end of the play is already determined undercut the apparent teleology of the hunt. With the ending predetermined, including Ike's response to it, the stories cut through the logic of causation and instead privilege recurrence, because it gives some sense of the collapse of time. The Ike stories appear to build to his act of repudiation, but that too is known to readers from the first page.

The sequence of stories centring on Ike highlight the tensions between the individual and the community and between action and deferral that distinguish cycles linked by a limited locality. The characters pursue the meaning and value of the plantation, its relation to the county, and its symbolic import for the South. In 'The Bear', Faulkner depicts the struggle of a long hunt. The cycle, like the hunt, requires – even demands – patience. One must follow its markers, track, and then wait. Like Old Ben himself, the cycle requires long deferrals and demands that one puts in the time.

Requiring interpretive skills and the ability to follow a path, the hunting scenes, intrinsically spatial, mirror the narrative form of *Go Down, Moses*.

The Gaps in the Ledger and McCaslin Kinship

The narrative form of *Go Down, Moses* parallels the hunt for kinship. The descendants of Lucius Quintus Carothers McCaslin all struggle with and for the legacy of their forefather. Although the myth of him is omnipresent in the stories, Lucius does not actually appear. Lucius figures as a lack in the text; all are searching for him, his heir, or his status as progenitor. The characters, in particular Ike, are hunting for some kind of meaning for the larger-than-life figure of their forefather. In this, they employ the same tracking and honing skills they use in hunting, whether it is for the bear or buried treasure. The absence of Lucius initiates a pattern of gaps in the McCaslin genealogy that make the exact familial relations uncertain. As the trope of hunting suggests, deferral, insinuation, and interpretation mark the narratives of kinship in the cycle.

That all of the kin relations are open to interpretation is a central crisis in *Go Down, Moses*. As we saw in Chapter 4, family trees often provide legitimacy and definition to filial relationships; however, 'in the case of the McCaslins, the diagram produces little gain in clarity. Rather than a clear line of descent, an orderly and hierarchical depiction of biological and social legitimacy, the McCaslin tree looks more like a tangled bush, or even a forest' (Evans 2008: 200–1). The McCaslin tree, although it begins from a single source, branches and breaks in unexpected ways, as Lucius has children by three women, two of whom are slaves and one of whom is also likely his daughter. The extent to which Lucius, Buck, or Buddy might have known that Tomasina was Lucius's own daughter is yet another mystery. As the generations grow, they cross and create new branches that defy the legitimacy offered by such genealogies and complicate any clear notion of how descent works in this family. As stories reveal new lines of genealogy and fresh connections among existing lines, the stories intimate that kinship is unknowable.

Perhaps in response to this nebulous web of relations, Lucius's white descendants become obsessed with the idea of his heir. His descendants assign avarice, ambition, cunning, and strength to the myth of Lucius, and, consequently, feelings of weakness and anxiety plague them. 'The Fire and the Hearth' identifies one possible heir:

Lucas Beauchamp. Carothers 'Roth' Edmonds goes head-to-head with Lucas and is bested. As he considers that Lucas is 'Impervious to time', Roth realises that 'the face which was not at all a replica even in caricature of his grandfather McCaslin's . . . had heired and now reproduced with absolute and shocking fidelity the old ancestor's entire generation and thought' (Faulkner 1990b: 114). Lucas possesses the qualities assigned to Lucius. In his treasure hunting, his maintenance of whiskey stills, and his children (he and his brother are the only heirs through the male line to reproduce), Lucas embodies the production that his white relatives romanticise. Lucas's strength is evident even in his name. Whereas Roth takes the diminutive of the original name, Lucas changes his given name, Lucius Quintus Carothers McCaslin Beauchamp, to strip himself of the appearance that he is a lesser version of the original. He resists the identity that his name implies. Bearing the whole name of the man who is both his grandfather and great-grandfather does not interest Lucas, and he accordingly makes the name his own by revising it. As Roth ponders the differences between himself and Lucas, the narrative voice switches to an internal monologue voiced by Roth:

> *He's more like old Carothers than all the rest of us put together, including old Carothers. He is both heir and prototype simultaneously of all the geography and climate and biology which sired old Carothers and all the rest of us and our kind, myriad, countless, faceless, even nameless now except himself who fathered himself, intact and complete, contemptuous, as old Carothers must have been, of all blood black white yellow or red, including his own.* (Faulkner 1990b: 114–15)

This internal monologue by Roth emblematises the extent to which his descendants romanticise Lucius as being a kind of first man. According to family lore, Lucius appears to come from nowhere and his wife remains unnamed, giving the impression that he alone sired the large clan.

This passage articulates a belief in the possibility of pure bloodlines, uncontaminated by biology, geography, or race. This belief energises and poisons the McCaslins, Beauchamps, and, perhaps most acutely, the Edmondses. Lucas, descended from Lucius's own daughter, has a purity of blood that, for Roth, transcends his racial subordination. His status as heir apparent, although heavily substantiated by the standards set forth in the story, is ultimately only provisional, as subsequent stories offer alternatives and contradictory visions of kinship. Roth's monologue makes clear the felt gap in the genealogy; in other words, Roth's statements express that important kinship lines are missing. Omissions, gaps, and exclusions figure significantly in *Go Down, Moses* in terms of both story and structure. Although the stories are largely autonomous, there are formal incongruities that disrupt their autonomy. Some stories have chapters, some have sections, some have both, and others have none. The anomalies and incongruities challenge the notion of structural unity, offering instead an imbalance between parts, which mirrors the McCaslin family tree, made up of unclear lines of descent and parentage and missing names and relationships.

Temporal gaps parallel the narrative gaps in McCaslin kinship causing crises in causality and exposition. Many questions remain unanswered: how is it that Buck and Sophonsiba eventually marry? Where does James go? What happens to Ike's wife? These questions indicate the gaps in plot; larger omissions emerge in terms of motivation, intention, and consequences: does love exist between Lucius and Eunice or between Lucius and Tomasina? To what extent is Tomey's Turl playing puppet master in the opening story? What is the nature of Buck and Buddy's domestic scene? And, what truly motivates Ike's repudiation of his inheritance? Is it guilt over the past, a desire to start fresh, or a disavowal of responsibility? Does his repudiation make any difference? On top of all of these questions are the myriad McCaslins who go unnamed and remain absent, including the clan's white matriarch and its youngest member. The cycle's structure relies on an open-endedness that reflects the lack of closure in the family lines. That so many of these questions go unanswered suggests that the stories' omissions replicate the fiction of kinship the McCaslins have created for themselves. They infuse their family history with grandeur, ignoring those elements that do not cohere within their accepted narrative. The white McCaslins especially omit any recognition of their biracial relatives and their ongoing interracial intimacies, as lovers, surrogate siblings, and parental figures.

Problems of kinship and of narrative coalesce in the fourth section of 'The Bear', wherein Ike reads the plantation ledgers that lead him to conclude that incest, death, and interracial intimacies founded his family.[3] Although Faulkner had written versions of other sections, the fourth section of 'The Bear' was an entirely new creation in 1941. Within the story, the fourth section appears chronologically out of order, as the subsequent and final section is set three years earlier. Faulkner later excluded the fourth section when including the piece in *The Big Woods* (1955), a collection of his so-called hunting stories, and Cowley suggested readers skip it if they wanted a coherent hunting story. The inclusion of this section in *Go Down, Moses* indicates how much meaning for the cycle as a whole derives from incongruity.

The fourth section of 'The Bear' returns the action of the story to the McCaslin farm and depicts the conversation in which Ike repudiates his inheritance and fights with Carothers McCaslin 'Cass' Edmonds, who serves as a surrogate father and brother to Ike. It contains some of the cycle's starkest statements on kinship. The ledgers expose that kinship powerfully conditions the characters' perceptions of themselves and the world. They reflect that it is impossible to adequately record kinship. Perhaps most significantly, they reveal that kinship relies on a fictive purity of origin and that subscribing to this narrative can be destructive. All of these revelations on kinship emerge as Ike reads the plantation ledgers wherein he finds 'evidence' of Lucius's actions. Alternative genealogies crop up in other stories, but Ike, and many readers, perceives the ledgers as a definitive family history.[4] Of the plantation ledgers, Ike

> realised that they probably contained a chronological and much more comprehensive though doubtless tedious record than he would ever get from any other source, not alone of his own flesh and blood but of all his people, not only the whites but the black ones too, who were as much a part of his ancestry as his white progenitors, and of the land which they had all held and used in common and fed from and on and would continue to use in common without regard to color or titular ownership. (Faulkner 1990b: 256)

The chronology of the ledgers contrasts with the oral histories told to Ike in the hunting camps and on the farm. This passage, in its references to chronology and comprehensiveness, signals Ike's desire to know the entire history of his family and the land, which here appear entwined, as the McCaslin ledgers also come to represent the entire South in Ike's mind: 'that chronicle which was a whole land in miniature, which multiplied and compounded was the entire South, twenty-three years after surrender and twenty-four from emancipation' (280–1). Ike's statements reveal his deep desire for a grand narrative that can clarify his family, home, region, and nation.

Ike approaches the ledgers with the expectation of finality and resolution, and these expectations colour his reading. The story excerpts and includes the ledger entries. They appear as italicised entries inserted into the text, thus recreating the process of Ike's reading. For instance, one entry summarises Eunice's life as, '*Eunice Bought by Father in New Orleans 1807 $650. dollars. Marrid to Thucydus 1809 Drownd in Crick Cristmas Day 1832*' (255). Other entries describe Eunice's death. The first, ostensibly written in Buddy's hand, states, '*June 21th 1833 Drownd herself*' (256). Another entry, this time by Buck, counters, '*23 Jun 1833 Who in hell ever heard of a niger drownding him self*' (256). Finally, Buddy again writes, '*Aug 13th 1833 Drownd herself*' (256). These ledger entries, among others which describe money left to Tomasina's descendants, convince Ike of Lucius's relationships with first Eunice and then their daughter Tomasina.

The inclusion of the entries leads to an impression of verisimilitude; however, the story also gives us grounds to be suspicious of the resolution Ike reaches. First, the ledgers do not appear chronologically. Some entries, such as the first included here, collapse large amounts of time into a single summation. Others list events after they happen, as in the debate between Buck and Buddy over the cause of death, an event that was not recorded until six months after the initial listing of Eunice's death. The obfuscation of chronology suggests that the ledgers are not as comprehensive or as legible as Ike initially makes them out to be. Moreover, the story only presents some of the notes from the ledgers; this selection mimics Ike's own reading practices. Although he claims omniscience, he selects from the information, omitting and disregarding what does not fit what he already believes to be there. The gaps in the ledgers reflect Ike's impulse to deliberately read for a predetermined meaning. Although there is evidence for his conclusions, the story's construction recreates the mania and purpose with which he reads the family chronicles. In this, Ike's reading in the fourth section of 'The Bear' parallels his attitudes toward the hunt in earlier sections. For Ike, the bear, the hunt, and the ledgers exist outside of time, as if they were predestined to happen. The verb tense, both retrospective and present (as in 'then he was twenty-one' [243]) and statements within the text itself (such as 'It was like the last act on a set stage' [216]) indicate that Ike approaches both as inevitable and himself as a mere actor completing the scene. Rather than resolving the unanswered questions about the family's genealogy, Ike's reading of the ledgers displays an ongoing uncertainty of kinship.

Ultimately, the evidence for Ike's discovery is meagre and spotty, based solely on selected entries from the ledgers and the bequest of money to Terrel's children. Despite its limitations, generations of readers have reached the same conclusion Ike does. The truth of Ike's discovery is less important than the process of interpretation he models (Evans 2008: 193–234). The practice of making meaning from selections is itself a model for the kind of reading that *Go Down, Moses* requires. Although Ike desperately wants to uncover a conclusive history of his family and the land, the ledgers only give him hints, insinuations, and contradictions. That Ike seeks the answer by discerning a clear genealogical line dooms him to failure, as the stories indicate the twists and turns that the family lines take. The cycle hints at a unity that it simultaneously denies. Thus, the cycle requires that we maintain multiple contingent readings as we move through the stories. It asks that we suspend final judgement and allow for both connection and heterogeneity. Rita Barnard argues that the disjointed form and the interminable sentences of the fourth section serve as metatextual rejoinders to the slave owner's ledger: 'the eschewal of such accounting is precisely the point: the complex, but elusive construction of the cycle as a whole offers a fittingly open-ended way of narrating an "injustice" that, in Faulkner's severe but accurate judgment, "can never be amortized"' (2005: 65). Ike's frantic and idiosyncratic reading of the ledgers mirrors the kind of reading the cycle requires; his readings also reflect the manic effects of denying and then accepting his patriarch's sordid history.

In summarising Faulkner's treatment of interracial intimacies, John N. Duvall concludes that 'What destroys whites in all of these narratives is their failure to acknowledge their literal and symbolic kinship with African Americans' (2005: 256). In *Go Down, Moses*, the effects of this denial are extreme. Lucius's white heirs struggle not only with the actual biological kinship with African Americans but also with the reality of having shared land, experiences, parents, and children. In 'The Fire and the Hearth', this denial comes as a rite of passage for a young Roth: 'Then one day the old curse of his fathers, the old haughty ancestral pride based not on any value but on an accident of geography, stemmed not from courage and honor but from wrong and shame, descended to him' (Faulkner 1990b: 107). Roth kicks Henry out of his bed, initiating an irreversible denial of the brotherly affection he had for Henry and the parental love he receives from Molly. Faulkner depicts this rejection as deforming all those it touches, and the notion of pure blood becomes a grotesque absurdity to which some characters cling. 'A family that insists upon pure blood, whatever that means,' Noel Polk argues, 'in effect insists on its own extinction, closing itself off through endogamy first (cousins and nieces and nephews) then through sibling incest, then twins of the opposite sex . . . then twins of the same sex, and finally the sterile isolation of masturbation' (2008: 72). In this summation, Polk captures the trajectory of the McCaslin fate: early generations are required to choose mates from the narrow local neighbourhood, as is the case with Buck and Sophonsiba Beauchamp or the domestic partnership of siblings, as with Buck and Buddy, until finally procreation is an impossibility, as it is for Ike who is 'uncle to half a county and a father to no one' (Faulkner 1990b: 3). Even when Roth reproduces, his denial of his interracial mistress ensures that the line ends with him. That James's granddaughter, who remains unnamed, does not tell Roth of their shared ancestor confirms that Roth's denial extends from 'the old haughty ancestral pride' (107).

For Ike, the appearance of this distant cousin instigates a crisis over kinship that distils his lifelong anxiety into a single encounter. Her appearance in 'Delta Autumn', the last story in the Ike-centred sequence, with her infant son confirms the twists and turns of the family lines. In the previous story, Ike has relinquished his rights and responsibilities to the land in favour of living in a small house, going on an annual hunt farther and farther into the big woods, and remaining childless. Many critics read Ike's repudiation as a noble acknowledgement of the sins of his grandfather. Conversely, Lucas, Ike's wife, and James's granddaughter read it as weakness – a selfish act of avoidance. The fact that Ike does little to acknowledge or alleviate the plight of his African American relatives confirms this latter interpretation and gives credence to the reading that Ike has not escaped the 'old haughty ancestral pride' (107), whatever his intentions might have been in relinquishing his inheritance. One complicating possibility is that Ike takes offence not at his grandfather's sin, which is suggested by the fact that he does not so much as mention this to Cass in section four of 'The Bear', but is instead offended by the generations that failed to see it, read this interpretation, and act in any way. In the absence of viable models, he chooses to renounce. Whatever his intentions at twenty-one, we know that by the time he is eighty, Ike panics in the face of continued interracial intimacy. As he talks with James's granddaughter, she begins to tell him who she is. He realises that this means she is interracial, although he initially reads her as white.

Temporality, kinship, and locality coalesce in Ike's imagination, instigating a crisis of identity for himself, his idea of the big woods, and even of the nation. Ike's realisation violates a faith in his own interpretive skills and upsets his worldview. Incredulity marks Ike's panic, registered in italics: '*Maybe in a thousand years or two thousand years in America*, he thought. *But not now! Not now!* He cried, not loud, in a voice of amazement, pity, and outrage: "You're a nigger!"' (344). His panic extends from his kin circle to encompass the entire world, and he reads it as a kind of self-fulfilling prophecy stemming from the destruction of the land: '*Chinese and African and Aryan and Jew, all breed and spawn together until no one has time to say which one is which nor cares*' (347). This scene reveals that Ike's interpretive practices are faulty and he knows it, causing a very grave crisis for his personal identity. His reaction is cut with ambivalence when he bequeaths General Compson's horn, his last inherited possession, to the infant, thus acknowledging some kinship by the transfer of property.

The Ancient Temporalities of the Present

The discourse of time reflects Ike's panic over the unreadable body. He has prepared himself for the eventuality of collapsed racial distinctions but projected this as occurring thousands of years into the future. When his worldview breaks down, he interprets it as a betrayal by time. He renders his anxiety over interracial intimacies as resulting in a lack of time for interpretation. Time and interpretive practice intersect in 'Delta Autumn' and all of the Ike-centred stories. His reading of the ledgers is nothing so much as an attempt to arrest and interpret the past in a desperate effort to determine the present and future. His spotty interpretation suggests that Ike lacks control over the relationship between interpretation and time; thus, 'one can read "The Bear" as a cautionary tale about reading the past, about using the past without agility, or without a keen sense of irony, without "sublimating the actual into the apocryphal," as Faulkner himself would put it' (Parini 2007: 168). Because Ike approaches the act of reading the ledgers as if he already knows what they contain, he lacks the ability to nuance the past and dooms himself to being dictated by the consequences of an apocryphal interpretation.

Just as locality and kinship create connections across the stories in *Go Down, Moses*, temporality also links the narratives, both in terms of structure and theme. In his short story cycles, Faulkner tends to sequence the stories by their main action in a roughly chronological progression. However, Faulkner experiments with time within the stories rather than within the cycle's general outline. For instance, section four of 'The Bear' occurs three years after the final section of the story. The opening of 'Was' expresses events that would take another century to pass after the main action of the story. Past and future events invade the present within each story, just as they do in his novels and other short stories. Thus, an obsession with temporality shapes his cycles. Faulkner does not assign years to the stories in *Go Down, Moses*; rather, references and allusions to key dates, such as Isaac's birth and Eunice's death, or historical events, such as World War II, gesture toward a timeline without cementing it. This avoidance of a definite timeline evinces a Faulknerian conception of time, which favours neither rigid linear progression nor open cyclicality. Rather, both notions of time determine the course of the narratives, the characters' responses to events, and the multiple understandings of history espoused by the characters and the works themselves.

Thus, Faulkner's short story cycle extends and further complicates our critical understanding of his conception of time. A year after the French translation of *The Sound and The Fury* appeared in 1938, Jean-Paul Sartre wrote that Faulkner's disavowal of chronology illuminates how 'It is man's misfortune to be confined in time' (1963: 226). Rather than chronology determining meaning in his characters' lives, they are bound by 'central themes' around which 'innumerable fragments of thought and act revolve' (Sartre 1963: 228) where key dramatic events filter every other event. In The *Sound and the Fury* (Faulkner 1990c), Sartre identifies Caddy's pregnancy, Benjy's castration, and Quentin's suicide as three such events. In *Go Down, Moses*, Ike's repudiation, Lucius's incest, and Zack's claim on Molly serve as similar 'emotional constellations' for the characters. Thus, selected events from the past bleed into and dictate the present. The Ike-centred sequence dramatises the extent to which the past invades the present for Ike from a young age. In 'The Old People', Sam Fathers, the only Native American who remains in the area, seems to possess infinite knowledge but is ultimately mortal. Often siting with Ike beside a fire, he tells stories of the old times: 'And as he talked about those old times and those dead and vanished men of another race from either that the boy knew, gradually to the boy those old times would cease to be old times and would become part of the boy's present, not only as if they had happened yesterday but as if they were still happening' (Faulkner 1990b: 165). This nostalgia reveals a desire to know his father and grandfather; more than that, however, these early childhood scenes establish in Ike a desire to keep reliving an idealised ritualised past and thereby control time.

The past's incursion into the present inspires the nearly interminable sentences of Faulkner's prose, particularly heightened in *Go Down, Moses*. In 'The Bear', Faulkner writes a 1,800-word sentence. Faulkner's famously long sentences reflect the ongoing motion of time that is so central to his fiction. Cowley recounts what Faulkner told him of this feature in his writing: '"My ambition," he said, "is to put everything into one sentence – not only the present but the whole past on which it depends and which keeps overtaking the present, second by second"' (1967: 663). The particular project of *Go Down, Moses* in terms of temporality is to establish a historical frame from which to view his entire canon. The characters' obsessions focus 'upon a time now lost once and for all – a time of unanimity, of invisible nature, and a time of origins, that is, before property, slavery, and profit, a time that hunters ritually try to revive at a certain season each year – and situates in a particular place (the big Woods, the land concession, Jefferson County)' (Glissant 1999: 46). *Go Down, Moses* exemplifies the temporality of consciousness that distinguishes Faulkner's style. The cycle also stands as an important amendment to it, as the cycle gives us a direct representation of one part of the past that so haunts his other works. The short story cycle, in its ability to balance cyclical and progressive understandings of history, is an ideal form for showing the paradoxical nature of the past.

In *Go Down, Moses*, time expands and contracts with stifling and liberating effects. When Sartre writes that man is 'time-bound', he refers to the ways in which time exceeds humanity's control and dictates consciousness. In its concluding statement, the opening story, 'Was', sets the stage for time as flexible. Buck, who has been held captive overnight at the Beauchamp house, states, 'It seems to me I've been away from home a whole damn month' (Faulkner 1990b: 29). The story buttresses the notion of time as a prison sentence in that the Beauchamps hold him captive and try to entrap him in marriage to Sophonsiba, which he sees as another kind of imprisonment of long duration. This caging juxtaposes Terrel's interminable sentence of servitude and separation from Tennie. Time takes on stifling properties in the context of marriage and enslavement in 'Was'. In contrast, in 'Pantaloon in Black', the brief history of his marriage collapses into a single moment for Rider: 'the dusk-filled single room where all those six months were now crammed and crowded into one instant, of time until there was no space left for air to breathe, crammed and crowded about the hearth, where the fire which was to have lasted to the end of them' (135–6). Time represents possibility in Rider's marriage, but that possibility is foreclosed by his wife's premature death. Time takes on spatial qualities above the hearth, which, in this story and in 'The Fire and the Hearth', measures the intensity and duration of marital commitment. The hearth, which burns throughout Lucas and Molly's long marriage, symbolises the power of time and devotion. Its fire 'was hot, not scorching, searing, but possessing a slow, deep solidity of heat, a condensation of the two years during which the fire had burned constantly above it, a condensation not of fire but of time, as though not the fire's dying and not even water would cool it but only time would' (50–1). This passage figures time as the only thing powerful enough to cool fire.

Among the white McCaslins, the idea of time as elemental stems from their belief in race as ancient and in racial purity. Roth believes his rejection of Henry and Molly is the result of an 'old haughty ancestral pride' (107) born of blood and some ancient truth rather than conditioned by his milieu, historical moment, and personal attitudes. Roth's response to Lucas in 'The Fire and the Hearth' bespeaks his belief in some essential, ancient truth to race distinctions, which he thinks he sees in Lucas: 'Without changing the inflection of his voice and apparently without effort or even design Lucas became not Negro but nigger not secret so much as impenetrable, not servile and not effacing, but enveloping himself in an aura of timelessness and stupid impassivity almost like a smell' (58). The story confirms Roth's sense that there is something timeless about Lucas. He seems younger than Edmonds and Mollie, who are both younger than himself, and everyone suspects that Lucas will outlast them, just as he outlasted the previous McCaslin generations before Roth. Lucas's resilience to time and his denial of subordination based on blackness cause Roth's anxiety, which he attempts to control by naming Lucas nigger. Faulkner exposes how deeply false and destructive these attitudes are, thereby resisting the model of identity Roth espouses.

A vague sense of his own long-lost purity gives rise to Roth's response to Lucas, and this sense of tainted whiteness deforms not just Roth but all of Lucius's white heirs. Through the repetition of their actions and beliefs across generations, Faulkner depicts a family doomed by their rigid faith in the honour of racial purity. Reading Lucas as impenetrable, the narrative voice in 'The Fire and the Hearth' breaks to Roth's internal monologue, '*I am not only looking at a face older than mine and which has seen and winnowed more, but at a man most of whose blood was pure ten thousand years when my own anonymous beginning became mixed enough to produce me*' (69). They insist on whiteness's superiority out of a fear of it being an afterthought of creation. Ike articulates a similar sense of his impurity and of the superiority of blackness in his conversation with Cass. In discerning what motivated his grandfather to leave one thousand dollars to Tomasina's children and grandchildren, he explains, '"He didn't want to. He had to. Because they will endure. They are better than we are. Stronger than we are"' (281). Although Tomasina and her descendants, including Lucas, are both black and white, such a distinction does not matter to either Ike or Roth, because of that supreme belief in an essential, transmittable difference and their paralysing knowledge of their own mortality.

Although both credit black bodies as being stronger and purer than themselves, their essentialising and actions are no less pernicious, especially to themselves, than their demonisation of the black characters have been. When Roth denies his child, again only giving money instead of acknowledgement, he repeats Lucius's actions. The actions and attitudes of the past repeat one hundred years later, and the volume's structure reflects the cyclical nature of the action. The belief in the ancient longevity of this difference validates for Ike and Roth their decision to do nothing; in Ike's case, his grand act is actually to do nothing. The title of the cycle, with its allusion both to the American slave spiritual and the biblical story of Moses's escape from slavery, evokes that duration and the sense of time implicit to the spiritual, the biblical story of Moses, and *Go Down, Moses*. Directions and lines pose a threat because their ends can be uncertain. After all, Moses had to go down into slavery to be delivered.

From the multiple stories, it can be difficult, if not impossible, to identify the cycle's ultimate stance on the relationship between temporality and race. Faulkner's own statements in support of the 'Go Slow' approach regarding desegregation further complicate this connection (Crawford 2008: 43–6). However, the treatment of the unequivocal deformation and sterility of the white McCaslins offers a symbolic, unmitigated condemnation of the white half of the family. The cycle dramatises the inherent relationship between time and ideologies of racial purity. Because any such purity can only go back so far, they must have a fictive point of origin; in the case of the

McCaslins, this origin is Lucius. As his personal history shows, the so-called origin is always a corrupted and often arbitrary moment. Although they come to different conclusions, Ike's reading of the ledgers and the stories the family tell about themselves indicate the extent to which any such narrative must rely on much that has been forgotten or omitted. Faulkner's treatment of the denial of interracial intimacies resonates with the idea of the grotesque in Anderson's *Winesburg*: 'It was his notion that the moment one of the people took one of the truths to himself, called it his truth, and tried to live his life by it, he became a grotesque and the truth he embraced became a falsehood' (Anderson 1999: 9). *Go Down, Moses* depicts the effects of holding tight to the 'truth' of racial purity on the characters. As Anderson describes, the characters embrace the truth of racial division so tightly it becomes a falsehood that renders them grotesque. The construction of identities based on a rigid belief in the one-drop rule takes on tragic dimensions in *Go Down, Moses*.

Gavin Stevens's famous line that 'The past is never dead. It's not even past' distils something elemental about Faulkner's fiction: collective and personal pasts define the truth of the present (Faulkner 1951: 92). These truths are always contingent, ephemeral, and multiple. *Go Down, Moses* resists any definitive judgement on the imbrications of temporality and racial identities. Rather, the cycle captures and repeats the ways in which temporality shapes the characters' multiple understandings of racial identity. Time becomes a metaphor for articulating responses to the colour line: time is a shield, salve, excuse, possibility, and cuckold. As such, temporality shows little regard for the conventional distinctions of the past, present, and future. *Go Down, Moses* dramatises the ongoing construction of identity; whether that identity is geographic, familial, or racial, it is never static, definite, or stable but always dynamic, provisional, and inconsistent.

Conclusions

Released in 1942, *Go Down, Moses* was published at a critical time in Faulkner's career. Not only was he struggling financially, he was also moving from the hyper-experimentation of his earlier fiction to the interest in the serial form and realism of the Snopes trilogy. *Go Down, Moses* dramatises how the divide between these interests is not so wide. The 1940s were also a transitional period for US modernism, and *Go Down, Moses* crystallises the tensions for Faulkner's fiction and modernist expression. With *Go Down, Moses*, and particularly 'With the creation of Isaac McCaslin,' James Early argues, 'Faulkner moves toward the central moral tradition of the realistic novel . . . in *Go Down, Moses* realism in characterisation creates a moral intensity unique in Faulkner's work' (1972: 19). Realism's interest in the production of human behaviour out of historical and material conditions is evident in Faulkner's treatment of Ike. That Faulkner blends realism in characterisation with modernist formal experimentation undermines the fallacies of objective, discernible truth that Faulkner considers inherent in more conventionally realistic narrative. The anxiety over European influence that Faulkner articulates in his essays on Anderson reflects the indebtedness of modernism to realist writers, from Europeans, such as Gogol, Flaubert, and Dickens, to American frontier humourists and realists, such as Longstreet and Twain (Cowley 1967: xxix).

Faulkner's fiction models the ways in which the cycle is modernist but also pulls from realism and portends postmodernism. If we most often understand modernism to be an impulse to understand, test, stabilise, and challenge the legitimacy of the word, the short story cycle is an essential component of this critical narrative. Stein's emphasis on gerunds, Hemingway's austere prose, Joyce's internal monologues, and Faulkner's interminable sentences all display an interest in the word as a sign and symbol. Although these modernists come to different ends, they begin from that same interest in the word. This interest in the possibilities and limitations of expression similarly shapes their work in the short story cycle, which articulates in form what these authors were after at the level of the word and the sentence: the constructions and perforations possible in language. The modernist short story cycle also intimates one of the defining moves of postmodern fiction 'to hide or at least obscure the mechanism of narration' (Ferguson 1991: 86). Of the modernists working in the cycle, Faulkner is perhaps the most explicit example of this prescient postmodernism, and, not surprisingly, he has been read as postmodernist. The short story cycle is critical to understanding the ways in which realism endures in modernism; more than that, the short story cycle represents a linchpin in understanding the continuity among realism, modernism, and postmodernism in American letters. The ongoing debate about period and stylistic distinctions shapes critical conversations of contemporary short story cycles and the new genres emerging from them.

Notes

1. See Lawrence H. Schwartz's *Creating Faulkner's Reputation: The Politics of Modern Literary Criticism* (1998).
2. For more comments on the form of *Go Down, Moses*, see Faulkner's letter to Haas from 28 April 1940 (Blotner 1976: 121–2) and also one to Bennett Cerf dated 28 July 1940 (Blotner 1976: 135).
3. Sally Wolff (2009) found that Faulkner had access to and drew inspiration from similar actual ledgers kept by the McCaroll/Francisco family, who were family friends.
4. Such alternative chronologies appear in 'The Fire and the Hearth', which recounts the entangled family lines, focusing on James, Fonsiba, and Lucas (Faulkner 1990b: 101–2). Another semi-comprehensive family history appears earlier in the story, which focuses more, although not exclusively, on the white McCaslin descendants (36–40).

Chapter 6

Atomic Genre

Bennie Salazar, a recurring character in Jennifer Egan's *A Visit from the Goon Squad* (2010), first fell in love with music for its raw energy. The band of his youth, The Flaming Dildos, roamed the San Francisco punk scene listening to others and hoping to be discovered. Decades later he is a jaded music executive trying to salvage the once-bright talents of a folksy sister duo. Having sold his start-up label to 'multinational crude-oil extractors', he listens to the duo play in a makeshift, basement studio and realises that the sisters' realness runs counter to so much else in his industry and life: 'Bennie knew that what he was bringing into the world was shit. Too clear, too clean. The problem was precision, perfection; the problem was *digitization*, which sucked the life out of everything that got smeared through its microscopic mesh. Film, photography, music: dead. *An aesthetic holocaust!*' (Egan 2011: 23). Bennie's frustration that technology is making everything too glossy, too sanitised extends from an ongoing anxiety about a loss of authenticity. Recording processes get more precise, and the studio's idiosyncrasies get lost. Life is messy; music should be too.

Anxieties about the seen and unforeseen losses that attend progress are a great source of angst in modern and contemporary literature. Bennie, in a story set in 2006, thinks this creeping loss is new or, at least, more terrible than what came before. The history of the short story cycle exposes that a desire for a lost authenticity occurs in its earliest moments and remains persistent. Kirkland, in 1837, laments that settlement ruins the natural beauty of Michigan and worries that increasing settlements will diminish the community of small-town Montacute. Jewett decries how increasing urbanisation makes small shipping towns such as Dunnet Landing obsolete. The mothers of Tan's *Joy Luck Club* worry that their daughters lack strong family ties because of transnational migrations. The astronauts in Bradbury's futuristic Martian tales long for small-town Illinois across the massive distance of space. Bradbury's cycle renders the holocaust actual and not only aesthetic when humans destroy Earth with the technology meant to keep them safe. Bennie's nostalgia for a lost process of production finds its most powerful analogue in Anderson's treatment of the incursion of the railroad onto the farms and town of Winesburg. The characters' anxieties about loss, the passage of time, and authenticity register in their alienation, inability to communicate, and desperation. Bennie Salazar would be at home in Winesburg.

As in *Winesburg*, nostalgia is powerful but ultimately false and even dangerous. Longing for the past is a career-killer in music, an industry committed to youth. As Bennie puts it, 'Nostalgia was the end – everyone knew that' (37). And yet, Bennie cannot escape nostalgia. He longs for a bygone era of undigitised 'Film, photography, music' (23). What Bennie does not realise is that the advent of each industry he names, seemingly aesthetically pure, ushered in anxieties about the loss of authentic expression. Film endangered booksellers and the stage. Photography threatened to make painting obsolete. The mass production of music rendered local arts vulnerable. Bennie's nostalgia for lost art parallels Anderson's treatment of the characters' responses to the railroad and industrialisation. Residents of Winesburg worry that life as they know it will be over and that there will not be anything real left, while the stories intimate that the perfect community they remember never existed. Throughout the history of the cycle, authors engage shifts in time to expose the persistent yet artificial sentimentality for the past.

That Bennie is a has-been punk kid is apt: he works in a genre that loses authenticity the moment it gains an audience. Bennie constructs a vision of the past conditioned by his disappointments in the present. A desire to restore what he has lost personally and professionally drives his present and future. Subsequent stories move into the past and future and undermine his feelings in this passage by exposing his memories as flawed and incomplete. Bennie's statement expresses an elemental impulse of Egan's volume: the passage of time renders our lives meaningful and meaningless. Or, as one of Bennie's ageing rock stars puts it: 'Time's a goon, right? Isn't that the expression?' (127).

Ultimately, the faulty logic embedded in Bennie Salazar's lament for a lost aesthetics is made possible by form: as the stories layer onto each other, they reveal nostalgia as false but do not simply dismiss it. When asked about her commitment to unity, Egan said, 'I was not concerned at all about tying up loose ends – *Goon Squad* is full of them! . . . the structural idea behind *Goon Squad* as a whole [is that . . .] – the reader knows more about the characters than they do about themselves, or each other, which (hopefully) adds a kind of resonance and poignancy – and sometimes irony – to their stories' (Wambold 2010). The stories' resistance to forming a unified whole mirrors the characters' inability to form legible identities. They are made of parts and pieces that gain meaning together but never unite to create coherent, stable identities. They are made up of fragments of memories that they have only partial access to, even as they think they know the entire memory; in much the same way, the stories offer glimpses into these characters' memories, lives, and desires only to later reveal those glimpses were fragmented and partial. The cycle allows the stories to actualise the ongoing, contentious making of meaning and identity from memory. Egan has described the book and its stories as atomised – in the vein that music production and consumption have atomised. The stories are discrete yet interconnected. That atomisation is sad, as it signals the limitations on producing a whole (album, vision, book, or product). But, it is also liberating. In a book about time, music, and identity, nothing could be more important than the pauses that happen in the in-between. Atomic implies that isolating the most basic part generates power, and it implies a logic in which a proposition, sentence, or formula cannot be analysed into a coherent structure. In this final chapter, I show how the short story cycle is an atomic genre as it gains explosive energy from individual stories.

The Problem with Labels

When *Goon Squad* was published in 2010, most of the reviewers laboured to define and name the ostensibly genre-bending volume. Most commonly called a novel, reviewers also named it a tale, mosaic, hybrid, novel-in-stories, linked story collection, not-quite-linked story collection, or simply book. It inspired a wild debate about what to call it in part because Egan had already developed a reputation as a writer who resists classification having published gothic, thriller, and realistic fiction. Egan admits, 'I have a hatred of familiarity . . . If I feel like I am doing something I've done before, it feels old and done' (Ciabattari 2010). She makes working in a new way the goal of each project. There is a generative principle in her very mode of conceiving and developing projects. *Goon Squad* represented for critics the apotheosis of her formal innovation.

Interviewers consistently ask Egan what to call the volume. She gives always insightful, occasionally conflicting answers. In one instance, she says,

> what I was trying to do – tell compelling stories about a multitude of characters whose lives intersect over many years – is as old as the novel form itself. I did realize that I was deviating from the standard model of 'connected stories,' though, because those books have a uniformity of voice and tone, and I wanted exactly the opposite – total diversity and variety of voice and tone and technique, yet fused together by the stories themselves into something with a big range. (Wambold 2010)

In this and other comments, Egan dismissed the idea that *Goon Squad* is a novel-in-stories or linked collection. This dismissal is, however, built on a false impression of the monotony of story cycles, which often include a great deal of range in voice, technique, and tone. Her comments illustrate the difficulty in discerning modes of fiction.

The link between the book's genre and decentralisation is a persistent theme in interviews and reviews during the immediate critical reception of *Goon Squad*. Stephan Lee (2011), for instance, asked, 'It seems as though the novel of loosely connected stories is on the rise. What is appealing to you about that structure? And do you think you will ever return to it?' His question implies that the volume consists of loosely connected stories. Egan's response is provocative: 'The structure itself has no innate appeal for me, honestly. I only used it because it made sense for this particular story about a group of decentralized people over many years. If the story I'd been writing had been more centralized, I would have gravitated toward a structure that manifested that' (Lee 2011). In this moment, she does not dismiss Lee's label but instead talks about centralisation. This comment aligns with a general tendency to turn to the form of the short story cycle when wanting to tell a big but decentralised set of stories.

Genre holds a fascination for readers and writers that is equal parts frustrating and exhilarating. Egan acknowledges, 'Actually, I don't really care too much about genre. I think it's a selling tool. Basically, it creates a kind of shorthand that makes some people's lives easier' (Michod 2010). And yet, Egan understands too that genre shapes readers' and the book industry's reactions: 'I felt more doubtful than usual with *Goon Squad*, because I knew that the book's genre wasn't easily named – Novel? Stories? Novel-in-stories? – and I worried that its lack of a clear category would count against it' (Lee 2011). Egan echoes a long-held anxiety that the bigness of novels equates to large ambitions. Her comments result from a common presumption that short stories, short story collections, and short story cycles are limited in ambition and artistry. Egan worries that the volume's resistance to neat categorisation would work against it for literary recognition and readership. That anxiety registers in the lengths interviewers and reviewers go to label it in nearly every publication following the cycle's release. In the case of *Goon Squad*, Egan's and others' initial worries could not have been more wrong. *A Visit from the Goon Squad*, among many others accolades, won the 2010 National Book Critics Circle Award and the 2011 Pulitzer Prize, landed on *The New York Times* and *The Los Angeles Times* bestseller lists, and was optioned by HBO.[1]

In searching for a descriptor, Egan often turns to metaphors. In 2009 before the publication and completion of *Goon Squad*, Egan said, 'What I would like to do is write a book of stories that leave some things open-ended but are connected in a sort of web' (Reilly 2009: 459). After the volume's release, she said that the characters are '"little islands far apart – I didn't see the land mass that connected them till later"' (Tillotson 2011). On another occasion, she modified one interviewer's label: 'The metaphor in my mind wasn't "linked," but "entangled"' (Ciabattari 2010). Metaphors of webs, land masses, and entanglement imply a deep structural model – even if it eludes typical genre labels. Because of the book's simultaneous deep, connecting structures that do not result in unity, short story cycle is the best, if imperfect, term for a volume that is novelistic and not. Calling it a short story cycle, Josh Lukin (2010) likens Egan to a 'punk Proust, hippie Dos Passos, a rock-and-roll Faulkner', placing the volume in a lineage of writers concerned with creating sprawling, diverse works based in a central cosmos but told in short forms both discrete and interconnected.

In addition to debates about genre, *Goon Squad* sparked conversations about the role of innovation in contemporary fiction. In a speech to the Northeastern Modern Language Association in March 2012, entitled 'Experimentation in Fiction: Notes from a Reluctant Practitioner', Egan states that she does not like the idea of experimentation because it seems to imply novelty and contemporariness. She argues that earlier centuries saw great experimental works like *Don Quixote* (1605–15) and *Tristram Shandy* (1759), which are wild, flexible grab bags. These and other early novels are postmodern in their rejection of verisimilitude, engagement with self-consciousness, interest in surfaces, and concern with their own creation. She locates the nineteenth century as the premiere period for such flexibility and swagger. Early novels address the reader directly and include voices from unlikely candidates, such as animals, that would today get them hailed as postmodern and new. Rather than focus on who pioneered these forms, Egan insists that there has been a longstanding mandate for writers: to tell stories in flexible ways. She argues that there is a false divide between convention and experimentation. The best works have synthesis.[2]

Placing herself in a lineage of sprawling, multivoiced novels, Egan's comments also inform the problems of naming and defining the short story cycle. The tension between independence and interdependences is especially crucial to short story cycles, because the form reinforces the insuperable divides we construct with each other and within ourselves – a theme central to Egan's volume and the genre as a whole. Egan has been reluctant to call *Goon Squad* a linked story collection or novel-in-stories because she argues that such volumes, whatever one calls them, are too tonally similar. This assumption fails to see the incredible diversity in the genre, which resembles in scope and form the diversity and experimentation she notes in the history of the novel.

The Messiness of Intention and Influence

Egan cites three guiding principles in crafting *Goon Squad*:

> One of them was that each piece had to stand strongly on its own: it had to be forceful individually. I wanted the whole to be more than the sum of its parts, but I didn't want them to lean on each other: I wanted them to enhance each other. The second was that each piece had to be completely different in terms of mood and world and voice. It ranges from sad to outright farce, and I really wanted to encompass all that in one book. And the third rule was that each piece had to be about a different person. There could be overlapping people, but there's only one chapter in which we look through a particular person's set of eyes. (Lukin 2010)

These three rules stress the autonomy – in terms of form, tone, and perspective – of each story. She resists the idea that the stories explain each other but instead claims that they complicate and extend each other. This commitment to diversity challenges the possibilities of narration as well as puts the burden of comprehension on the reader.

Goon Squad resulted, in part, from Egan's own experiences as a reader. When she conceived of the project, she had been reading Marcel Proust's seven-volume *In Search of Lost Time* (1913–27) and watching *The Sopranos* (1999–2007). Reading Proust over many years with a group, all of them experiencing life changes, Egan, then in her late thirties, questioned whether she could write about time in the twenty-first century. 'Proust accomplished his heroic task in a sort of real time way', Egan notes. She 'especially loved Proust's ability to capture the transformation and reversals that happen over time, the way that outcomes are so often unexpected and in fact almost the opposite of what you would expect. The biggest question for me was how to capture the sweep and scope of those transformation and reversals without taking thousands of pages to do it. It's a technical question – how do you do that?' (Alford 2012). *The Sopranos* modelled how to write time on a large scale in a contemporary mode that is both decentralised and compelling. *The Sopranos* engages time to show the characters' development and stasis, as well as the sometimes illuminating, often capricious, and always unrelenting force of time. Both Proust's opus and *The Sopranos* are about investigating the effects of the passage of time on people. In *Goon Squad*, Egan draws from their treatment of fragmentation, antiheroes, surface and subtext, and trenchant historical contextualisation – all done through long narrative arcs told in discrete segments.

A third major influence on Egan's conception was that of the concept album – a big musical story told in parts, each of which is tonally different but shares sufficient recurring themes and motifs. Egan divides her volume into A and B sides. There is no table of contents, and the stories are both numbered and titled. In the final story of the A side, Bennie's former band mate, Scotty, who was once the most charismatic and talented of The Flaming Dildos but is now impoverished, visits Bennie at the height of his success. In this moment of reunion, Scotty 'experienced several realizations, all in a sort of cascade: (1) Bennie and I weren't friends anymore, and we never would be. (2) He was looking to get rid of me as quickly as possible with the least amount of hassle. (3) I already knew that would happen. I'd known it before I arrived. (4) It was the reason I'd come to see him' (Egan 2011: 100–1). Egan confirms that youth cannot be regained. There exists now a gap in their ability to connect. The list gives the appearance of clarity but its contents and the metaphor of the cascade reveal an utter, overwhelming lack of mutual and self-understanding. Scotty attempts to make sense of the gaps through an analogy to music: '"I came for this reason: I want to know what happened between A and B."' Scotty explains, '"A is when we were both in the band, chasing the same girl. B is now"' (101). The implication is that the A side of life is brief and full of memories but that the B side, the *longue durée* of their personal histories, is more meaningful. This divide between A and B lends the story an apparently clear framework, but the stories themselves belie that easy unity. Often, Egan dramatises the A side of experience in the B side of the book. Thus, Egan's temporality obscures a clear progression. Scotty longs for a legible causality that is occasionally possible but always partial, because of the great expanse of time and the fallibility of memory.

The cycle's epigraph announces Proust's influence and the cycle's overriding concern with how the past shapes the present:

> 'Poets claim that we recapture for a moment the self that we were long ago when we enter some house or garden in which we used to live in our youth. But these are most hazardous pilgrimages, which end as often in disappointment as in success. It is in ourselves that we should rather seek to find those fixed places, contemporaneous with different years.'
> . . .
> 'The unknown element in the lives of other people is like that of nature, which each fresh scientific discovery merely reduces but does not abolish.' (Egan 2011: n.p.)

Following the epigraph, Egan's stories reject the nostalgia that leads the characters back to earlier moments in their lives, especially youth. When they return to places or relationships expecting them to be the same as they once were, they realise that the sameness cannot be and often is not wanted. As Scotty and Bennie do, Egan's characters continually chase an elusive moment in the past only to find it as flawed as the present. Proust's passage suggests that we contain the recognition and memory within ourselves and that suffices.

The second part of the epigraph about the ultimate inability to know another aligns with the ways Egan's characters attempt to understand each other. The stories trace how they fail to ever completely uncover or decipher the 'unknown element' – even in the most

Atomic Genre   149

intimate relationships: childhood friends, first loves, marriages, and parents and children. If any of Egan's characters can hope to understand each other, it is those who share a passion for music. Music inspires a common language and temporality (akin to Proust's idea of 'fixed places, contemporaneous with different years'). Shared love of music originates from a desire to communicate verbally, musically, and bodily. It is linguistic and beyond language. Ironically, too, music, as an industry, has been ravaged by the changes of the late twentieth and early twenty-first centuries. Music and literature combined create the perfect medium to render time's power to illuminate, erode, create, and destroy.

In accordance with the idea of a concept album, Egan began with a rule that each story must be told differently yet contribute to a greater whole. In her lecture, she noted that she tried and failed to write a story in epic poetry and as an off-off Broadway theatre show. Apart from these non-starters, the volume contains stories told in first, second, and third person adopting and adapting the forms of realist fiction, journalism, speculative fiction, vignettes, near-novellas, and PowerPoint. The structure resulted from a combination of intuition and trial and error. She wanted to let go of chronology and instead mimic the feeling of curiosity. In an interview with Heidi Julavits (2010), Egan explains that the web expanded when she 'got curious' about Bennie Salazar who is mentioned briefly in the opening story which led to 'The Gold Cure', and then started thinking about his marriage, which led to the story 'A to B', and that led to realising that Stephanie's brother is the narrator of 'Forty-Minute Lunch'. *The Sopranos* prompted the realisation that 'we're all peripheral to other people and central to ourselves' (Julavits 2010), and the stories mimic that tension between centrality and periphery, as the series of stories related to Bennie demonstrates. As she worked on these stories individually, Egan had an epiphany, 'realizing Sasha, from "Found Objects," was the same person as the protagonist of "Good-bye, My Love." I couldn't believe I had written two stories about women who steal wallets without realizing they were one person' (Julavits 2010). The realisation about Sasha recurring in her ostensibly separate stories indicates how Egan composed the volume: 'the whole writing process seemed to be about thinking I would write just one more piece about this constellation of people' (Cox 2010).

Like so many other cycles and collections, portions of *Goon Squad* appeared in print well before the volume's completion.[3] Egan asserts that she 'had no sense that they linked up at all. And then I started working on "Found Objects," and it all kind of followed from there in a strange way because I wasn't even planning to work on this book' (Julavits 2010). It seems that she initially conceived of these pieces as separate and that she later adapted and revised them to resonate and have consistency with the other volumes in the story, sometimes renaming characters or relationships or changing details to make them fit the world of the book. The length of the composition process, the duration of reading Proust or watching *The Sopranos*, and the decline of albums mirror the sheer and crushing weight of time:

> I knew as far back as 2001 that I would write a book called *A Visit from the Goon Squad*, though I had no idea what kind of book it would be . . . As I worked on it, I kept wondering, 'Who is the goon?' I liked the sense that there are many answers. And then I found myself writing 'Time is a goon,' and realized that of course that's true – time is the stealth goon, the one you ignore because you are so busy worrying about the goons right in front of you. (Ciabattari 2010)

'The Stealth Goon': Time

The first story ends with a meditation on the passage of time. As Sasha sits in her therapist's office, she hears 'the faint hum that was always there when she listened, and these minutes of Coz's time: another, then another, then one more' (Egan 2011: 18). The hum of time reminds Sasha of what she loses with its passage: the ability to connect or change. Sasha is a kleptomaniac, who steals ostensibly insignificant objects which are actually meaningful. What she chooses to steal often reveals a deep desire for connection – she steals only from people, never stores. Stealing derives from an impulse to record her life in these 'Found Objects', which gives the story its title. The title evokes an artistry implicit in her sleight of hand. She reflects on 'the pride she took in these objects, a tenderness that was only heightened by the shame of their acquisition. She'd risked everything, and here was the result: the raw, warped core of her life' (15). She has slipped her latest acquisition, a scrap of faded paper that reads 'I BELIEVE IN YOU' (17), from Alex, a one-night stand. This relic from his wallet, a link to his past, reflects her unspoken impulse to make meaning from theft, itself a symbolic absence. Storytelling, desire, and petty thieving coalesce in Sasha's therapy sessions when she hears that hum of time.

She wants to tell Coz, her therapist, that she is changing and that she is fixed, but instead she requests, 'Don't ask me how I feel' (18). Sasha's stunted communication, both on and off the couch, reveals her alienation and time's compounding effect. When Sasha reappears in the penultimate story, 'Great Rock and Roll Pauses', told from her daughter's point of view, she has changed. She no longer steals. She is married with children in a lovely house, and she makes sculptures and scrapbooks from found objects. The objects in her life are relics of her life rather than others'. Her story is recorded by her daughter, signifying that she has a future. But, Egan does not give us the story of those changes. Sasha's growth happens in the gaps between stories. In fact, the other Sasha-related stories focus on the years before 'Found Objects'. Using gaps in time and storytelling, Egan dramatises how Sasha's problems of communication have not entirely vanished but have instead been transformed with time and changes in circumstances. Egan's engagement with non-linear time and storytelling enables a treatment of perspective and experience that intimates that the characters' basic problems remain with them forever. However, the articulations and implications of those problems – as in Sasha's stunted ability to connect – change as time passes.

The cycle's use of non-linear narratives actualises the necessity of dealing with the past, even when such attempts prove vexed. Egan explains her personal vision of time: 'I don't experience time as linear. I experience it in layers that seem to coexist. I feel like 20 years ago was really recent even though I was much younger and had a different kind of life. Yet at the same time I feel like I'm still kind of there' (Julavits 2010). The cycle's main action spans from 1973 to 2021, with references to the past and the future that thwart any definite identification of when a story happens. The past is both a reality and a construction of the present. There exists cyclical resonance but not clear causality. Egan's description of time as layered is apt – multiple versions of the past, present, and future coexist.

Egan had initially thought the stories would move backwards in time, but that proved too rigid and too chronological for capturing the recursive nature of time:

> I didn't see it as a novel, exactly, but more as a series of lateral 'moves' ... For a long time I imagined that the book would simply move backwards, because the early chapters were unfolding that way, but the plan was complicated, first, by the emergence of chapters

that took place in the future, and second, by my horrified discovery, when I read the book through in backwards order, that the result was lumbering and flat. It was at this point that I realized I needed to let go of linear chronology entirely, and that backwards was still linear. (Igarashi 2011)

The organisation of the cycle fulfils the search for satisfaction by sequencing the stories around moments of trauma and character revelation that resonate from one story to the next. For instance, Sasha's conflation of sex, communication, and time in the first story resonates with Bennie's search for a 'gold cure' to solve his impotence, energise his music career, and connect with his son in the second story. Egan repeatedly jumps forward or backward in time to predict or explain characters' actions in the present – often, these moments concern how the story's moment of illumination derives from deeper webs of kinship and community.

However, the main chronology abjures any clean linearity. For example, following the main plot of each story takes the reader from 2006 in the second story to the late 1970s in the third to trace Bennie's problems post-divorce to his experience with The Flaming Dildos, which does so much to explain his doomed relationships and love for music. But it is later stories, which include points of view from his band mate Scotty, his wife, and his brother-in-law, that really flesh out just how damaged his relationships and psyche are – to a degree that even he does not realise. These stories take place in the time gaps between the second and third stories, and the final story even projects his future. Egan's use of layered time reminds us, however, that progress is beside the point; all of these moments are true and important, outside of some larger narrative of development. *Goon Squad* renders the passage of time quotidian and monumental, personal and public.

The stories' invocation of time often identifies time by its relation to moments of violence and crisis. For example, the third-person narrator of 'Safari' locates the time of the story as being twenty years after the Korean War, which Lou, Bennie's mentor and another music industry executive, barely escaped. Lou has taken two of his children, from a long string of broken marriages, on safari where they sing and dance with warriors. In a move typical of the volume, the narrator locates the time of the story by a glimpse into a violent future: 'Thirty-five years from now, in 2008, this warrior will be caught in the tribal violence between the Kikiuyu and the Luo and will die in a fire. He'll have had four wives and sixty-three grandchildren by then' (Egan 2011: 61), one of whom will go on to Columbia University, become an inventor, and marry Lulu, a character from another story who, we learn, carries herself with majesty befitting a warrior princess. This passage, packed with information, is typical, and yet the figure and conflict do not recur in the stories. The passage signals how pervasive trauma is and intimates the caprice with which we decide whose trauma matters. After all, this moment, with all of its import, is a footnote in the familial drama of a privileged scion of a music industry titan taking his family on an African adventure vacation. They are both doomed patriarchs, but it is Lou's story that matters most here. Egan makes this point about narrative inequities even as she acknowledges the lasting trauma happening in Lou's family that will culminate in the suicide of his beloved son.

Flashbacks and flash-forwards perforate any ability to say with certainty when a story happens. Egan explains, 'The tension is between the incremental and inexorable passage of time, and the leaping, shuttering quality of consciousness. The two do not match up. One result of that is that time is passing gradually, but we experience its effect as very sudden. Our perception of time is full of all of these gaps' (Michod 2010). In 'The Gold Cure', time is an obstacle – Bennie's sister duo are 'pushing thirty' (Egan 2011: 19) – and an unwelcome interloper. Bennie keeps getting 'caught in a loop' (21) remembering and recording embarrassing traumatic moments from his past, like trying to kiss a nun. The present forces him to stop getting caught up in the past. As he listens to the sisters in a basement studio built by their father, he falls in love with their sound, lamenting contemporary music production. He realises, surrounded by three generations of this family, that they are just bad. Time is a goon in several ways. He mistakes how long ago he discovered them – it has been five years, not two. And, his devotion to them becomes clear when we learn that he first heard them four days after September 11th. They embody the connection he longs for after the trauma of that day: they are organic, familial, unsullied. Even their studio resembles the warm, dark comfort of a womb.

September 11th ruptured time in the lives of the characters, and the book is, in many ways, a contemplation of that day and its aftermath. The simultaneity of loss and the spectacle of violence resemble the fractured temporality in so many other short story cycles: the vision and violence of earthly destruction in Bradbury's *The Martian Chronicles*, the tsunami that splinters Hema and Kaushik in Lahiri's cycle, the creation of simultaneous yet insuperably divided blood lines by American slavery in *Go Down, Moses*, and the loss of any belief in progress after World War I in *Winesburg* and *In Our Time*. In all of these cycles, some moment of systemic trauma stills, speeds up, and warps temporality. For *Goon Squad*, the attacks on September 11th loom in the cycle's chronology as somehow a lack and a presence – emblematised in the name assigned to the space: the Footprint. Bennie's brother-in-law captures the messed-up state of the world in the first story of the 'B side': '"I go away for a few years and the whole fucking world is upside down . . . Buildings are missing. You get strip-searched every time you go to someone's office. Everybody sounds stoned, because they're emailing people the whole time they're talking to you. Tom and Nicole are with different people"' (123). The changes wrought by 9/11 are many: there is the literal devastation of the cityscape, a constant reminder of what is lost and also an everyday sight; the increase in quotidian surveillance; the proliferation of handheld computers and the attendant alienation in social relations. At the same time, the collapse of a Hollywood power couple ironically signals that other 'tragedies' have occurred. The things he knew a few years ago are gone. Most unsettling to the narrator is that people just go on and change. Bennie's brother-in-law has summarised the changes of a few years in a few, crushing sentences. Time is brutal in its indifference and speed.

Desiring Provisionality

In *Goon Squad*, breaks in time mirror gaps in genealogy. The stories are replete with severed biological family connections. Sasha's dad left when she was six. Scotty's mom went away for 'the first time' (45) when he was in the fifth grade. Lou's family consists more of fission than fusion: 'Lou is one of those men whose restless charm has generated a contrail of personal upheaval that is practically visible behind him: two failed marriages and two more kids back home' (60). Egan's stories link the early loss of a family member to problems in adolescence and adulthood, often manifesting their long-term effects in theft, promiscuity, and death. It is not all bleak, though. Throughout the stories, the characters seek to restore or form new kinship ties through shared experience and desire. The stories dramatise how the characters desire acceptance into a group or a family. They are looking for stability, seeking others to grant them their provisional identity.

Music becomes one of the primary ways the characters generate formative kinship, which, as I delineate in Chapter 4, is ongoing, participatory, and chosen. Formative kinship can supplement biological ties but goes further than biology in cementing and creating positive, productive kinship. As The Flaming Dildos bounce from club to club, their shared love of music moulds them into a surrogate family. They care for each other, know each other's weaknesses and vulnerabilities, and provide solace and pain. All, excepting Alice, come from some measure of broken families, and the Dildos provides a space based on shared passion, genuine friendship, and an investment in moving forward together. It is no wonder then when it falls apart that both Bennie and Scotty cite its demise as a trauma that alters the rest of their lives.

Being a part of a band or fostering the growth of other musicians creates a pleasure in work, an antidote to the alienated, uncreative labour that threatens to swallow them all. Bennie, for instance, experiences euphoria because he is part of the musical process with the sisters: 'a sensation of pleasure filled his whole torso the way a snowfall fills up a sky. Jesus, he felt good. He'd been delegating too much. Hearing the music get *made*, that was the thing: people and instruments and beaten-looking equipment aligning abruptly into a single structure of sound, flexible and alive' (29). Bennie's pleasure derives from the generative and connecting experience of making sound, which juxtaposes the stifling and solitary work inside the office. Music provides a means to create formative kinship, even if it is partial or momentary. Sasha and Bennie have worked together over ten years at this moment, and being in the space of music inspires him to consider how much he both loves and 'feel[s] a swell of gratitude and appreciation'. He reflects that 'He rarely thought of Sasha as an independent person, and beyond a vague awareness of boyfriends coming and going (vague first out of respect for her privacy, lately out of indifference), he knew few specifics of her life' (27–8). Bennie and Sasha know each other intimately and not at all, which seems to be requisite for a good family: to love and appreciate another while also recognising just how partial our knowledge of another is. These moments of formative kinship ultimately prove transitory for the characters, because desire has a way of upsetting such moments of stability.

Desire is often the origin and undoing of family. Egan depicts the coeval presence of desire and loss in forming identity because of the characters' ongoing need to be recognised by another – an impulse ultimately behind Sasha's kleptomania, Bennie's quest for a cure to his impotence, and Scotty's search for the Bennie of his childhood. Judith Butler describes the ways in which desire and grief begin from this same impulse:

> Let's face it. We're undone by each other. And if we're not, we're missing something. If this seems so clearly the case with grief, it is only because it was already the case with desire. One does not always stay intact. It may be that one wants to, or does, but it may also be that despite one's best efforts, one is undone, in the face of the other, by the touch, by the scent, by the feel, by the prospect of the touch, by the memory of the feel. And so when we speak about my sexuality or my gender, as we do (and as we must), we mean something complicated by it. Neither of these is precisely a possession, but both are to be understood as modes of being dispossessed, ways of being for another, or, indeed, by virtue of another. (Butler 2004: 19)

All of the characters are seeking 'ways of being for another' – whether this is through music or through family connections. The abandonment by a parent early in life leaves an incessant need to be recognised by another, as is clear with Sasha and Scotty. Egan dramatises Butler's idea that we undo and depend upon each other, which is why trauma and desire are so often linked in the cycle.

Sasha and Bennie create a kind of family based in time, music, and the liminal space they occupy between domestic and professional spheres – all of which is persistently threatened by unwanted desire. At the end of the 'The Gold Cure', Bennie thinks, 'What he felt for Sasha was love, a safety and closeness like what he'd had with Stephanie [his ex-wife] before he'd let her down so many times that she couldn't stop being mad' (Egan 2011: 38). Sasha provides the comfort and intimacy of family, and he flirts with the idea of letting sexual desire spill out. Sasha deftly dismisses him, instead giving him 'a chaste kiss, a kiss between brother and sister, mother and son' (38). The conflation of wife, lover, friend, sister, and mother is an important one for Bennie, who has often asked women to be all of these things to him at once. Sasha cannot allow Bennie's desire because, as she reminds him, 'We need each other' (38). Desire would poison their tenuous but powerful kinship.

The Flaming Dildos – whose very name playfully yet sincerely conjures a potentially dangerous sexual drive – provides a kinship network without the labels and commitments that would trouble

Bennie's later relationships. In the vein of Egan's impulse to order the stories based on an expectation of surprise and satisfaction, the third story, 'Ask Me If I Care', following 'The Gold Cure', recounts the heyday of the Dildos from Rhea's first-person perspective. Rhea is one of three girls who follow the band. The story traces a web of adolescent desire: Rhea wants Bennie who desires Alice who longs for Scotty who pines for Jocelyn. The group's shared love of music generates kinship that they can maintain only so long as all of that desire remains suspended. The group falls apart, leaving all of them nostalgic and traumatised for a lost family, when desire gets acted upon by Jocelyn. Her affair with Lou triggers a chain reaction that splinters Bennie from Scotty, when Scotty turns to Alice for consolation. Bennie's desire for Alice has everything to do with her blond whiteness, family stability, and private-school background.

Bennie's lifelong pursuit of WASPy blondes results from his anxieties about his background. Egan describes having read 'an essay by Stanley Crouch, challenging literary writers to be less timid about crossing racial lines. I felt like he was speaking directly to me . . . So I let Bennie be racially ambiguous, which seemed in keeping with his wishes. Bennie wanted to create himself anew, as so many Americans do' (Maran 2010). Bennie measures the success of his self-refashioning by accumulating signs of his affluence, which he constructs as markedly different from his past. His anxieties of identity manifest themselves in his move to the affluent suburb of Crandale Country Club, his ongoing pursuit of the wealthiest and blondest woman around, and his worries about his and his son's hair. As a teenager, he fashions his hair into a Mohawk and 'smiles at [the cholos] but never answers' (Egan 2011: 42). Jocelyn consoles the pining Rhea with her observation that 'The good news is, rich girls won't go with cholos. So he'll never get Alice, period-the-end' (42). Being punk allows him to brand himself differently than others, including friends and family, would. He remains fascinated by validating his authenticity as he seeks to gain access to exclusive music scenes and women, but the question lingers: 'When does a fake Mohawk become a real Mohawk? Who decides? How do you know if it happened?' (46). Being able to switch ethnic signifiers is, to Bennie, the ultimate privilege. Alice, the first such girl who rejects him, sets Bennie on a course to chase women who embody that privilege for the rest of his life. He hopes that proximity to whiteness will lend him the cultural capital and sense of belonging he associates with it.

The story that opens the B-side of the cycle is called 'A to B' (also the title of an album by Bennie's first discovery); this transition piece shows the longstanding effects of Bennie's desire. The story's main action takes place in the thick of his marriage and is told from the third-person, limited point of view of Stephanie, his wife. Of the stories that largely feature Bennie already discussed, 'A to B' falls chronologically after 'Ask Me If I Care' (the third story), a few years before 'X's and O's' (the fifth story), and well before 'The Gold Cure' (the second story). Such disjunctions upset any clear causality and yet in 'A to B' Bennie chases the same legitimacy he craved as a teen: 'It was Bennie who had chosen Crandale, and in some deep way Stephanie understood why: they'd flown in private jets to islands owned by rock stars, but this country club was the farthest distance Bennie had traveled from the dark-eyed grandmother in Daly City. He'd sold his record label last year; how better to mark success than by going to a place where you didn't belong?' (113). Country club communities, such as Crandale, appear welcoming with their wide lawns and parties, but they thrive on exclusion – by class, by membership to the right groups, and by appearance. Bennie is a tragic hero as he chooses the very place where his success will be dismissed.

As Bennie seeks to validate himself through work and home, sexual desire remains the primary mode of gaining access that is more than provisional. Bennie feels watched at the pool, and at parties, he is asked, '"What kind of name is Salazar?"' (116). Although he has 'perfected an arsenal of charms to obliterate that scepticism, especially in women' (116), Bennie becomes unhinged when his crusty neighbours suspect, to his face, that he might be Al-Qaeda. He realises that all brownness is a threat to many of these people who, in the wake of September 11th, wrap all of their latent racism into amorphous fears about terrorism. His wife, Stephanie, too longs for access and so befriends Kathy, the epitome of Crandale society and the wife of the man who suspected Bennie of being a terrorist. The final, important action of the story, Bennie's desire for Kathy, happens off the page. And yet, Stephanie has known how this story would end: 'It took no imagination at all to see how everything had converged: pain; revenge; power; desire. He'd slept with Kathy. Of course' (134). Bennie's infidelity is confirmed in the seemingly innocuous golden bobby pin Stephanie finds; it is the one sign of whiteness Stephanie does not have. That bobby pin – with its associations to neatness, health, perfect coordination – is a metonym for Bennie's aspirations. His longing for the whitest woman around began long before Stephanie; could not be mollified by his wife, son, or work; and threatens to doom all of his relationships – romantic, familial, or friendly. He suffers from a gap; whether socially or self-inflicted, his stories reveal how he continually endeavours to fill it through sex.

In the multi-part story, 'Safari', the narrator attempts to offer a theory about the association between absence and longing. Told in the third person but often taking on the knowledge and perspective of Mindy, a graduate student in anthropology, the story defines the ways that loss and desire interconnect. Mindy acts as a kind of participant/observer; she is the younger lover of Lou and surrogate maternal figure to his two children. As a budding scholar, she sees theory in all she does. She identifies Lou's daughter as having '*Structural Resentment*'; consequently, she must do 'everything in her limited power to distract him from said girlfriend's presence, her own nascent sexuality being her chief weapon' (64). In contrast, the beloved son will show signs of '*Structural Affection* . . . because he hasn't learned to separate his father's loves and desires from his own' (65). Both children respond to the already partial absence of their father through desire. His daughter will dance provocatively and drink to excess. His son will later have sex with Jocelyn, his father's lover with whom he shares a birthday.

Mindy is not wrong in her assessment, but her theories do not capture the complexity between family, loss, and desire. The atomic structure of the cycle pokes holes in the grand narrative of Mindy's theorising. It is another metafictional moment when Egan seems to warn her readers not to expect or accept tidy readings and summations. In quiet moments, 'Mindy has even wondered if her insights on the link between social structure and emotional response could amount to more than a rehash of Lévi-Strauss – a contemporary application. She's only in her second year of coursework' (64). Her structures cannot adequately explain the son's later death, nor can they explain Lou's desire for ever-younger women. The theory can also not quite explain how this safari will be, despite its disappointments, 'a story they'll tell for the rest of their lives' (71) searching each other out on Facebook and Google. Their relationships are a mess, their moments of harmony are fleeting, and they harbour anger and longing. However, this safari is a formative moment for each of them, giving them a provisional family and identity by being recognised by another – which is implicit in the very act of watching on a safari. Such moments sustain the characters through the absence of a parent, the end of a relationship, or the death of a sibling.

PowerPoint and the Pleasure of Pauses

In 2008, Egan was captivated by news analysis that linked Obama's turnaround in the campaign for the presidency to a PowerPoint. She was curious how the brand had become generic and yet knew somehow in watching the coverage that it had – that everyone held a set of assumptions about what PowerPoint means and does. She began reading and writing in PowerPoint: 'I did read a lot of corporate PowerPoint presentations to get me into the mood, and I found them fascinating in the way everything becomes fascinating when it starts bending in the direction of fiction' (Cox 2010). She was particularly interested in the corporate aesthetics of this ubiquitous presentation program. But, she could not write a successful story in it. Her first attempts, done in a corporate-type voice with rectangle drawings, were stale and flat. She sold her book without the story, but she was fixated.

A solution came when she realised another problem. She wanted to write about Sasha, whose future was not yet forecast but whose past hung over the cycle. However, she did not want Sasha to be the focus. With two months for all of her revisions, she decided to return to PowerPoint to solve the Sasha problem. She also realised she could write about the desert – which she had wanted to do – through PowerPoint. Instead of writing in the voice of someone who would typically use PowerPoint, she recognised that she needed to write in a less conventional voice, and that story became the now-famous 'Great Rock and Roll Pauses'. As Egan notes, it is a very conventional story in which very little happens. In PowerPoint action is impossible so the form made the self-reflection and sweetness of the story possible. PowerPoint is a productive form for the story because it is atomised; discrete forms are separated from each other, which mirror the structural organisation of *Goon Squad*. The book is about time, music, and the pauses in each, and PowerPoint reflects those themes in its very form.[4]

'Great Rock and Roll Pauses' concerns Lincoln, a boy who cannot bridge the gap of communication, but it is told from the point of view of his sister, Alison. She often tries to communicate his feelings for him, but she often fails to communicate with her mother. In this, the story meditates on the problems of communication within an otherwise present, loving family. It is a counterpoint to 'Safari' in many ways. PowerPoint 'allowed', according to Egan, 'to do, in the boldest way, the thing I was trying to do already: to write incorporating gaps and interruptions, to try and elude the straightjacket of chronology that writers always struggle with' (Michod 2010). As Luscher suggests, the pleasure of reading short stories and cycles derives largely from the aesthetic pleasures of looseness that depend upon a reader's imagination (1989: 158). In PowerPoint, there is an ongoing tension between the particularity of a slide, an illuminated moment, and the development of an overarching narrative.

In this story, Egan employs and disrupts the conventions of linear fiction through PowerPoint. Alison Blake's PowerPoint assumes the voice and recordkeeping qualities of a journal, which is a typically chronological mode, although the past and future seep into the narrative revealing the porousness of temporality. Alison divides her narrative into four subchapters: 'After Lincoln's Game', 'In My Room', 'One Night Later', and 'The Desert'. In these titles and divisions, she emphasises time's passage, music, family, and place. Each chapter slide and the table of contents slide depict the titles inside arrows, lending the story a sense of progression. Egan's ideas about the gaps inherent to slideshows resonate with the idea that fragmentation requires that one must first perfect conventional form. She recognised that PowerPoint forces one to 'break down a particular thought, or fictional moment, into its most basic structure, and then illustrate that structure. I finally reached my true apotheosis as a PowerPointer when I began creating my own slide graphic out of shapes, rather than using templates' (Julavits 2010). Only 'in the middle of that piece [did she realise] that PowerPoint does offer an achronological option, for multiple chronologies' so that 'it epitomizes this really extreme way of the all the principles I'd been working on' (Julavits 2010). A PowerPoint can be progressive while also suspending a moment, gesturing forward and back, or creating a sideways temporality. Alison's story is an aesthetic rendering of the beauty and pain of continuity and disconnection.

Alison's slide 'Mom's Art' (Egan 2011: 265) emblematises the parallels between different modes of artistic production. Sasha, onetime midwife to rock and roll albums, now makes scrapbooks from her family's lives and sculptures from 'found objects' (the title of the first story and a callback to her kleptomania, of which her daughter remains unaware). Making and promoting records is not far distant from scrapbooking and the art of being a mother. Knowing when to record, restrain, or encourage are necessary for all three tasks. Sasha has found a way to record her life through and with the objects of others and herself. Even as her daughter mocks her, she articulates the art's founding principle: 'She says they're precious because they're casual and meaningless' and then in an overlapping hexagon, '"But they tell the whole story if you really look"' (265). She finds meaning in minutiae – a quality that connects her to both her children. Lincoln, who seems to be on the autism spectrum (although this – like Bennie's ethnicity – is only hinted at, never stated), is fascinated by and finds beauty in the pauses in songs. Alison attempts to communicate the beauty he sees in the gaps, while failing to recognise the continuities in front of her: her PowerPoint mirrors her mother's sculpture and scrapbooking. They find art in the mundane and particular. They are interested in process, intention, and effect. And, they all have this tremendous ability to ignore truths in front of them. Alison misses just what an art mothering is, even as she pays homage to Sasha in her derision. Alison's simultaneous blindness and perception mirror Sasha's when she was stealing – she cited it as giving her agency and individuality while it actually stripped her of power. Mother and daughter are strikingly similar, but there exists a gap between them. In this slide, Egan distils the cycle's treatment of creative expression: music, collage, and writing. All generate meaning from the spaces between sound and form much like the cycle.

The story is, at its core, rather conventional in its examination of growing up and the lack of communication and understanding in the most intimate of connections, family. Egan symbolically renders the overlapping but distinctive construction of this family by using a Venn diagram. In the centre, the biggest circle reads 'US'. Alison represents each member in separate, connected circles with a description of their relation to her. The separation of the circles disrupts the unity of this nuclear family. Alison relates and reacts to the distance within her family by mocking her mother, admiring her father, and attempting to communicate on Lincoln's behalf. Her sentimental longing for her often absent father manifests itself in anger at her too-present mother. For all her omnipresence, Sasha remains unknowable to Alison, which she realises only when looking at a picture of a younger version of Sasha. Alison describes each element of the photo, observing 'Mom's mouth is smiling, but her eyes are sad' and concluding 'She looks like someone I want to know, or maybe even be' (258). Alison is in the liminal space of adolescence and is already more like her mother than she knows – whose world-weary adolescence remains unknown to Alison. For instance, Sasha is a 'found object' by an uncle feeling distanced from his immediate family; in these parallels, the cycle builds recurrence without exactitude.

The twin traumas of growing up and loss connect Sasha and Alison in ways only the reader understands. The story narrates the processes by which Alison comes to terms with the complexity of her family and her own anxieties that she will grow up and leave them, realising 'Living here all together was so sweet' (299). Lincoln loves the pauses because they seem like the end of something, but then the song goes on, which offers consolation as they all worry about the future and past. In a slide titled, 'Mom's Reason for Not Talking about that Time', Alison replicates Sasha's oblique statements: 'I don't trust my memories'; 'It feels like another life'; 'It's all so imbued with my own struggles' (259). Each quote appears in a bubble inside a funnel. The grey space around the bubbles fills in what the clichés only allude to: that the early 1990s were a time when Sasha was trapped by her empty affairs and kleptomania. What we know is that these were responses to the trauma of her childhood and adolescence, which include being left by her father, three suicide attempts, and the death of beloved friend. It is this friend, Rob, whose death haunts and drives Alison's dad, Drew, to work incessantly as a doctor. He longs to save others as compensation for a life he could not save. Rob is a picture in Sasha's wallet; he looms over and in the family's relationships. Drew was there when Rob drowned – the full story of which we get in a second-person narrative from Rob in the tenth story 'Out of Body'. Drew believes that 'keeping secrets can kill you' (272) but rarely expresses the details or feelings of his loss, instead sublimating them into impossible rescue attempts with his patients. Rob's death is one of the most substantial gaps in the story; Alison can only narrate its aftermath. But, the memory of this gap recurs.

To understand the nature of connection and gaps, Lincoln and Alison turn to music and writing, which coalesce in the story, actualising a major theme in the cycle. Music and writing allow the characters to explore the power and problems of expression, which are ultimately tied to the pressures of time. Alison and Lincoln attempt to know their parents' pasts while their parents worry about the kids' futures. Drew especially struggles against the narrative of how his relationship with his son would be. Autism is a disorder of time and communication. Or, rather, it is a disorder that compels other people to reorient communication and time, requiring patience and multiple modes of exchange. Problems of expression that attend being on the spectrum concern the gap between what one wants to say and what is understood. By not naming Lincoln's condition, Egan plays with the faulty social expectation that one element of a person – whether it is an ethnicity, disorder, or trauma – is the only thing that constitutes identity.

Lincoln's passion for music connects him to Sasha. Music is its own language, and the two communicate their feelings about each other through the content of songs. When they talk about Bowie's motives or the effects of a pause, they are really communicating about how well they know and love each other. Drew lacks access to this language. He questions, 'Should we be encouraging this?' and 'How is this helping him to connect to other kids?' Sasha responds, 'It connects him to the world' (277). The unspoken anxiety is how Lincoln will negotiate the world when his parents are not there – a universal concern for any parent but one with special meaning for parents of children with autism.

Drew cannot see the connection between music and social ability. In a heartbreaking sequence, Drew attempts to push forward in direct ways, which Egan shows in graphics of scales and wheels, registering the mechanical mode of Drew's address. Drew erupts in yelling, and Lincoln falls into a weeping ball. Sasha intercedes and interprets: 'The pause makes you think the song will end. And then the song isn't really over, so you're relieved. But then the song does actually end, because every song ends, obviously, and **THAT. TIME. THE. END. IS. FOR. REAL**' (281). The capitalisation, bold face, and proliferation of end punctuation confirm that this is the explicit meaning. But, like all explanations, it is both a truth and not the whole truth. Not articulating the meaning of the pauses held more meaning for Lincoln. Stating its purpose so baldly partly misses the point. Represented in a large dialogue balloon, this moment crystallises just how much families depend on interpretation and silence for stability and coherence. The next slide is a large, empty dialogue balloon, titled 'A Pause While We Stand on the Deck' (282). Alison is an effective narrator because she is a mediator, knowing (mostly) when to speak and be silent. She comes to recognise that as difficult as being part of a family is, hers is much better than most alternatives. The cycle as a whole dramatises how silence and interpretation happen and the effects of when they do not.

PowerPoint allows Egan, through Alison's narration, to illustrate what cannot be expressed in language. For instance, the devastating silence within the fight is rendered in the empty dialogue balloon, which breaks and then restores the family's connection. Ironically, given her artistic sensibilities, Sasha cannot envision PowerPoint as writing. Annoyed that Alison is making slides in her journal, her mother pleads, 'Why not try *writing* for a change?' and later 'I mean writing a *paper*' (253). The use of italics implies a sense of what proper writing entails. Again, nostalgia creeps into moments where characters debate artistic authenticity. Like Bennie, Sasha does not contextualise her nostalgia in relation to her own promotion of musicians who may have been faulted for not playing *real* music. Sasha is especially troubled by the gaps: 'I see a lot of white. Where does the writing come in?' (253). Alison, however, knows the power white space and graphics can have. Just as her parents do, Alison repeats clichés that reveal truth and react to debates about the best mode of expression. She does so in a series of dialogue bubbles on the next page, saying things like 'Add a graphic and increase your traffic!' and 'Charts should illuminate, not complicate' (254). Alison mounts a defence of graphics – they generate more audience, they say things in ways words cannot – through playful slogans. Silences and pauses have generative power. White space is also writing. Short story cycles rely on narrative white space for meaning. The gaps between stories express what cannot be articulated: the repressed desires in *Winesburg*, the interracial intimacies and denial of them in *Go Down, Moses*, and the disappointed ambitions in *The Joy Luck Club*.

In *Goon Squad*, the creative possibilities of silence find expression in the desert, which is the title and setting of the last subchapter. The desert has the appearance of absence but actually contains a thriving ecosystem beautiful in its austerity and colour. Significantly, the desert is the space where Alison and Dad retreat after the fight, communicate, and find a way to build better relationships. As a subchapter, 'The Desert' is both autonomous and connected. The desert 'Starts Where Our Lawn Used to Be' (286), signifying its separation and proximity. It contains Sasha's sculptures and snakes, reflecting the comfort and threat within and beyond the family's home. Alison notes in concentric circles that 'The whole desert is a pause' and that 'The desert is quiet and busy' (287). In drawing parallels to Lincoln's world, she makes the pauses meaningful to her father, pointing out that they do work – they provide contrast to all of the noise. Death and loss permeate the landscape and conversation, but from the traumas something new is born. In the once-lush landscape, new animals come to live. New energies provide power. Drew finds new ways to connect. He can narrate a new relationship with his son.

The silence and the emptiness of PowerPoint's graphics illustrate the story's (and cycle's) climactic moment. Drew draws Lincoln out of bed to listen to the desert's silence, represented by a black, empty page outlined as a dialogue box. The blackness mirrors the night and the clandestine communication of father and son (302). The section culminates in the repetition of the Venn diagram from the opening.

Here, however, there is no title. The circles are emptied of content and interchangeable. The family has found a way to come together, rendered in the absence of text. The story shifts then to presenting, without commentary, the graphics Lincoln had wanted to create. In four graphs, Alison illustrates the 'Haunting Power', 'Necessity', 'Timing', and 'Persistence' of pauses – qualities which Lincoln possesses and the family needs (305–8). It is a deeply optimistic ending. It implies that each family member contributes to realising Lincoln's vision and making something tangible. Alison's mediation, Mom's musical knowledge, Dad's technological expertise, and Lincoln's multiple ways of seeing create lovely, complex objects. The short story, in its compression, makes meaning from what goes unspoken. The PowerPoint concludes with a conventional 'The End' but this too is just a pause as the cycle continues.

Writing a Cyclical Future

As Egan discovered in using PowerPoint, the future need not be a terrifying prospect. The final story articulates anxieties about the future of music, communication, family, and space, and it ties together a few but not all of the loose threads as it includes or alludes to Bennie, Scotty, Sasha, Scotty, Lulu, and Alex. When asked about what connects the stories, Egan replied, 'it was the combination of the first and last stories that really anchored it for me: a young woman steals a wallet while on a first date with a guy she met online, and 15-or-so years later, that guy, now a husband and father tries to remember that same date from his early years in New York. Those bookends always filled me with hope' (Lee 2011). The final story, 'Pure Language', takes place in the early 2020s and is told from Alex's point of view; he is the minor character who Sasha sleeps with in 'Found Objects'. As Egan explains, he becomes the main character and the centre of his own familial and temporal drama in the final story. He connects with Lulu, the self-possessed daughter of another story's narrator, to generate buzz for a kids' concert, put on by Bennie and Scotty, to take place where the Twin Towers fell. The space, known as the Footprint, evokes the empty fullness of the desert in the previous story. The final story offers an argument about all the nostalgia and anxieties about authenticity: work with what you got. Performing for kids in the aftermath of a loss that is personal and collective is not perfect, but it is also not desolate. Bennie and Scotty are, after all, making music together again. Egan's final story confirms the optimistic tone of 'Great Rock and Roll Pauses', but it also delineates the collapse of a world and story as we had known it. After all, in the end Bennie and Alex go looking for Sasha in her old apartment, trying to reconnect with some lost presence of their past and feeling euphoric about finding not just her but their past selves, their youth. As he comes down from the 'careening hope', Alex hears 'the hum, always that hum, which maybe wasn't an echo after all, but the sound of time passing' (340). The story concludes by cycling back to the image of time as humming at the end of the first story.

Problems of language fuel the cycle's final moments, indicated by the story's title, 'Pure Language'. Lulu, with her typical indifferent and accurate insight, observes that language is exhausting and exhausted: 'All we've got are metaphors, and they're never exactly right. You can't ever just *Say. The. Thing*' (321). With its end stops and capitalisation, this moment echoes the earlier one from Sasha about the power of pauses. Here, Lulu expresses frustration about the emptiness of language and its trouble at getting at reality. For Lulu, the vexed nature of language, the need for speed, and the creation of handheld communication culminate in a revolution in language and expression about which many feel ambivalent or very negative. Alex, for instance, attempts to limit his child's exposure to this new language but also feels that it might best express his sentiments about using this technology to his sceptical wife, '*Nu job in th wrks – big $ pos. pls kEp opn mind*' (325). Lulu's generation increasingly speaks in this new text language, which condenses, omits obscenities, and vents. Of course, it reflects the growing use of text messaging in contemporary culture, and the laments its often vapid content inspires.

What I find most striking is how modernist Lulu and the story are. In tackling the insufficiency of language in response to forces of increasing urbanisation and technology, Lulu sounds like Picasso or Pound as she explains why old metaphors do not work any more: '"No one says 'viral' anymore . . . I mean, maybe thoughtlessly, the way we still say 'connect' or 'transmit' – those old mechanical metaphors that have nothing to do with how information travels. See, reach isn't describable in terms of cause and effect anymore: it's simultaneous"' (317). Lulu thinks she is making language new, and she is, but she is also repeating a response to modernity that dates back over a century. As Benedict Anderson ([1983] 1991) famously argues, fiction and print media reflect that experience is happening and being communicated simultaneously. Like Bennie at the beginning, Lulu thinks of her moment and insight as unique, but it continues a long pattern of thinking about technological change. What has changed is the degree to which simultaneity is happening. Alex's wife, Rebecca, resembles an academic studying modernism: 'Her new book was on the phenomenon of word casings, a term she'd invented for words that no longer had meaning outside quotation marks. English was full of these empty words – "friend" and "real" and "story" and "change" – words that had been shucked of their meaning and reduced to husks. Some, like "identity," "search," and "cloud," had clearly been drained of life by their web usage' (323–4). Her research has an eerie similarity to Paul Fussell's *The Great War and Modern Memory*, which includes a chart of words that no longer have the same meaning after World War I – words like comrade become friend; valour becomes bravery after the fact (2013: 22–3).

That the concert is to be set in the Footprint connects this new mode of expression to trauma and meaningful absence, which is a classic move of high modernism. Egan invests the city with the uncanny alienation found in Pound, the scarred landscapes of Hemingway, and the playful, meaning-laced language of Stein. In this final story, Egan suggests that modernist thought and expression presents a viable mode for reacting to the forces and trauma transforming contemporary America. Egan's treatment of trauma and language ultimately gets filtered through very personal themes. The final stories come back to family dramas and issues of desire. 'Pure Language' and 'Great Rock and Roll Pauses' also come back to the meaning of place – the Footprint and the desert are awe-inducing, nostalgia-infused, but they are also signifiers that critique. The desert was once a golf course; the Footprint, now a music venue, is a sign of a corporate culture that eradicates sophisticated music. However, their paradoxical significations do not mean that these spaces are without happiness and meaning. Rather, this future (or present, depending on how one looks at it) is not dystopic but achingly familiar. The atomic form of the cycle creates a twenty-first-century modernism in Egan's *A Visit from the Goon Squad*.

In April 2011, HBO optioned the book for a possible television show. HBO also recently optioned the rights to Faulkner's oeuvre and has already produced a five-hour adaptation of Ford Madox Ford's tetralogy *Parade's End* (1924–8). Modernism is having a resurgence on the small screen that is, I think, part of a general flowering of really great writing on television (the most common comparison for the long-form narratives of television remains the nineteenth-century novel – which is another connection to Egan's cycle). Inspired as she was by

The Sopranos, Egan admits that she 'did consciously ask the question of whether there would be a way to write a novel that would have the same lateral feeling of a television series – the same kind of sense of movement in all directions, but not necessarily forward' (Itzkoff 2011). The cycle lends itself to television and has had an impact on the way television often tells stories in episodic yet long narrative forms. Although the move from book to the small screen has now reportedly 'fizzled' (Alter 2013), *Goon Squad* has great potential as a television adaptation, because of the gaps and pauses between the stories. Those gaps leave space to tell new stories that expand out indefinitely from the original text. The connection between television and print fiction resembles the expanding worlds of Faulkner, Erdrich, Díaz, and Alvarez, suggesting once again the generative power of the form.

Notes

1. Another short story cycle, Elizabeth Strout's *Olive Kitteridge*, was recently adapted for HBO in 2014. The series, which won eight Emmy awards, drew renowned actors and was structured as a four-part interconnected miniseries.
2. This paragraph is paraphrased from Egan's lecture, 'Experimentation in Fiction: Notes from a Reluctant Practitioner' (2012).
3. The following stories, either in part or whole, appeared prior to *Goon Squad*: 'The Gold Cure' in *Granta*; 'Forty-Minute Lunch: Kitty Jackson Opens Up About Love, Fame, and Nixon' as 'Forty-Minute Lunch' in *Harper's*; 'Ask Me If I Care', 'Found Objects', and 'Safari' in *The New Yorker*; 'Out of Body' and 'You (Plural)' in *Tin House*; and 'Selling the General' in *This Is Not Chick Lit*. Talking with Julavits (2010), Egan mentions that 'four of them were written years and years ago': 'You (Plural)', 'Good-bye, My Love', 'Forty-Minute Lunch', and 'X's and O's'.
4. Paraphrased from 'Experimentation in Fiction: Notes from a Reluctant Practitioner' (Egan 2012).

Coda

Novellas-in-Flash and Flash Cycles

In an interview to publicise *A Visit from the Goon Squad*, Jennifer Egan confessed to being a nut for literary criticism in her college years, explaining that 'literary theory satisfied a deep love that I have for big, encompassing narratives about the world and how it works – which are usually, in the end, more creative visions unto themselves than illuminating explanations' (Cox 2010). This coda is a creative vision for a new direction in the genre: the cycle told in flash fiction. With flash fiction on the rise since at least the 1980s, many contemporary writers turn to flash to tell connected yet diffuse stories centred on a character, theme, or setting, akin to the long tradition of the short story cycle. Like all big, encompassing narratives, this coda is just a sampling, because genre often eludes our ability to be fully inclusive. When scholars attempt to define and describe an ostensibly new or unfamiliar genre, as has been the case with the short story cycle and now the flash cycle, pressure to limit or narrow how that genre works persists.

Popular and critical reception, from Amazon reviews to published monographs, reflect this pressure to name exactly what is and what is not a flash cycle, which explains why names for the genre have proliferated to account for the many variations on it, including the flash fiction novel, the novella-in-shorts, the flash novella, the vignette novel, and novella-in-flash (Beckel and Rooney 2014: vii). Rose Metal Press, whose mission is to publish hybrid words, released an anthology of five novellas-in-flash in 2014. The collection, titled *My Very End of the Universe*, includes novellas-in-flash ranging from 5,000 to 12,000 words. Like longer form short story cycles, the five novellas-in-flash that make up *My Very End of the Universe* are 'composed entirely of standalone flash fiction pieces organized into a full narrative arc' (Beckel and Rooney 2014: vii). Like cycles 'many gaps and separations and new-yet-continuing stories force the reader to play closer attention – to not get lulled – while also creating a whole fictional reality' (Beckel and Rooney 2014: xiii). The editors, Abigail Beckel and Kathleen Rooney, write in their introduction that they prefer the term novella-in-flash because the volumes retain three characteristics common to the novella: (1) 'extended conflict and character development'; (2) 'accumulation and accretion to create a single, unified effect'; and (3) 'conclusions that often hover on the edge of major change' (2014: xii). Their insistence on unity sounds like early attempts to defend the story cycle as a genre under the influence of New Criticism; however, the flash cycles themselves often belie such unity as their comments on the gaps and lack of narrative resolution indicate. Like the story cycle, the novella-in-flash enjoys a longer history than is generally acknowledged. Beckel and Rooney cite Evan S. Connell's *Mrs. Bridge* (1959) and its sequel *Mr. Bridge* (1969), Joan Didion's *Play It as It Lays* (1970), and Mary Robison's *Why Did I Ever* (2001), who originally wrote her book on hundreds of notecards (Pokrass 2014a: 52), as influences on the current explosion in the genre.

The authors within the collection each contributed a preface to their pieces, reflecting on how and why they chose this form. For Tiff Holland, author of *Betty Superman* (2011, 2014a), the collection's first novella-in-flash, the big nature of her protagonist meant that she needed shorter, more manageable doses to capture her personality. Holland concludes her preface with the observation: 'every subject makes its own form. I just try to pay attention' (2014b: 9). Other authors of flash cycles echo this sentiment. Meg Pokrass, author of *Here, Where We Live* (2014, 2014b), compares the form to quilt-making in that an artist places meaningful scraps from the past alongside a recently acquired piece to create a new whole, the effect of which depends on the connections between the pieces. Her metaphor recalls a more traditional short story cycle: *How to Make an American Quilt* (1991) by Whitney Otto. Pokrass observes that the novella-in-flash reflects how memory and experience work: 'We humans frequently have very little perspective on our own stories as we are living them. The novella-in-flash, divided into tiny bits of action, mirrors life this way. I do not believe that life as it is being lived has a "narrative arc" – and, if it does, it does not become clear until a person is gone' (2014a: 51). The fragmented nature of human consciousness evinces the imprint of modernism on contemporary fiction. The problem of articulating subjectivity in narrative form persists into the novella-in-flash, which, according to Aaron Teel, author of *Shampoo Horns* (2012, 2014b), best mirrors how we make meaning from memories: 'When a succession of moments has receded far enough away, the memories that remain are mixed up and weird, disconnected, out of time – they come to me in flashes' (2014a: 101). Such claims as these authors make reveal an affinity between subjects and forms that embrace hybridity and multiplicity.

In this anthology, and in the genre as a whole, issues of family, domesticity, and community recur; the heightened brevity yet layered stories mirror how kinship arises from the telling of familiar stories. Such oft-told stories, which mix truth and fiction, comprise family life, distilling each member to a set of anecdotes and observations that illuminate the complex inner workings of each person. For instance, Jenny Offill's 2014 *Dept. of Speculation* traces the origins and history of a romantic relationship from dating to motherhood to marital strife. In her *New York Times* review, Roxane Gay writes that in Offill's

> shimmering fragments of prose . . . Seemingly significant information is doled out in inscrutable doses. Each fragment is satisfying or not, and exists unto itself but also, clearly, as part of something bigger. 'Dept. of Speculation' moves quickly, but it is also joyously demanding because you will want to keep trying to understand the *why* of each fragment and how it fits with the others. (Gay 2014)

Offill's treatment of new motherhood is an honest, compassionate rendition of those inexplicable months. The writerly narrator confesses of her new child, 'The days with the baby felt long but there was nothing expansive about them. Caring for her required me to repeat a series of tasks that had the peculiar quality of seeming both urgent and tedious. They cut the day into little scraps' (Offill 2014: 25–6). This is one of the flash pieces that make up Offill's book, and, as the passage indicates, the prose too has a sense of urgency and tedium befitting the themes of parenting and marriage.

Gay, an advocate for the form in the tradition of Mencken and Cowley with whom I began this book, wrote the introduction to Matthew Salesses's flash cycle *I'm Not Saying, I'm Just Saying* (2013) about a man who discovers he has a five-year-old son and questions whether fidelity to partner and stability to son are things he wants or even can do. Gay frames the reading of these pieces in terms of their connection to flash fiction, which she identifies by its 'compression – using few words to tell a story that is not constrained, in scope, by brevity' (2011: 11). Of the 115 'explosive fragments' that constitute the cycle, Gay writes that they must be considered 'both as a sum and all parts' (2011: 12). In both books, a single narrative voice connects flash fictions that chart the narrator's experiences with quotidian and traumatic events in the context of romantic love and family. This trend has also been popular among nonfiction writers who construct memoirs in flash: *The Argonauts* (2015) by Maggie Nelson, *Revolution: The Year I Fell in Love and Went to Join the War* (2011) by Deb Olin Unferth, and *The Two Kinds of Decay* (2008) by Sarah Manguso, among others, signalling yet another revision to strict generic distinctions.

The interweaving of the quotidian and traumatic are of paramount importance to two other flash cycles: *Lotería* (2013) by Mario Alberto Zambrano and *We the Animals* (2011) by Justin Torres. Both Zambrano and Torres are graduates of the Iowa Writers' Workshop, and both use the cycle in flash to narrate coming-of-age stories of second-generation immigrants in the United States. Sandra Cisneros's classic *The House on Mango Street* (1984) provides a blueprint for these volumes: semi-autobiographical portraits of young people who realise that their ethnicity, families, and individualism create an uneasy clashing of forces internally and externally. Like Cisneros's cycle, these volumes depict that ongoing process in staccato-esque pieces that range from paragraphs to pages, experimenting with voice and content along the way. The flash form lends itself to the kind of provisional identity-making that reflects processes of maturation and migration for an exceptional child inside and outside their homes, communities, and nations.

Zambrano's volume takes as its structural motif the Mexican card game Lotería. The preface, called 'Rules of the Game', describes Lotería as 'Mexican bingo' but this game of chance is rendered not in numbers but images. A sung riddle – sometimes a conventional one; sometimes one made up by the dealer – accompanies each image, and players mark their cards. These images accompany each of the short pieces that make up the volume. The narrator, Luz María Castillo, flips over the cards and narrates, in non-linear fashion, the events and memories that led her to be in custody of the state. The image preceding each story often appears as a figure or motif in the fragmented narrative it accompanies, but it does not always do so. Luz takes comfort in the cards, and the seemingly random yet meaningful flipping of them not only draws her back to happy family memories but always gives her an analogy for finding order in seeming chaos. The stories resemble a journal addressed to God as she awaits her case worker and her fate. 'La Araña', the spider, is the opening card and narrative fragment, casting a malevolent, mysterious tone over the opening story:

> This room has spiders.
> ¿Y? It's not like You don't see them. The way they move their legs and carry their backs and creep in the dark when you're not looking. (Zambrano 2013: 1)

The notion that dangerous, unwelcome forces occupy the same space as us is a harbinger of the trauma at the centre of the flash cycle. From the opening story, eleven-year-old Luz warns us 'It's not like I'm a piece of news in the Chronicle [you] can pick up and read. It's not like that. If anything, it's a *telenovela* with a *ranchera* in the background playing so loud you can't even hear your thoughts anymore' (Zambrano 2013: 5). The stories proceed then to narrate the daily life of her childhood – family parties, television evenings, sister squabbles, and parental fights that turn into all-out war.

The fragmented structure replicates the fissures of childhood memories of trauma, and the journal form allows Zambrano to trace how Luz eventually gets back to the night that sent her to the state institution and her dad to jail. In the story called 'La Estrella', the star, Luz recounts how the police, on a tip from her sister, also named Estrella, came to arrest their father for the suspected murder of their mother. Luz, in disbelief and out of a sense of loyalty to their father, fired the family's gun and shot her sister – perhaps accidentally, perhaps not. The story concludes that all she can remember after seeing her sister's body are the stars. Singular, yet connected, the stars are another motif for the flash cycle. *Lotería* is a beautiful book – as a physical object – with thick, rough-cut pages and gorgeous colour images of the cards. *Lotería* is more novelistic than many other flash cycles in that the narrative action reads like a mystery culminating in a climactic evening, whereas many of these books avoid such narrative arcs in favour of parallel storylines.

Torres's volume also employs an adolescent narrator of a second-generation immigrant American family, but this time the narrator begins as first-personal plural, as the title, *We the Animals*, intimates. Over the course of the flash pieces, the narrative voice narrows onto the youngest brother – gay, artistic, defiant, questioning – who is both a part of and apart from his two older brothers. His sexuality and writing exclude him from fraternity even as the brothers remain protective of him to the end. The flash cycle experiments with collective and singular narrators to reflect the kinds of community that embrace and marginalise a person simultaneously. *We the Animals* narrates the story of three brothers who have a Puerto Rican father and a white mother. Their parents were very young when the children were born, and their earliest formative experiences, told in the plural narrative voice, have to do with the children's insatiable desire in an often economically and emotionally unstable home:

> We wanted more. We knocked the butt ends of our forks against the table, tapped our spoons against our empty bowls; we were hungry. We wanted more volume, more riots. We turned up the knob on the tv until our ears ached with the shouts of angry men. We wanted more music on the radio; we wanted beats; we wanted rock. We wanted muscles on our skinny arms. We had bird bones, hollow and light, and we wanted more density, more weight. We were six snatching hands; six stomping feet; we were brothers, boys, three little kings locked in a feud for more. (Torres 2011: 1)

This is how Torres opens the book in a three-page vignette called 'We Wanted More'. Announcing the frantic energy that characterises the narrators, the boys as characters, and the flash pieces themselves, Torres begins with fervour and ends with fire. Along the way, he shows the slow burn of adolescence as the parents separate and reconcile, as the boys compete for blankets and love, and as the central narrator comes into his own as an individual separate from yet linked to his brothers. In this, the form mirrors the family dynamic it explores, asking how one person can make an individual identity from the fragments and debris of family life.

The youngest brother knows that his sexuality and artistry unite and distance him from his brothers, that his mixed ancestry unites and keeps him distanced from Puerto Ricans, and that his diverging ambitions distance him from all of the boys he grew up with:

> They felt proud to be the kind of boys they were – boys who spat in public, boys who kept their gaze on the floor or fixed on a space above your head...
>
> They were not scared, or disappointed, or fragile. They were possible. Soon they'd be sailing right over them ditches. Soon they'd be handling that cash. They'd decide. They'd forge themselves consequential. They'd sing the mixed breed.
>
> And me now. Look at me. See me there with them, in the snow – both inside and outside their understanding. See how I made them uneasy. They smelled my difference – my sharp, sad, pansy scent. They believed I knew a world larger than their own. They hated

me for my good grades, for my white ways. All at once they were disgusted, and jealous, and deeply protective, and deeply proud. (Torres 2011: 104–5)

In this passage, the third-person plural renders the brothers separate. No longer 'we'; now 'they'. They are together, united by their defiance, heterosexuality, bombast, and ambitions different than their youngest brother. His academic gifts and his same-sex desire alienate him from his brothers and yet time, kinship, and love make them proud and protective of him. Four stories from the end and the fissures that ensue, this flash piece offers a respite and a moment of formative kinship and provisional identity. In so doing, it aligns with the sense that novellas-in-flash hover on the edge of a major change but do not follow that change through to a happy or sad ending. Instead, we remain suspended.

Writers use flash to transform conventional novelistic practices such as teleology and character development as well as conventional characteristics of the short story such as character revelation and nuanced setting. Flash cycles illuminate how genre itself is an ever-changing force that, according to Tzvetan Todorov, inverts, displaces, and combines elements of established forms to create new ones (1990: 15). The onus is put on readers to make meaning, fill in the gaps, and anticipate the major changes that may or may not happen if another story were to be written. As the genre expands, readers will have flexibility to construct their own reading practices. A reader can sample, savour every morsel, or binge and devour these books at once. The flash cycle or novella-in-flash – by whatever name we call it – acknowledges that experience and truth are never singular or easily legible but are always multiple and always morphing.

And yet, as I read these contemporary flash pieces, I am reminded of the nineteenth-century sketchbooks from which the modernist story cycles emerged. It would seem that everything old is new again. Indeed, the very issues of ethnicity, region, and domesticity that animate nineteenth-century volumes from Sui Sin Far, Sarah Orne Jewett, and the rest are highly akin to these flash fiction pieces. Even the turn to shorter story forms hearkens back to these earliest volumes. What we might perceive as an epochal shift toward flash fiction is just an extension of the ancient story cycle tradition. From the mid-nineteenth century, authors have sought a form that addresses the provisionality that saturates modern life – from national formations, to ethnic belonging, to familial structures, to our very notion of what it means to belong to a place or time. The sense of vertigo ushered in by the cultural upheavals wrought by industrialisation, urbanisation, and travel find a corollary in the broken-yet-connected form of the cycle. In its resistance to singularity and conclusion, the cycle offers a mode that parallels the contingency writers find in modern life.

Selected American Short Story Cycles

I am grateful to Susan Garland Mann and Maggie Dunn and Ann Morris, who have previously assembled bibliographies in the genre.

Irving, Washington. *The Sketch Book of Geoffrey Crayon, Gent.* 1820.
Longstreet, Augustus Baldwin. *Georgia Scenes.* 1835.
Lee, Eliza Buckminster. *Sketches of a New England Village, in the Last Century.* 1838.
Hawthorne, Nathaniel. *The Legends of the Province-House.* 1838–9.
Kirkland, Caroline Matilda. *A New Home – Who'll Follow? Or Glimpses of Western Life.* 1839.
Hawthorne, Nathaniel. *Mosses from an Old Manse.* 1846.
Melville, Herman. *The Piazza Tales.* 1856.
Jewett, Sarah Orne. *Deephaven.* 1877.
Cable, George Washington. *Old Creole Days.* 1879.
Garland, Hamlin. *Main-Travelled Roads.* 1891.
Chopin, Kate. *Bayou Folk.* 1894.
Jewett, Sarah Orne. *The Country of the Pointed Firs.* 1896.
Freeman, Mary E. Wilkins. *The People of Our Neighborhood.* 1898.
Chesnutt, Charles W. *The Conjure Woman.* 1899.
Crane, Stephen. *Whilomville Stories.* 1899.
Austin, Mary. *The Land of Little Rain.* 1903.
Gale, Zona. *Friendship Village.* 1908.
Stein, Gertrude. *Three Lives.* 1909.
James, Henry. *The Finer Grain.* 1910.
Far, Sui Sin. *Mrs. Spring Fragrance.* 1912.
Anderson, Sherwood. *Winesburg, Ohio.* 1919.
Frank, Waldo. *City Block.* 1922.
Toomer, Jean. *Cane.* 1923.
Hemingway, Ernest. *In Our Time.* 1925.
Barnes, Djuna. *Ladies Almanack.* 1928.
Steinbeck, John. *The Pastures of Heaven.* 1932.
—. *The Red Pony.* 1933.
Hughes, Langston. *The Ways of White Folks.* 1934.
Steinbeck, John. *Tortilla Flat.* 1935.

Selected American Short Story Cycles

Saroyan, William. *My Name Is Aram*. 1937.
Wright, Richard. *Uncle Tom's Children*. 1938.
Faulkner, William. *The Unvanquished*. 1938.
—. *The Wild Palms*. 1939.
—. *The Hamlet*. 1940.
—. *Go Down, Moses*. 1942.
Caldwell, Erskine. *Georgia Boy*. 1943.
Welty, Eudora. *The Wide Net and Other Stories*. 1943.
Steinbeck, John. *Cannery Row*. 1945.
Faulkner, William. *Knight's Gambit*. 1949.
Mori, Toshio. *Yokohama, California*. 1949.
Welty, Eudora. *The Golden Apples*. 1949.
Asimov, Isaac. *I, Robot*. 1950.
Bradbury, Ray. *The Martian Chronicles*. 1950.
Salinger's *Nine Stories*, J.D. 1953.
O'Connor, Flannery. *A Good Man Is Hard to Find*. 1955.
Bradbury, Ray. *Dandelion Wine*. 1957.
Cheever, John. *The Housebreaker of Shady Hill and Other Stories*. 1959.
Connell, Evan S. *Mrs. Bridge*. 1959.
Updike, John. *The Olinger Stories*. 1964.
Baldwin, James. *Going to Meet the Man*. 1965.
O'Connor, Flannery. *Everything That Rises Must Converge*. 1965.
Barth, John. *Lost in the Funhouse: Fiction for Print, Tape, Live Voice*. 1968.
Gaines, Ernest. J. *Bloodline*. 1968.
Connell, Evan S. *Mr. Bridge*. 1969.
Coover, Robert. *Pricksongs and Descants*. 1969.
Malamud, Bernard. *Pictures of Fidelman: An Exhibition*. 1969.
Momaday, N. Scott. *The Way to Rainy Mountain*. 1969.
Didion, Joan. *Play It as It Lays*. 1970.
Updike, John. *Bech: A Book*. 1970.
Barth, John. *Chimera*. 1972.
Adler, Renata. *Speedboat*. 1974.
Kingston, Maxine Hong. *The Woman Warrior: Memoirs of a Girlhood among Ghosts*. 1975.
Oates, Joyce Carol. *Crossing the Border: Fifteen Tales*. 1976.
Eisner, Will. *A Contract with God and Other Tenement Stories*. 1978.
Major, Clarence. *Emergency Exit*. 1979.
Updike, John. *Too Far to Go: The Maples Stories*. 1979.
Banks, Russell. *Trailerpark*. 1981.
Carver, Raymond. *Cathedral*. 1983.
Naylor, Gloria. *The Women of Brewster Place*. 1982.
Cisneros, Sandra. *The House on Mango Street*. 1984.
Doctorow, E. L. *Lives of the Poets: Six Stories and a Novella*. 1984.
Erdrich, Louise. *Love Medicine*. 1984.
Kincaid, Jamaica. *Annie John*. 1985.

Banks, Russell. *Success Stories*. 1986.
Chavez, Denise. *The Last of the Menu Girls*. 1986.
Dybeck, Stuart. *Coast of Chicago*. 1986.
Minot, Susan. *Monkeys*. 1986.
Oates, Joyce Carol. *Marya: A Life*. 1986.
Suleri, Sara. *Meatless Days*. 1989.
Tan, Amy. *The Joy Luck Club*. 1989.
Kincaid, Jamaica. *Lucy*. 1990.
O'Brien, Tim. *The Things They Carried*. 1990.
Alvarez, Julia. *How the García Girls Lost Their Accents*. 1991.
Cisneros, Sandra. *Woman Hollering Creek and Other Stories*. 1991.
Jen, Gish. *Typical American*. 1991.
Otto, Whitney. *How to Make an American Quilt*. 1991.
Butler, Robert Olen. *A Good Scent from a Strange Mountain*. 1992.
García, Christina. *Dreaming in Cuban*. 1992.
Houston, Pam. *Cowboys Are My Weakness*. 1992.
Johnson, Denis. *Jesus' Son*. 1992.
Jones, Edward P. *Lost in the City*. 1992.
Watanabe, Sylvia. *Talking to the Dead*. 1992.
Alexie, Sherman. *The Lone Ranger and Tonto Fistfight in Heaven*. 1993.
Hendrie, Laura. *Stygo*. 1994.
Hongo, Garett. *Volcano: A Memoir of Hawai'i*. 1995.
Nunez, Sigrid. *A Feather on the Breath of God*. 1995.
Bacho, Peter. *Dark Blue Suit and Other Stories*. 1996.
Butler, Robert Olen. *Tabloid Dreams*. 1996.
Díaz, Junot. *Drown*. 1996.
Pietrzyk, Leslie. *Pears on a Willow Tree*. 1996.
Watson, Brad. *The Last Days of the Dog-Men*. 1996.
Yamanaka, Lois-Ann. *Wild Meat and the Bully Burgers*. 1996.
Estep, Maggie. *Soft Maniacs: Stories*. 1999.
King, Stephen. *Hearts in Atlantis*. 1999.
Phillips, Dale Ray. *My People's Waltz*. 1999.
Proulx, Annie. *Close Range: Wyoming Stories*. 1999.
Vreeland, Susan. *Girl in Hyacinth Blue*. 1999.
Bloom, Amy. *A Blind Man Can See How Much I Love You*. 2000.
Cronin, Justin. *Mary and O'Neil*. 2001.
Robison, Mary. *Why Did I Ever*. 2001.
Parker, Amy. *Beasts & Children: Stories*. 2002.
Boswell, Marshall. *Trouble with Girls*. 2003.
Braver, Adam. *Mr. Lincoln's Wars: A Novel in Thirteen Stories*. 2003.
Dybeck, Stuart. *I Sailed with Magellan*. 2003.
Gwyn, Aaron. *Dog on the Cross: Stories*. 2003.
Kusel, Lisa. *Other Fish in the Sea*. 2003.
Cook, K. L. *Last Call*. 2004.
Day, Cathy. *The Circus in Winter*. 2004.

Jaime-Becerra, Michael. *Every Night Is Ladies' Night: Stories*. 2004.
Bakopoulos, Dean. *Please Don't Come Back from the Moon*. 2005.
Forbes, Charlotte. *The Good Works of Ayela Linde: A Novel in Stories*. 2006.
Mason, Bobbie Ann. *Nancy Culpepper: Stories*. 2006.
Barry, Rebecca. *Later, at the Bar: A Novel in Stories*. 2007.
Litman, Ellen. *The Last Chicken in America: A Novel in Stories*. 2007.
Lahiri, Jhumpa. *Unaccustomed Earth*. 2008.
Pollock, Donald Ray. *Knockemstiff*. 2008.
Strout, Elizabeth. *Olive Kitteridge*. 2008.
Sanow, Anne. *Triple Time*. 2009.
Cardinale, Joseph. *The Size of the Universe*. 2010.
Casey, Patrick Thomas. *Our Burden's Light*. 2010.
Chuculate, Eddie. *Cheyenne Madonna*. 2010.
Egan, Jennifer. *A Visit from the Goon Squad*. 2010.
Hitt, James. *Carny: A Novel in Stories*. 2010.
Moyer, Kermit. *The Chester Chronicles*. 2010.
Walsh, M. O. *The Prospect of Magic*. 2010.
Duke, Beth. *Delaney's People: A Novel in Small Stories*. 2011.
Fink, Jennifer Natalya. *Thirteen Fugues*. 2011.
Hoffman, Alice. *The Red Garden*. 2011.
Torres, Justin. *We the Animals*. 2011.
Alther, Lisa. *Stormy Weather and Other Stories*. 2012.
Díaz, Junot. *This Is How You Lose Her*. 2012.
Pritchard, Sara. *Help Wanted: Female*. 2013.
Salesses, Matthew. *I'm Not Saying, I'm Just Saying*. 2013.
Stonich, Sarah. *Vacationland*. 2013.
Zambrano, Mario Alberto. *Lotería*. 2013.
Beckel, Abigail and Kathleen Rooney (eds), *My Very End of the Universe: Five Novellas-in-Flash and a Study of the Form*. 2014.
Chiusano, Mark. *Marine Park*. 2014.
Klay, Phil. *Redeployment*. 2014.
Offill, Jenny. *Dept. of Speculation*. 2014.
Scheiber, Barbara. *We'll Go to Coney Island*. 2014.
Beattie, Ann. *The State We're in: Maine Stories*. 2015.
Marra, Anthony. *The Tsar of Love and Techno: Stories*. 2015.
Ruiz-Camacho, Antonio. *Barefoot Dogs: Stories*. 2015.
Majka, Sara. *Cities I've Never Lived in: Stories*. 2016.

Works Cited

Alford, Robert (2012), 'Celebrating the Possibilities of Fiction: A Conversation with Jennifer Egan', *Pop Matters*, 21 February, <http://www.popmatters.com/column/154523-celebrating-the-possibilities-of-fiction-a-conversation-with-jennife/> (last accessed 24 May 2017).
Alter, Alexandra (2013), 'TV's Novel Challenge: Literature on the Screen', *The Wall Street Journal*, 22 February, <https://www.wsj.com/articles/SB10001424127887323478004578306400682079518> (last accessed 24 May 2017).
Alvarez, Julia (2000), 'A Note on the Loosely Autobiographical', *New England Review*, 21.4: 165–6.
— (2005), *How the García Girls Lost Their Accents*, New York: Plume.
Anderson, Benedict [1983] (1991), *Imagined Communities: Reflections on the Origin and Spread of Nationalism*, London: Verso.
Anderson, Sherwood (1917), Letter to Waldo Frank, 15 January, Box 6, Folder 243, Sherwood Anderson Papers, The Newberry Library, Chicago (last accessed 1 July 2013).
— (1919), Letter to Ben Huebsch, 12 November, Box 7, Folder 325, Sherwood Anderson Papers, The Newberry Library, Chicago (last accessed 1 July 2013).
— (1942), *Sherwood Anderson's Memoirs*, ed. Paul Rosenfeld, New York: Harcourt, Brace.
— (1984), *Sherwood Anderson: Selected Letters*, ed. Charles E. Modlin, Knoxville: University of Tennessee Press.
— (1989), *A Story Teller's Story*, London: Penguin.
— (1999), *Winesburg, Ohio*, ed. Glen A. Love, Oxford: Oxford University Press.
Anzaldúa, Gloria (1999), *Borderlands/La Frontera: The New Mestiza*, San Francisco: Aunt Lute Books.
Banks, Russell (1996), *Trailerpark*, New York: Harper.
— (2003), Interview by Richard Klin, *January Magazine*, June, <http://januarymagazine.com/profiles/rbanks.html> (last accessed 1 November 2010).
Barak, Julie (1998), '"Turning and Turning in the Widening Gyre": A Second Coming into Language in Julia Alvarez's *How the García Girls Lost Their Accents*', *MELUS*, 23.1: 159–76.

Barnard, Rita (2005), 'Modern American Fiction', in Walter Kalaidjian (ed.), *The Cambridge Companion to American Modernism*, Cambridge: Cambridge University Press, pp. 39–67.
Barry, Rebecca (2007), *Later, at the Bar: A Novel in Stories*, New York: Simon & Schuster.
— (2008), *Later, at the Bar: A Novel in Stories*, trade paperback edn, New York: Simon & Schuster.
Beckel, Abigail and Kathleen Rooney (2014), 'Introduction', in Abigail Beckel and Kathleen Rooney (eds), *My Very End of the Universe: Five Novellas-in-Flash and a Study of the Genre*, Brookline, MA: Rose Metal, pp. vii–xx.
Bell, Millicent (1993), 'Introduction', in Millicent Bell (ed.), *New Essays on Hawthorne's Major Tales*, Cambridge: Cambridge University Press, pp. 1–35.
Blotner, Joseph (ed.) (1976), *The Selected Letters of William Faulkner*, New York: Random House.
Bostrom, Melissa (2007), *Sex, Race, and Family in Contemporary American Short Stories*, New York: Palgrave.
Bowden, Mary Weatherspoon (1981), *Washington Irving*, Boston: Twayne.
Boym, Svetlana (2001), *The Future of Nostalgia*, New York: Basic Books.
Bradbury, Raymond (1950), *The Martian Chronicles*, Garden City, NY: Doubleday.
— (1997), *The Martian Chronicles*, rev. edn, New York: Harper.
Brooks, Cleanth (1983), *First Encounters*, New Haven, CT: Yale University Press.
Brown, Ellen A. and Patricia Hernlund (1978), 'The Source for the Title of Stephen Crane's *Whilomville Stories*', *American Literature*, 50.1: 116–18.
Butler, Judith (2004), *Undoing Gender*, New York: Routledge.
Chin, Frank (2005), 'Come All Ye Asian American Writers of the Real and the Fake', in Kent A. Ono (ed.), *A Companion to Asian American Studies*, Malden, MA: Blackwell, pp. 133–56.
Ciabattari, Jane (2010), 'The Book on Aging Rockers', *The Daily Beast*, 29 June, <http://www.thedailybeast.com/articles/2010/06/29/jennifer-egan-interview-a-visit-from-the-goon-squad> (last accessed 6 August 2014).
Cowley, Malcolm (ed.) (1967), *The Portable Faulkner*, New York: Random House.
Cox, Christopher (2010), 'Jennifer Egan', The Paris Review, 25 June, <https://www.theparisreview.org/blog/2010/06/25/qa-jennifer-egan/> (last accessed 6 August 2014).
Crawford, Margo Natalie (2008), *Dilution Anxiety and the Black Phallus*, Columbus: Ohio State University Press.
Curry, Martha (1980), 'Sherwood Anderson and James Joyce', *American Literature*, 52.2: 236–49.
Davis, Rocío G. (2002), *Transcultural Reinventions: Asian American and Asian Canadian Short-Story Cycles*, Toronto: TSAR Publications.

Day, Cathy (2004), *The Circus in Winter*, Orlando: Harcourt.
— (2008), Interview by Bryan Furuness, August, <http://www.hobartpulp.com/web_features/an-interview-with-cathy-day> (last accessed 1 November 2010).
Delville, Michel (1998), *The American Prose Poem: Poetic Form and the Boundaries of Genre*, Gainesville: University Press of Florida.
D'hoker, Elke (2013), 'The Short Story Cycle: Broadening the Perspective', *Short Fiction in Theory and Practice*, 3.2: 151–9.
Doane, Mary Ann (2002), *The Emergence of Cinematic Time: Modernity, Contingency, The Archive*, Cambridge, MA: Harvard University Press.
Dubey, Madhu (2003), *Signs and Cities: Black Literary Postmodernism*, Chicago: University of Chicago Press.
Dunn, Maggie and Ann Morris (1995), *The Composite Novel, the Short Story Cycle in Transition*, New York: Twayne; Toronto: Maxwell Macmillan Canada.
Duvall, John (2005), 'Regionalism in American Modernism', in Walter Kalaidjian (ed.), *The Cambridge Companion to American Modernism*, Cambridge: Cambridge University Press, pp. 242–60.
Early, James (1972), *The Making of Go Down, Moses*, Dallas: Southern Methodist University Press.
Egan, Jennifer (2011), *A Visit from the Goon Squad*, New York: Anchor.
— (2012), 'Experimentation in Fiction: Notes from a Reluctant Practitioner', 43rd Annual Northeast Modern Language Association, 16 March.
Erdrich, Louise (2005), *Love Medicine*, New York: Harper.
Evans, David H. (2008), *William Faulkner, William James, and the American Pragmatic Tradition*, Baton Rouge: Louisiana State University Press.
Faulkner, William (1939), *The Wild Palms*, New York: Random House.
— (1951), *Requiem for a Nun*, New York: Random House.
— (1978), *Knight's Gambit*, New York: Vintage.
— (1990a), *As I Lay Dying*, New York: Vintage.
— (1990b), *Go Down, Moses*, New York: Vintage.
— (1990c), *The Sound and the Fury*, New York: Vintage.
— (1991), *The Unvanquished*, New York: Vintage.
— (2004a), 'A Note on Sherwood Anderson, 1953', in *Essays, Speeches & Public Letters*, ed. James B. Meriwether, New York: Modern Library, pp. 3–11.
— (2004b), 'Sherwood Anderson, 1925', in *Essays, Speeches & Public Letters*, ed. James B. Meriwether, New York: Modern Library, pp. 246–54.
Ferguson, James (1991), *Faulkner's Short Fiction*, Knoxville: University of Tennessee Press.
Ferguson, Suzanne (1996), 'The Short Stories of Louise Erdrich's Novels', *Studies in Short Fiction*, 33: 541–55.
Fetterly, Judith and Marjorie Pryce (1992), *American Women Regionalists, 1850–1910*, New York: Norton.

Forkner, Benjamin (2012), 'Short Story Cycles of the Americas, A Transitional Post-Colonial Form: A Study of V. S. Naipaul's *Miguel Street*, Ernest Gaines's *Bloodline*, and Gabriel Garcia Marquez's *Los Funerales De Mama Grande*', Dissertation, Louisiana State University.

Friedman, Lawrence M. (2004), *Private Lives: Families, Individuals, and the Law*, Cambridge, MA: Harvard University Press.

Friedman, Susan Stanford (2006), 'Periodizing Modernism: Postcolonial Modernities and the Space/Time Borders of Modernist Studies', *Modernism/Modernity*, 13.3: 425–33.

Fussell, Paul (2013), *The Great War and Modern Memory*, Oxford: Oxford University Press.

Gay, Roxane (2013), 'Introduction', in Matthew Salesses, *I'm Not Saying, I'm Just Saying*, Lexington, KY: Civil Coping Mechanisms, pp. 11–12.

— (2014), 'Bridled Vows: Jenny Offill's "Dept. of Speculation"', *The New York Times*, 7 February, <https://www.nytimes.com/2014/02/09/books/review/jenny-offills-dept-of-speculation.html?_r=0> (last accessed 1 October 2016).

Giles, Paul (2007), 'The Deterritorialization of American Literature', in Wai Chee Dimock and Lawrence Buell (eds), *Shades of the Planet: American Literature as World Literature*, Princeton: Princeton University Press, pp. 39–61.

Glendon, Mary Ann (1996), *The Transformation of Family Law: State, Law, and Family in the United States and Western Europe*, Chicago: University of Chicago Press.

Glissant, Édouard (1999), *Faulkner, Mississippi*, trans. Barbara Lewis and Thomas C. Spear, New York: Farrar, Straus, and Giroux.

Hagood, Taylor (2008), *Faulkner's Imperialism: Space, Place, and the Materiality of Myth*, Baton Rouge: Louisiana State University Press.

Hawthorne, Nathaniel (2003), *Mosses from an Old Manse*, ed. Mary Oliver, New York: Modern Library.

Hegeman, Susan (1999), *Patterns for America: Modernism and the Concept of Culture*, Princeton: Princeton University Press.

Herring, Scott (2009), 'Regional Modernism: A Reintroduction', *Modern Fiction Studies*, 55.1: 1–10.

Holland, Tiff (2014a), *Betty Superman*, in Abigail Beckel and Kathleen Rooney (eds), *My Very End of the Universe: Five Novellas-in-Flash and a Study of the Genre*, Brookline, MA: Rose Metal, pp. 15–44.

— (2014b), 'Written in Stone: How Subject Dictated Narrative Form', in Abigail Beckel and Kathleen Rooney (eds), *My Very End of the Universe: Five Novellas-in-Flash and a Study of the Genre*, Brookline, MA: Rose Metal, pp. 3–9.

Hoskins, Andrew (2004), 'Television and the Collapse of Memory', *Time Society*, 13.1: 109–27.

Howells, William Dean (1910), *My Literary Passions: Criticism and Fiction*, New York: Harper & Brothers.

Hsu, Hsuan L. (2005), 'Literature and Regional Production', *American Literary History*, 17.1: 36–69.
Igarashi, Yuka (2011), 'Interview: Jennifer Egan', *Granta*, 18 March, <https://granta.com/interview-jennifer-egan/> (last accessed 6 August 2014).
Ingram, Forrest L. (1971), *Representative Short Story Cycles of the Twentieth Century: Studies in a Literary Genre*, The Hague: Mouton.
Irving, Washington (1930), *The Sketch Book of Geoffrey Crayon, Gent.*, New York: Longman.
Itzkoff, Dave (2011), 'Egan Discusses Plans for TV "Goon Squad"', *The New York Times*, 22 April, <http://query.nytimes.com/gst/fullpage.html?res=9D03EFDF1331F931A15757C0A9679D8B63> (last accessed 6 August 2014).
James, William (1884), 'On Some Omissions of Introspective Psychology', *Mind*, 9.33: 1–26.
Jewett, Sarah Orne (2000), *The Country of the Pointed Firs and Other Stories*, New York: Modern Library.
Joseph, Philip (2007), *American Literary Regionalism in a Global Age*, Baton Rouge: Louisiana State University Press.
Julavits, Heidi (2010), 'Jennifer Egan', *Bomb Magazine*, Summer, <http://bombmagazine.org/article/3524/jennifer-egan> (last accessed 6 August 2014).
Kadmos, Helena (2014), '"Look what they done to this ground, girl!": Country and Identity in Jeanine Leane's *Purple Threads*', *Journal of the Association for the Study of Australian Literature*, 14.3: 1–11.
Kelley, Margot (2000), 'Gender and Genre: The Case of the Novel-in-Stories', in Julie Brown (ed.), *American Women Short Story Writers: A Collection of Critical Essays*, New York: Garland, pp. 295–310.
Kennedy, J. Gerald (1988), 'Towards a Poetics of the Short Story Cycle', *Journal of the Short Story in English*, 11: 9–25.
— (1995), *Modern American Short Story Sequences: Composite Fictions and Fictive Communities*, Cambridge: Cambridge University Press.
Kern, Stephen (1983), *The Culture of Time and Space 1880–1918*, Cambridge, MA: Harvard University Press.
Kirkland, Caroline Matilda (1990), *A New Home – Who'll Follow? Or Glimpses of Western Life*, ed. Sandra A. Zagarell, New Brunswick, NJ: Rutgers University Press.
Kogen, Lauren (2006), 'Once or Twice Upon a Time: Temporal Simultaneity and the *Lost* Phenomenon', *Film International*, 4.2: 44–7, 50–5.
Lahiri, Jhumpa (2008), *Unaccustomed Earth*, New York: Knopf.
Lee, Eliza Buckminster (1838), *Sketches of a New England Village, in the Last Century*, Boston: James Munroe.
Lee, Stephan (2011), 'Jennifer Egan on "Goon Squad", "Los Angeles Times" Brouhaha, and Her Next Novel', *Entertainment Weekly*, 2 April, <http://ew.com/article/2011/04/02/jennifer-egan-interview-goon-squa/> (last accessed 6 August 2014).

Lévi-Strauss, Claude [1949] (1969), *The Elementary Structures of Kinship*, trans. James Harle Bell and John Richard von Sturmer, ed. Rodney Needham, rev. edn, Boston: Beacon.

Lister, Rachel (2007), 'Female Expansion and Masculine Immobilization in the Short Story Cycle', *Journal of the Short Story in English*, 48: 43–58.

Lordi, Emily J. (2006), 'Endnotes', in *Billy Budd and the Piazza Tales*, New York: Barnes & Noble, pp. 321–30.

Love, Glen A. (1999), 'Introduction', in Sherwood Anderson, *Winesburg, Ohio*, ed. Glen A. Love, Oxford: Oxford University Press, pp. vii–xxvi.

Lovelady, Stephanie (2005), 'Walking Backwards: Chronology, Immigration, and Coming of Age in *My Ántonia* and *How the García Girls Lost Their Accents*', *Modern Language Studies*, 35.1: 28–37.

Luis, William (2000), 'A Search for Identity in Julia Alvarez's: *How the García Girls Lost Their Accents*', *Callaloo*, 23.3: 839–49.

Lukin, Joshua (2010), 'Part of Us that Can't Be Touched', *Guernica*, 1 July, <https://www.guernicamag.com/egan_7_1_10/> (last accessed 6 August 2014).

Lundén, Rolf (1999), *The United Stories of America: Studies in the Short Story Composite*, Amsterdam: Rodopi.

Luscher, Robert M. (1989), 'The Short Story Sequence: An Open Book', in Susan Lohafer and Jo Ellyn Clarey (eds), *Short Story Theory at a Crossroads*, Baton Rouge: Louisiana State University Press, pp. 148–67.

— (2013), 'Down the Road from *Winesburg*: The Spatiotemporal Aesthetics of the Short Story Sequence in Donald Ray Pollock's *Knockemstiff* and Laura Hendrie's *Stygo*', *Short Fiction in Theory and Practice*, 3.2: 193–210.

Lynch, Gerald (2001), *The One and the Many: English-Canadian Short Story Cycles*, Toronto: University of Toronto Press.

McClintock, Anne (1995), *Imperial Leather: Race, Gender and Sexuality in the Colonial Context*, New York: Routledge.

McCullough, Kate (1999), *Regions of Identity: The Construction of America in Women's Fiction, 1885–1914*, Stanford: Stanford University Press.

Mann, Susan Garland (1989), *The Short Story Cycle: A Genre Companion and Reference Guide*, New York: Greenwood.

Maran, Meredith (2010), '"Goon Squad": Jennifer Egan's Time Travel Tour de Force', *Salon*, 13 June, <http://www.salon.com/2010/06/13/jennifer_egan_interview_ext2010/> (last accessed 6 August 2014).

March-Russell, Paul (2009), *The Short Story: An Introduction*, Edinburgh: Edinburgh University Press.

Meisenheimer, Jr., D. K. (1997), 'Regionalist Bodies/Embodied Regions: Sarah Orne Jewett and Zitkala-Ša', in Sherrie A. Inness and Diana Royer (eds), *Breaking Boundaries: New Perspectives on Women's Regional Writing*, Iowa City: University of Iowa Press, pp. 109–23.

Melville, Herman (2006), *Billy Budd and the Piazza Tales*, New York: Barnes & Noble.

Michod, Alec (2010), 'The Rumpus Interview with Jennifer Egan', *The Rumpus*, 23 June, <http://therumpus.net/2010/06/the-rumpus-interview-with-jennifer-egan/> (last accessed 6 August 2014).
Moretti, Franco (1987), *The Way of the World: The Bildungsroman in European Culture*, London: Verso.
Morrison, Toni (1993), *Playing in the Dark*, New York: Vintage.
Mucher, Walter J. (2002), 'Being Martian: Spatiotemporal Self in Ray Bradbury's *The Martian Chronicles*', *Extrapolation*, 43.2: 171–87.
Nagel, James (2001), *The Contemporary American Short-Story Cycle: The Ethnic Resonance of Genre*, Baton Rouge: Louisiana University Press.
Nowotny, Helga (1994), *Time: The Modern and Postmodern Experience*, trans. Neville Plaice, Cambridge: Polity.
Offill, Jenny (2014), *Dept. of Speculation*, New York: Knopf.
Pacht, Michelle (2009), *The Subversive Storyteller: The Short Story Cycle and the Politics of Identity in America*, Newcastle upon Tyne: Cambridge Scholars.
Parini, Jay (2007), 'Afterword: In the House of Faulkner', in Joseph R. Urgo and Ann J. Abadie (eds), *Faulkner's Inheritance: Faulkner and Yoknapatawpha, 2005*, Jackson: University Press of Mississippi, pp. 160–9.
Poe, Edgar Allan (1984), 'Review in *Godey's Lady's Book*, November 1847', in *Essays and Reviews*, New York: Penguin, pp. 577–84.
Pokrass, Meg (2014a), 'Breaking the Pattern to Make the Pattern: Conjuring a Whole Narrative from Scraps', in Abigail Beckel and Kathleen Rooney (eds), *My Very End of the Universe: Five Novellas-in-Flash and a Study of the Genre*, Brookline, MA: Rose Metal, pp. 47–53.
— (2014b), 'Here, Where We Live', in Abigail Beckel and Kathleen Rooney (eds), *My Very End of the Universe: Five Novellas-in-Flash and a Study of the Genre*, Brookline, MA: Rose Metal, pp. 55–98.
Polk, Noel (2008), *Faulkner and Welty and the Southern Literary Tradition*, Jackson: University Press of Mississippi.
Ponder, Melinda M. (1990), *Hawthorne's Early Narrative Art*, Lewiston, NY: Edwin Mellen.
Pratt, Mary Louise (1991), 'Arts of the Contact Zone', *Profession*, 91: 33–40.
Reilly, Charlie (2009), 'An Interview with Jennifer Egan', *Contemporary Literature*, 50.3: 439–60.
Salesses, Matthew (2013), *I'm Not Saying, I'm Just Saying*, Lexington, KY: Civil Coping Mechanisms.
Sartre, Jean-Paul (1963), 'Time in Faulkner: *The Sound and the Fury*', in Fredrick J. Hoffman and Olga W. Vickery (eds), *William Faulkner: Three Decades of Criticism*, New York: Harcourt, pp. 225–32.
Sawhney, Hirsh (2008), 'No Place Like Home', *The Guardian*, 7 June, <https://www.theguardian.com/books/2008/jun/07/fiction1> (last accessed 20 April 2017).

Scholes, Robert and A. Walton Litz (1996), 'Epiphanies and Epicleti', in James Joyce, *Dubliners*, ed. Robert Scholes and A. Walton Litz, New York: Penguin, pp. 247–50.

Schwartz, Lawrence H. (1998), *Creating Faulkner's Reputation: The Politics of Modern Literary Criticism*, Knoxville: University of Tennessee Press.

Singer, Marc (2001), 'Moving Forward to Reach the Past: The Dialogics of Time in Amy Tan's *The Joy Luck Club*', *Journal of Narrative Theory*, 31.3: 324–52.

Skei, Hans H. (1985), *William Faulkner: The Novelist as Short Story Writer*, Oslo: Universitetsforlaget.

— (1999), *Reading Faulkner's Best Short Stories*, Columbia: University of South Carolina Press.

Sollors, Werner (1995), 'Ethnicity', in Frank Lentricchia and Thomas McLaughlin (eds), *Critical Terms for Literary Study*, 2nd edn, Chicago: University of Chicago Press, pp. 288–305.

Somogyi, Barbara and David Stanton (1991), 'Amy Tan: An Interview', *Poets and Writers*, 19.5: 24–32.

Spears, Tim (2005), *Chicago Dreaming: Midwesterners and the City, 1871–1919*, Chicago: University of Chicago Press.

Suárez, Lucía M. (2004), 'Julia Alvarez and the Anxiety of Latina Representation', *Meridians*, 5.1: 117–45.

Tan, Amy (1989), *The Joy Luck Club*, New York: Ivy.

Teel, Aaron (2014a), 'A Brief Crack of Light: Mimicking Memory in the Novella-in-Flash', in Abigail Beckel and Kathleen Rooney (eds), *My Very End of the Universe: Five Novellas-in-Flash and a Study of the Genre*, Brookline, MA: Rose Metal, pp. 99–105.

— (2014b), 'Shampoo Horns', in Abigail Beckel and Kathleen Rooney (eds), *My Very End of the Universe: Five Novellas-in-Flash and a Study of the Genre*, Brookline, MA: Rose Metal, pp. 107–69.

Thompson, E. P. (1967), 'Time, Work-Discipline, and Industrial Capitalism', *Past & Present*, 38: 56–97.

Tillotson, Kristin (2011), 'A Very Goon Year for Jennifer Egan', *Star Tribune*, 6 September, <http://www.startribune.com/a-very-goon-year-for-jennifer-egan/128426023/> (last accessed 6 August 2014).

Todorov, Tzvetan (1990), *Genres in Discourse*, New York: Cambridge University Press.

Tönnies, Ferdinand (1957), *Community and Society*, trans. and ed. Charles P. Loomis, East Lansing: Michigan State University Press.

Torres, Justin (2011), *We the Animals*, New York: Mariner.

Trussoni, Danielle (2007), 'Bad Behavior within Reason', *The New York Times*, 6 May, <http://query.nytimes.com/gst/fullpage.html?res=9F06E7DC133EF935A35756C0A9619C8B63> (last accessed 15 January 2008).

Wagner, Tamara Sylvia (2005), 'Realigning and Reassigning Cultural Values: Occidentalist Stereotyping and Representations of the Multiethnic Family in Asian American Women Writers', in Guiyou Huang (ed.), *Asian American Literary Studies*, Edinburgh: Edinburgh University Press, pp. 152–75.

Wambold, Sarah (2010), 'A Visit from the Goon Squad [Texas Book Festival Interview]', *Austinist*, 16 October, <http://austinist.com/2010/10/04/jennifereganpieter_m_van_hattem_the.php> (last accessed 6 August 2014).

Wang, Dorothy (1989), 'A Game of Show Not Tell; *The Joy Luck Club*', *Newsweek*, 17 April, p. 69A.

Weber, Max (1998), *The Protestant Ethic and the Spirit of Capitalism*, trans. Talcott Parson, Los Angeles: Roxbury.

Weekes, Karen (2002), 'Identity in the Short Story Cycles of Lori Moore', *Journal of the Short Story in English*, 39: 1–10.

Weinstein, Cindy (2004), *Family, Kinship, and Sympathy in Nineteenth-Century American Literature*, Cambridge: Cambridge University Press.

Whalan, Mark (2007), *Race, Manhood, and Modernism in America: The Short Story Cycles of Sherwood Anderson and Jean Toomer*, Knoxville: University of Tennessee Press.

White, Ray Lewis (1972), *Sherwood Anderson/Gertrude Stein: Correspondence and Personal Essays*, Chapel Hill: University of North Carolina Press.

Williams, Raymond (1982), 'Class and Region in the Novel', in Douglas Jefferson and Graham Martin (eds), *The Uses of Fiction*, Milton Keynes: Open University Press, pp. 59–68.

Wolff, Sally (2009), 'William Faulkner and the Ledgers of History', *Southern Literary Journal*, 62.1: 1–16.

Wood, James (2008), *How Fiction Works*, New York: Farrar, Straus and Giroux.

Zagarell, Sandra A. (1988), 'Narrative of Community: The Identification of a Genre', *Signs: Journal of Women and Culture in Society*, 13.3: 498–527.

— (1990), 'Introduction', in Caroline Matilda Kirkland, *A New Home – Who'll Follow? Or Glimpses of Western Life*, ed. Sandra A. Zagarell, New Brunswick, NJ: Rutgers University Press, pp. xi–xliii.

— (2007), 'Reflections: Narrative, Community, Narrative of Community', in Roxanne Harde (ed.), *Narratives of Community: Women's Short Story Sequences*, Newcastle upon Tyne: Cambridge Scholars, pp. 433–48.

Zambrano, Mario Alberto (2013), *Lotería*, New York: HarperCollins.

Zauhar, Frances M. (2007), 'Sarah Orne Jewett and the Community of American Authors', in Roxanne Harde (ed.), *Narratives of Community: Women's Short Story Sequences*, Newcastle upon Tyne: Cambridge Scholars, pp. 411–31.

Index

Alvarez, Julia, 9, 87–97, 99–101, 107–8, 111, 169
Anderson, Benedict, 167
Anderson, Eleanor, 120
Anderson, Sherwood
 correspondence, 12, 31–4
 influence on other writers, 12, 37–40, 42, 45–6, 48–9, 50–1, 54–8, 60–1, 66–8, 120–1, 138
 influenced by other writers, 13, 33–4
 Mary Cochran, 33
 Memoirs, 12
 A Storyteller's Story, 13
 Winesburg, Ohio, 1–2, 5–6, 10–11, 12–14, 27–36, 37–8, 142, 154, 165
Anzaldúa, Gloria, 62; *see also* Borderland
The Atlantic, 117

Balzac, Honoré de, 7, 18
Banks, Russell, 3, 38–43, 45–6, 50, 51, 55, 56–8
Barak, Julie, 8
Barnard, Rita, 57, 131
Barry, Rebecca, 3, 38, 43–51, 55–8
Baudelaire, Charles, 4
Beckel, Abigail and Kathleen Rooney, 170–1
bildungsroman, 4, 28–9, 40, 125
Bloom, Amy, 20, 111n3
Boccaccio, 7
Borderland, 62–3, 71; *see also* Anzaldúa, Gloria
Bowden, Mary Weatherspoon, 18
Boym, Svetlana, 23, 26, 66
Bradbury, Ray, 60–78, 81, 83, 141–2, 153
Brooks, Cleanth, 118, 125
Butler, Judith, 156
Butler, Robert Olen, 9

Caldwell, Erskine, 111n1
capitalism, 13–14, 29, 64–8, 110
Carver, Raymond, 2
Cather, Willa, 35
Chaucer, Geoffrey, 7
Chin, Frank, 89
Chippewa *see* Ojibwe
Chodorow, Nancy, 112n5
Cisneros, Sandra, 173
Cold War, 74–7
Colliers, 117
colonialism *see* imperialism
Connell, Evan S., 111n1, 171
contact zone, 62–3, 81, 85;
 see also Pratt, Mary Louise
Cowley, Malcolm, 1–2, 113, 116, 125, 129, 135, 172
Crane, Stephen, 23–4
Curry, Martha, 34

Danticat, Edwidge, 7
Davis, Rocío, 4, 9
Day, Cathy, 3, 38, 43, 49–58
Delville, Michel, 4
D'hoker, Elke, 4
Díaz, Junot, 9, 21, 111n3, 169
Didion, Joan, 171
Dinnerstein, Dorothy, 112n5
Don Quixote, 145–6
Dos Passos, John, 10, 108–9
Du Bois, W. E. B., 35
Dubey, Madhu, 57
Dunn, Maggie and Ann Morris, 2–3
Duvall, John N., 131
Dybeck, Stuart, 59

Early, James, 139
Egan, Jennifer, 2, 141–69, 170
Erdrich, Louise, 9, 61–3, 77–86, 87, 90, 169
Esquivel, Laura, 7

ethnicity, 7–8, 9, 53, 61–3, 68–72, 77–81, 87–94, 97, 107–11, 157–9, 173–6
Evans, David H., 119, 121, 123

family *see* kinship
family law, 94
Far, Sui Sin, 21, 109–11, 176
Faulkner, William, 10, 168–9
   Absalom, Absalom!, 119
   As I Lay Dying, 109, 114, 119
   The Big Woods, 129
   correspondence, 115–16, 118, 140n2
   Go Down, Moses, 1, 34, 113–40, 153–4, 165
   Knight's Gambit, 1–2, 113
   'A Note on Sherwood Anderson, 1953', 120–1
   'Sherwood Anderson, 1925', 120
   The Sound and the Fury, 108, 119, 134
   The Unvanquished, 1, 34, 113, 116, 117
   The Wild Palms, 114, 116
feminism, 96–7
Fetterly, Judith and Marjorie Pryce, 109
flash cycle, 170–7
flash fiction, 4, 170
Flaubert, Gustave, 7, 61
Ford, Ford Madox, 168
Forkner, Benjamin, 4
frame narrative, 19–20, 35
Frank, Waldo, 31, 32, 34, 35
Frank O'Connor International Short Story Award, 111n2
Franklin, Benjamin, 64–5
Freeman, Mary Wilkins, 21–3
Friday, Nancy, 112n5
Friedman, Lawrence M., 94, 112n4
Friedman, Susan Stanford, 22
Fussell, Paul, 168

Gale, Zona, 21–3
García, Christina, 87
Garland, Hamlin, 21
Gaskell, Elizabeth, 14
Gay, Roxanne, 172–3
gemeinschaft, 16, 22, 32, 39, 47, 55
gender, 7–8, 50–3, 87–9, 94–7, 101–2, 107–11
gesellschaft, 16, 39, 55; *see also* industrialisation
Giles, Paul, 14–15

Glendon, Mary Ann, 112n4
Glissant, Édouard, 114, 122

Haas, Robert K., 115–16
Harper's, 23, 117
Hawthorne, Nathaniel, 6, 18, 19–21
HBO, 145, 168
Hegeman, Susan, 35
Hemingway, Ernest, 1–2, 5, 10, 12, 34, 37, 139, 154, 168
Herring, Scott, 35–6
Holland, Tiff, 171
Homer, 7
Hoskins, Andrew, 72
Howells, William Dean, 15
Hsu, Hsuan L., 27
Huebsch, Ben, 33
Hughes, Langston, 35
Hurston, Zora Neale, 35

immigration *see* migration
immigration law, 92–4
imperialism, 62–72, 77–81
industrialisation, 13–16, 19–29, 64–8, 79–81, 142, 177; *see also* gesellschaft
Ingram, Forrest L., 3–4
International Meridian Conference, 65
interstitial temporalities, 62–3, 67–81, 85, 115
Iowa Writers' Workshop, 173
Irving, Washington, 17–18, 21, 25

James, William, 83
Jewett, Sarah Orne, 14, 21–7, 28, 36, 47, 109, 141, 176
Joyce, James, 4–7, 34, 139
Julavits, Heidi, 149

Kadmos, Helena, 8
Kelley, Margot, 8, 87–8
Kennedy, J. Gerald, 2, 18, 108–9
Kern, Stephen, 79
Kincaid, Jamaica, 9, 87
Kingston, Maxine Hong, 87, 89, 111n2
kinship, 87–100, 107–11, 113–16, 118–20, 124, 126–33, 154–60, 172
   formative kinship, 89, 100–6, 115, 155, 176
Kirkland, Caroline, 15–17, 22, 24, 28, 32, 36, 39, 47, 52, 141
Kogen, Lauren, 72

Korean War, 152
künstlerroman, 28

Ladies Home Journal, 23
Lahiri, Jhumpa, 21, 87–9, 91, 93–5, 103–6, 111, 153
Lee, Elizabeth Buckminster, 17
Lee, Stephan, 144
Lévi-Strauss, Claude, 97, 106, 110, 159
limited locality, 14, 22, 25, 34–6, 38–43, 46–7, 61, 91, 115, 120–6
Lister, Rachel, 8
Longstreet, Augustus Baldwin, 17, 139
Los Angeles Times, 145
Lovelady, Stephanie, 99
Loving v. Virginia, 94
Luis, William, 99
Lukin, Josh, 145
Lundén, Rolf, 3, 8
Luscher, Robert, 2, 40, 161
Lynch, Gerald, 8

McClintock, Anne, 91, 107
McCullough, Kate, 88, 109
Malory, Thomas, 7
Manguso, Sarah, 173
Mann, Susan Garland, 4
March-Russell, Paul, 5
Master of Fine Arts programs, 8, 173
Masters, Edgar Lee, 13, 33
Meisenheimer, Jr., D. K., 109
Melville, Herman, 10–11, 19–21
Mencken, H. L., 1–2, 172
migration, 87–94, 99–102, 109–11, 173–6
Minot, Susan, 9
Mitford, Mary Russell, 7, 17
modernism, 1–2, 5–7, 9–11, 12–15, 27–36, 42, 56–9, 108–9, 138–9, 141–2, 167–8, 171
Moretti, Franco, 28
Mori, Toshio, 9
Morrison, Toni, 10, 114–15
Mucher, Walter J., 63–4, 73
Munro, Alice, 7
My Very End of the Universe, 170–2

Nagel, James, 4, 9, 92
narratives of community, 13–14; *see also* limited locality
nation, 7–9, 12, 14–18, 21–4, 35–6, 61–5, 76–7, 80–1, 87–98, 109–11, 120–2, 176–7
National Book Award, 111n2

National Book Critics Circle Award, 111n2, 145
Naylor, Gloria, 87, 111n2
Nelson, Alice Dunbar, 109
Nelson, Maggie, 173
The New York Times, 145
The New Yorker, 104
Northeastern Modern Language Association, 145
nostalgia, 17, 21, 43–56, 65–8, 110, 122–4, 134–5, 141–2, 148, 164–8
  critical nostalgia, 22–7, 38, 60–1
novel, 8–11, 12, 15, 19–20, 25, 33–5, 39, 44–5, 57, 60–1, 90, 108–9, 115–16, 119, 143–6, 151–2, 176
novella-in-flash *see* flash cycle

O. Henry, 5
Obama, Barack, 160
O'Brien, Tim, 5, 9
Offill, Jenny, 172
Ojibwe, 9, 62, 77, 80–1, 84
oral storytelling, 58
Otto, Whitney, 171
Our Bodies, Ourselves, 95
Ovid, 7

Pacht, Michelle, 4
Panchatantra, 7
Picasso, Pablo, 167
pluralism, 7–8, 16
Poe, Edgar Allan, 6
Pokrass, Meg, 171
Polk, Noel, 131–2
Pollock, Donald Ray, 58–9
Porter, William Sydney *see* O. Henry
postmodernism, 7, 57–8, 139, 145–6
Pound, Ezra, 1, 35, 56–7, 167–8
PowerPoint, 149, 160–6
Pratt, Mary Louise, 62–3; *see also* contact zone
prose poetry, 4
Proust, Marcel, 145, 147–50
provisional identities, 6–7, 61, 115, 120, 127–8, 138, 154–9, 173, 176–7
Pulitzer Prize, 145

race, 41–2, 71–2, 114–17, 120–38, 157–9
railroads, 19, 27, 54–5, 65, 142
realism, 7, 13, 17, 18–21, 30, 56–9, 138–9, 143; *see also* verisimilitude

regionalism, 13–27, 34–6, 56–9, 120–3
Robison, Mary, 171
romanticism, 18–21
Rose Metal Press, 170–2

Salesses, Matthew, 172–3
Salinger, J. D., 2
Sartre, Jean-Paul, 134–5
Sawhney, Hirsh, 89
September 11th terrorist attacks, 153–4, 158, 166–8
short story, 5–6, 15
short story cycle
   definitions and terminology, 1–5, 12–13, 19, 32–6, 60, 90, 143–6
   history, 4–9, 14–19
   previous publication, 18–20, 23–4, 60, 104, 116–18, 149–50
   revision, 60, 86n2, 104, 116–18, 128–9, 149–50, 160
   within short story collections, 20–1, 88
simultaneity, 72–82, 85, 91, 153
Singer, Marc, 89, 92
sketchbooks, 4, 13–18, 35, 63, 73–4, 109–11, 176–7
The Sopranos, 147, 149–50, 168–9
Stein, Gertrude, 4, 13, 33–4, 139, 168
Steinbeck, John, 12–13, 34, 37
Strout, Elizabeth, 169n1
Suárez, Lucía M., 93
Suleri, Sara, 9

Tan, Amy, 3, 61, 87–96, 98–9, 101–3, 107, 109, 111, 141, 165
Teel, Aaron, 171–2
Thompson, E. P., 64
A Thousand and One Nights, 7
Todorov, Tzvetan, 176
Tönnies, Ferdinand, 16; *see also gemeinschaft; gesellschaft*

Toomer, Jean, 12, 34–5, 37
Torres, Justin, 173–6
Tristram Shandy, 145–6
Trujillo, Rafael, 92–3, 100
Trussoni, Danielle, 44
Turgenev, Ivan, 7, 18, 34

Unferth, Deb Olin, 173
United States Civil War, 21, 23, 51–4, 60–1, 114
Updike, John, 20, 111n1
urbanisation, 13–14, 26–7, 176–7

verisimilitude, 22, 130, 146
Vietnam War, 5
Vonnegut, Kurt, 10

Wagner, Tamara Sylvia, 88
Wang, Dorothy, 90
Weber, Max, 64–5, 84
Weekes, Karen, 8, 87
Weinstein, Cindy, 109
Welty, Eudora, 34, 109
Whalan, Mark, 4, 30
Whitman, Walt, 10–11
Williams, Raymond, 24
Williams, William Carlos, 35
Wilson, Edmund, 1–2
Wolff, Sally, 140n3
Wood, James, 61
Woolf, Virginia, 108–9
Works Progress Administration, 51
World War I, 5, 27, 154, 168
World War II, 114, 134

Zagarell, Sandra, 13–14
Zambrano, Mario Alberto, 173–4
Zauhar, Frances M., 25
Zitkála, Šá, 109
Zola, Émile, 7

EU representative:
Easy Access System Europe
Mustamäe tee 50, 10621 Tallinn, Estonia
Gpsr.requests@easproject.com

www.ingramcontent.com/pod-product-compliance
Lightning Source LLC
Chambersburg PA
CBHW051117230426
43667CB00014B/2623